IMAGES
of America

ANAMOSA PENITENTIARY

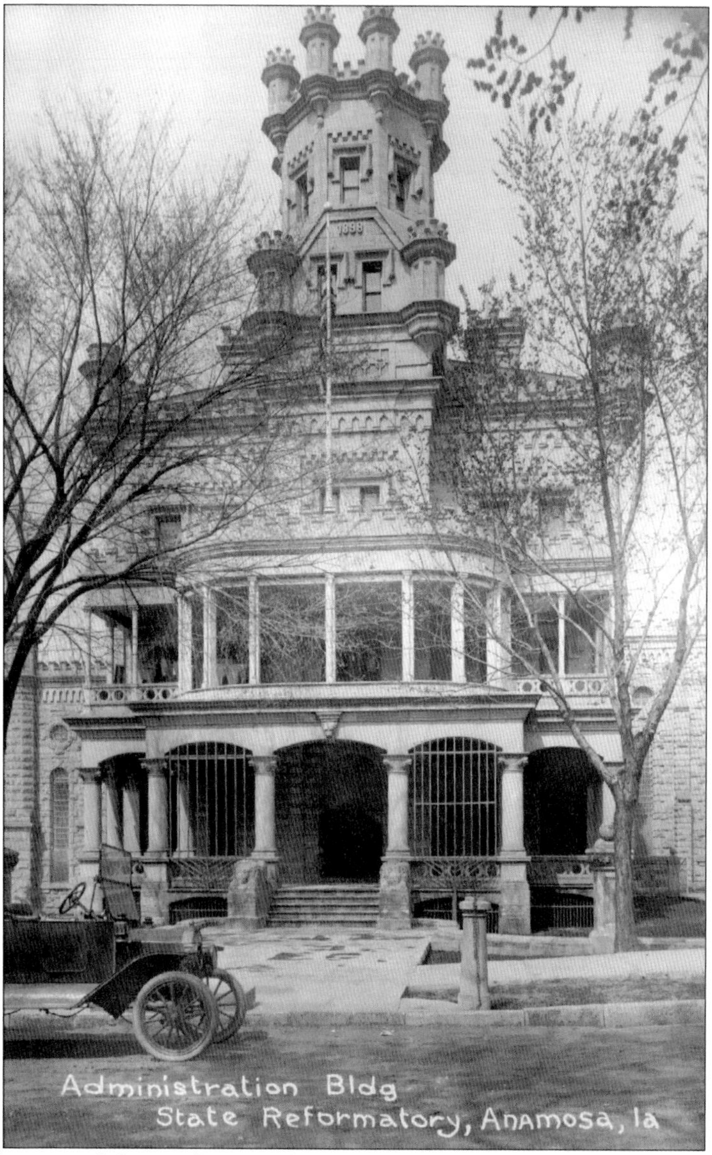

This postcard image of the warden's residence and administrative offices probably dates about 1915. With the exception of one-story additions built onto both sides, the building looks much the same today. (Courtesy Anamosa Penitentiary Museum.)

On the Cover: The cover depicts a group of elderly inmate workers along the south cell house. This is the only known photograph of Anamosa prisoners wearing striped shoes. The inscription on the back of the picture states "Papa's men, Christmas '94" and is signed "Mary." Note that the supervisor must have borrowed his shoes from the inmates, as they are also striped. (Courtesy Anamosa Penitentiary Museum.)

IMAGES
of America

ANAMOSA PENITENTIARY

Richard Snavely and Steve Wendl

ARCADIA
PUBLISHING

ISBN 978-0-7385-7779-1

Published by Arcadia Publishing
Charleston, South Carolina

Printed in the United States of America

Library of Congress Control Number: 2009938748

For all general information contact Arcadia Publishing at:
Telephone 843-853-2070
Fax 843-853-0044
E-mail sales@arcadiapublishing.com
For customer service and orders:
Toll-Free 1-888-313-2665

Visit us on the Internet at www.arcadiapublishing.com

To the dedicated staff of the Anamosa Penitentiary,
past, present, and future.

Contents

Acknowledgments

Many resources and individuals have helped make this project possible. A majority of the images have been provided by the Anamosa State Penitentiary Museum. A large number of images have been given to the museum over the years by generous supporters, for which we are grateful. Historical information has been gleaned from many sources, including numerous volumes of *Report to the Legislature* published by the State of Iowa, *A History of the Anamosa State Penitentiary* by Dellis Swartzendruber, and Bertha Finn's "Iowa State Men's Reformatory—Here Since 1872," published in *Anamosa, A Reminiscence*. Ernie Rairdin scanned many of the images. Unless otherwise noted, all images appear courtesy of the Anamosa State Penitentiary Museum. Credits noting the Paul C. Juhl Collection refer to the Iowa State Historical Society (ISHS).

INTRODUCTION

They just don't build prisons the way they used to. Nowadays, state-of-the-art prisons are efficient but drab, a sterile jumble of concrete and fences topped with razor ribbon. Few would be called beautiful. In fact, most prisons, old or new, just aren't much to look at.

But over a century ago, in a small town on the Iowa prairie, a beautiful prison was built. Some might argue that in a deeper sense, a beautiful prison is an oxymoron, that from a cultural and moral standpoint, prisons can never be beautiful. Perhaps, from that perspective, they are right. But the architects of the world would see it differently. Is it the near-perfect symmetry of the prison's frontage, with the 110-foot administration building dominating the center, contrasted by long, low cell houses on each flank? Is it the exquisitely detailed turrets and crenellations that lend a castle-like appearance, stirring both admiration and dread, especially in those who are about to be imprisoned there? Let those who doubt that prisons can be beautiful come to Anamosa first, before passing judgment.

Beauty, however, was the last thing on the minds of the Iowa governor and state lawmakers in the late 1860s, when Iowa was still a very young state and more practical concerns dominated their thoughts. The only prison, at Fort Madison in extreme southeastern Iowa, was overcrowded. A new facility was needed, preferably in the northern part of the state. Expense was, of course, a major concern. It would be very useful if the new prison were located near a rock quarry to supply the raw building material. Inmates could be used to quarry the stone and build the structure. The ideal prison location should also have enough timber at hand, water power available, and railroad service.

Several Iowa communities were considered, including McGregor, Charles City, and Marshalltown. However, Anamosa proved to be the strongest contender. It was a rapidly growing community located on the Wapsipinicon River in east central Iowa and was served by the Dubuque Southwestern Railroad. Ample timber was readily available, and Anamosa was prepared to donate land for the prison. Perhaps the biggest factor favoring Anamosa, however, was its fortunate proximity to some of the largest and finest limestone quarries anywhere. Various quarries were available for purchase and would provide a nearly limitless supply of stone to build the new prison and, importantly, to use for other state buildings as well. In fact, a profit could be turned by selling to private concerns. This perfect storm of serendipitous circumstances sealed the deal for Anamosa and, in 1872, the Iowa legislature voted to establish the new prison at Anamosa. The accurate, but unimaginative official title of the new facility was "Additional Penitentiary."

And so it began, the long and intimate relationship between prison and small town, identities intertwining so thoroughly over the years that mentioning the name Anamosa to any Iowan brings the instant response, "Oh, the prison town."

The penitentiary, like Rome, was not built in a day. In fact, it took 70 years before major construction was complete and the prison assumed the look and shape familiar to visitors today. Private contractors were used at first to erect a wooden stockade fence enclosing an 11-acre tract and to build a small structure that would house the first convicts, who arrived May 13, 1873. This group, 20 in number, was supposed to be the fledgling workforce that would start building the prison in earnest. However, prison officials grumbled that, among the 20, only 16 were "able to do a day's work." Nonetheless, Anamosa now had prisoners, and its population would only grow. By 1885, 281 inmates were in residence.

The prison took shape in fits and starts. Major problems were encountered and overcome. There were too few convicts to work the stone and too few staff to supervise the convicts. Appropriations from the legislature were insufficient, and there was no provision for a doctor or deputy warden. There were escapes and accidental construction deaths. Quicksand was encountered while building the wall. And so it went.

The quarry was about a mile away. Inmate work crews either walked or rode a handcar to the site daily. There they would toil from sunup to sundown, cutting massive limestone blocks from the hillside. The blocks would then be transported to the prison on rail flatcars, entering the prison via the west train gate. Inside, each stone was cut and shaped to final dimensions, after which other inmate crews labored to fit each stone into the gigantic jigsaw puzzle that became their prison.

Over the years, Anamosa dutifully shouldered whatever additional burdens the state required of it. Insane prisoners were housed in their own ward at Anamosa for many years. Female inmates were also incarcerated here, separated by interior walls from the male and insane prisoners, until their own prison was established in Rockwell City in 1918. It was almost as though there were three separate prisons inside the walls.

When the nationwide prison reform movement gathered steam after the turn of the century, Anamosa was asked to retool itself into a specialized facility for younger offenders. Thus, the prison became the reformatory, holding this designation for the next 90 years. First offenders under age 31 went to Anamosa; others went to Fort Madison. In 1945, after a riot at the juvenile facility in Eldora, Anamosa developed an Eldora Annex, housing 85 of the most incorrigible youths for the next two years.

An emphasis on treatment programs, education, and vocational training for the younger men became the mission and philosophy of the institution for most of the 20th century. In more recent times, Anamosa was at the forefront of national correctional trends. During the 1960s and 1970s, as the concept of community-based corrections grew, Anamosa was instrumental in developing the first work release halfway houses in Eastern Iowa. Anamosa became the first reception center in 1981, receiving and processing all admissions to the Iowa prison system (with almost no additional staffing), until that function was moved to the Iowa Medical and Classification Center near Iowa City in 1983.

In 1997, the state legislature, acknowledging the changing population makeup at Anamosa, officially designated the facility the Anamosa State Penitentiary. The prison had come full circle. More maximum-security beds were needed. With changing times came changing roles, and Anamosa resumed its original role of state penitentiary without missing a beat. The years had accustomed them to change and resiliency.

The prison was originally nicknamed "The White Palace Of The West," a tribute to the gleaming white limestone construction. Although the years have dulled the shine somewhat, its dedication to protecting Iowans remains undimmed. Thousands of souls have met and mingled in this spot. Here are some of the images and stories from this old and, yes, beautiful place.

One

The White Palace

How does one go about building a new prison? This was the Herculean task facing the board of commissioners, who had been appointed by the Iowa legislature. These three men, William Ure, Foster L. Downing, and Martin Heisey, began by inspecting quarry sites in Anamosa. They then traveled to nine eastern states and Canada to tour existing prisons and gather ideas from them, not just about physical design, but also regarding discipline and treatment of prisoners. Ultimately, after much consultation and careful deliberation, the prison and quarry sites were selected.

Architectural drawings were supplied by L. W. Foster and Company of Des Moines and called for a 636-foot-by-933-foot structure that would eventually hold 500 prisoners. In 1873, work began. Although private contractors were initially used to build the stockade fence and erect temporary buildings, the idea from the beginning was to use inmate labor for the vast majority of the work, so that the state would never have to be at the mercy of contractors. The first permanent building was started in September 1873, with prisoners No. 7, D. J. Wie, and No. 14, Ed Sheridan, laying the first stone.

Despite the commissioners selecting a building site they considered to be healthy and well drained, quicksand—a major obstacle—was encountered while building the prison wall in the northwest corner of the grounds in 1882. It was too late to turn back, so a solution had to be devised. A pile driver was used to drive large timbers into the mire, until they reached bedrock. The timbers were driven as thick as they could stand, then sawed off. A 100-foot distance had to be dealt with in this way. A layer of cement was then poured across the top and the wall built on top of that.

Transporting and maneuvering such gigantic stones was not without risk. At least four inmates were killed in two separate construction accidents. By the beginning of World War II, major construction was largely complete. The "White Palace of the West" was a reality.

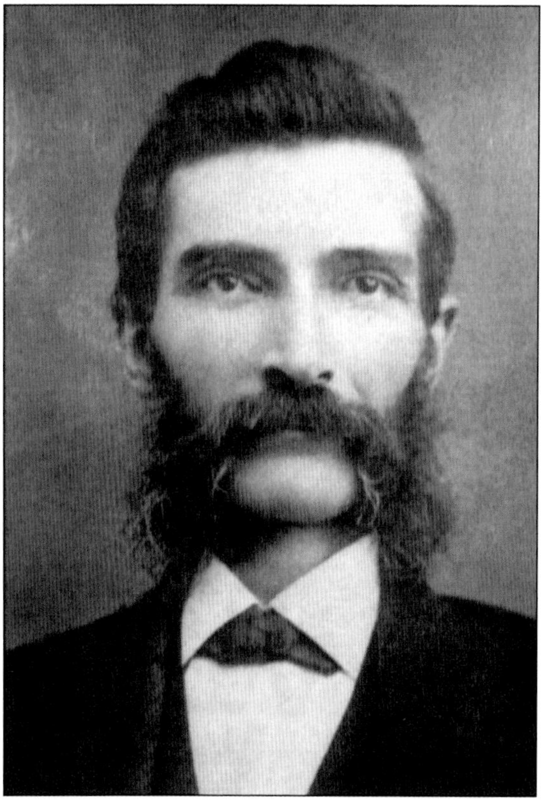

John McKean was born in Pennsylvania in 1835 and came to Iowa in 1854, where he was later elected to the Iowa Senate. He introduced the legislation that established the Additional Penitentiary at Anamosa. Later, when confronted by constituents about why he did not bring a college to the town instead, he prophetically explained that colleges close all the time, but prisons endure.

Believed to be the architect's early design, the drawing below appeared in the 1872 Andreas Atlas. While the final design contained many differences, several features in this rendering became reality. The warden's residence/administration building is much the same, but without the front portico. The center building (behind the warden's residence), the water tower in the center of the yard, and Shop No. 1 (far left corner) can be seen in the eventual construction.

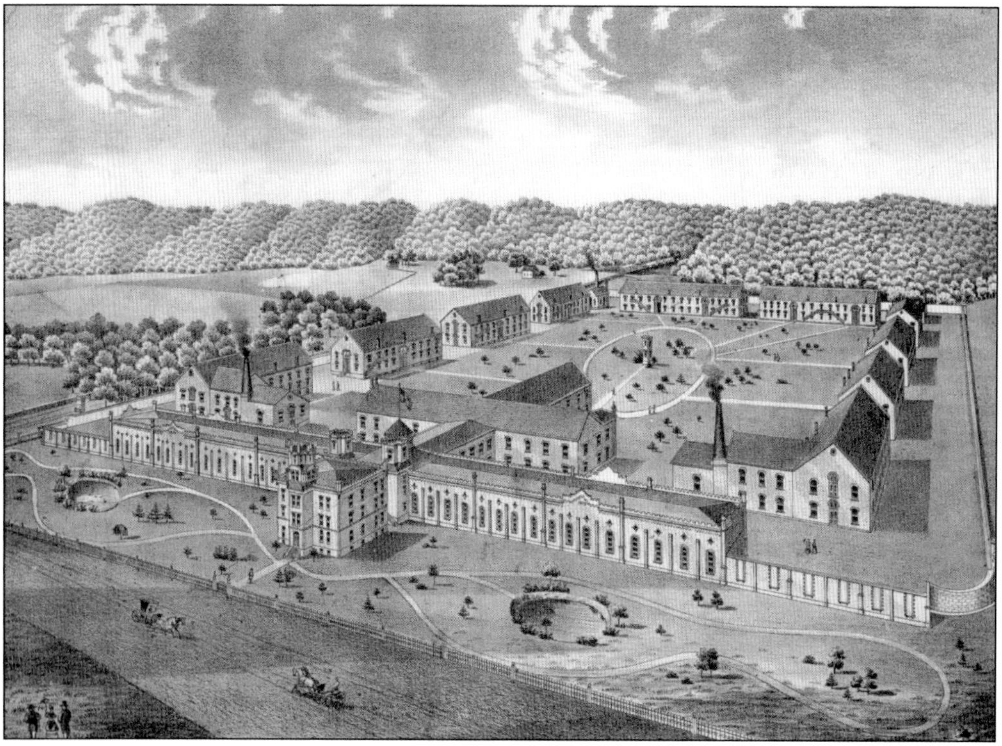

This 1875 photograph is the oldest known image of the Additional Penitentiary. The small building with the circular window held the wooden cells that housed the first inmates. The inmates then constructed Shop No.1, the largest building. By January 1875, the roof was completed, and within a year the building housed the dining hall, kitchen, chapel, and 81 stone cells. (Courtesy Paul C. Juhl Collection SHSI.)

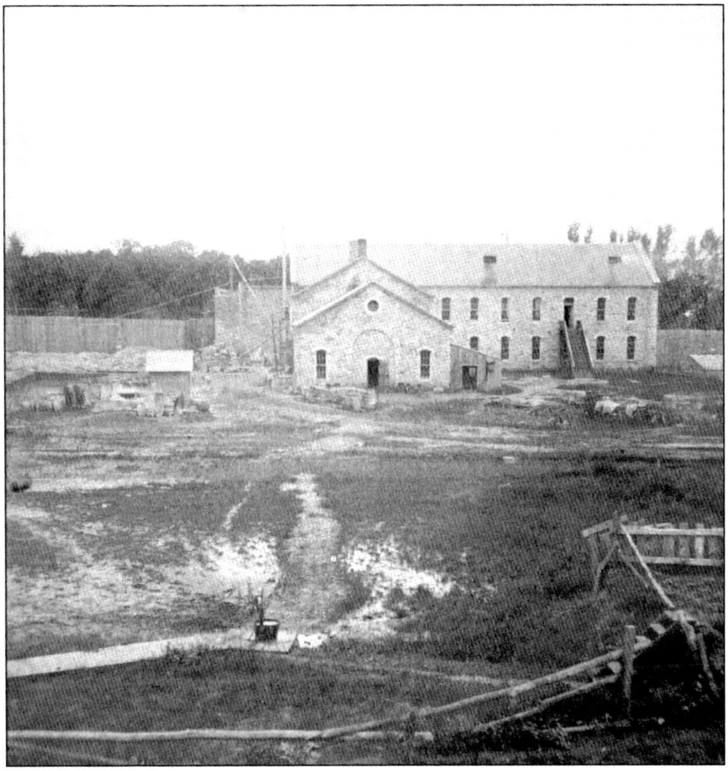

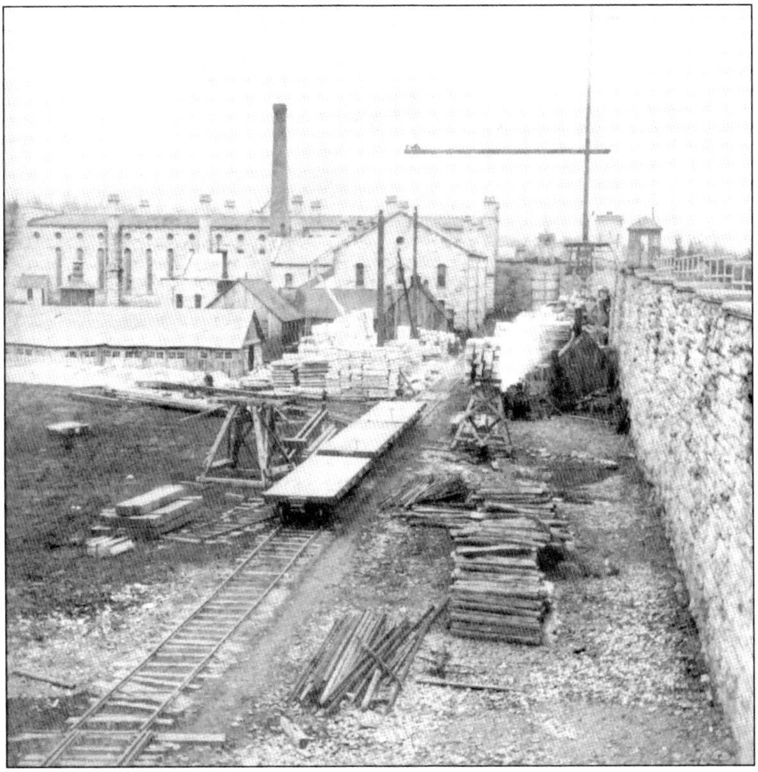

This early 1880s image looks east from the west wall. The south cell house (far background) that opened in 1881 appears complete. The long building (foreground left) is the stone cutting shop.

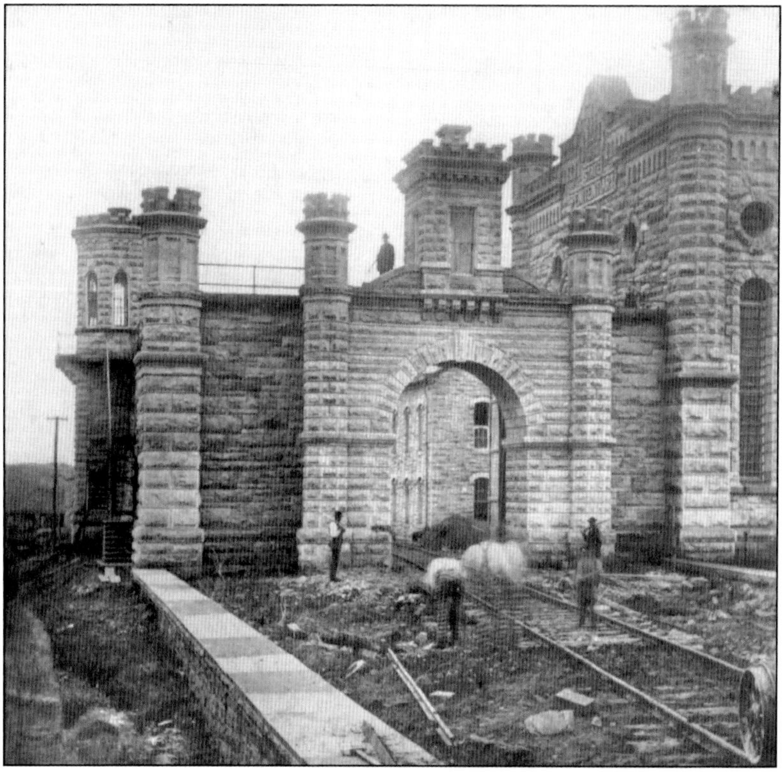

This early 1880s image shows construction in front of the east train gate. The south cell house on the right appears to be finished, but the insane hospital and the female department are not started. The gate into the prison is wide open, but a close examination of the photograph reveals at least three guns being held by the staff to maintain security.

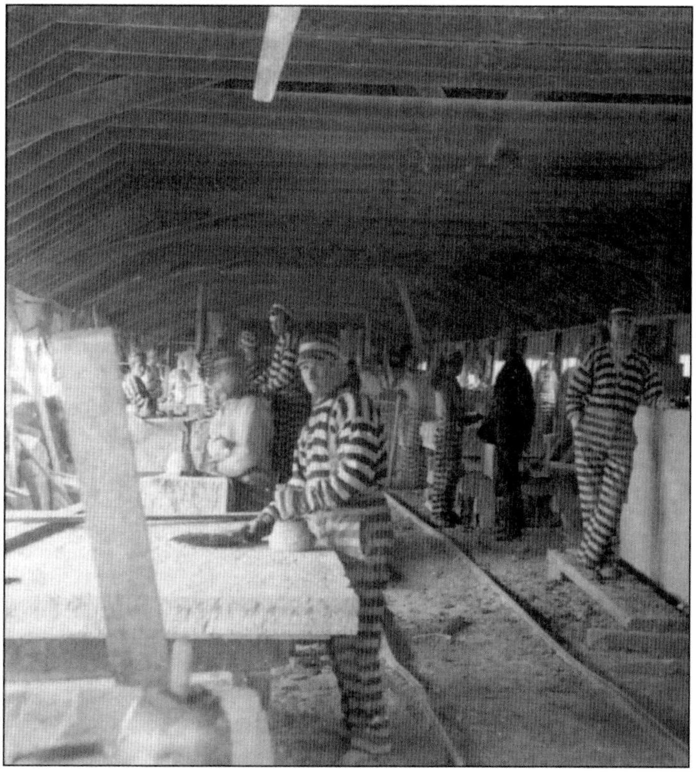

The interior of the stone cutting shop was busy even during the winter months. Large blocks of stone were brought to the workers by a rail cart that was pushed along the tracks in the floor. Heavy stone mallets helped chisel the stone into the proper shape.

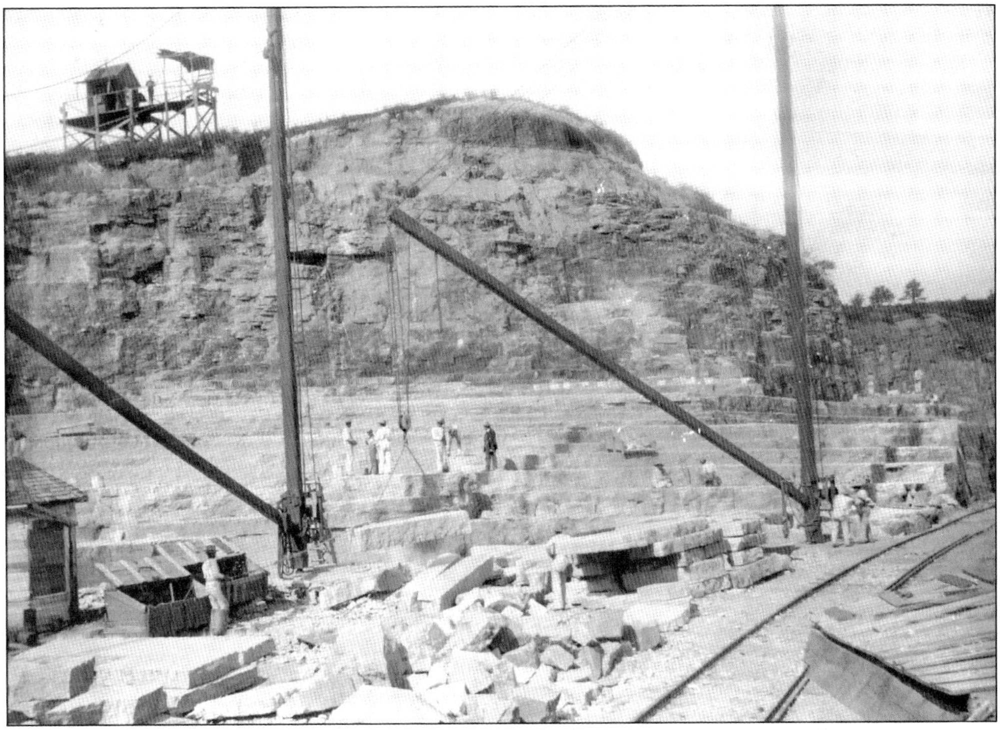

The penitentiary was located in Anamosa primarily due to its proximity to the stone quarries near Stone City. A rail line transported the stone and the inmate workers, the latter by handcars or by walking along the tracks. Crews of 50 or more workers went to the quarry daily. The large cranes lifted the blocks of stone, while gun guards supervised from the hill above.

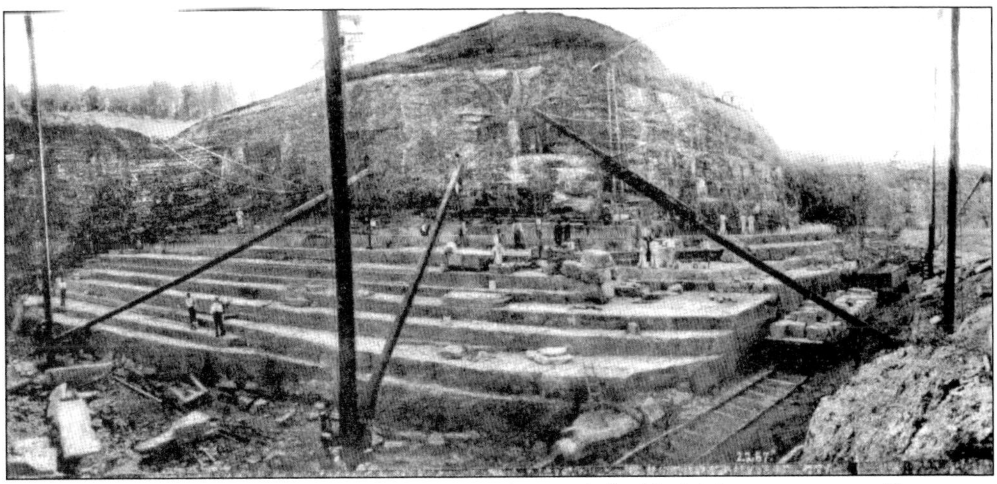

The stone quarried in the Anamosa area is a soft, evenly bedded dolomite, a type of limestone popular for construction.

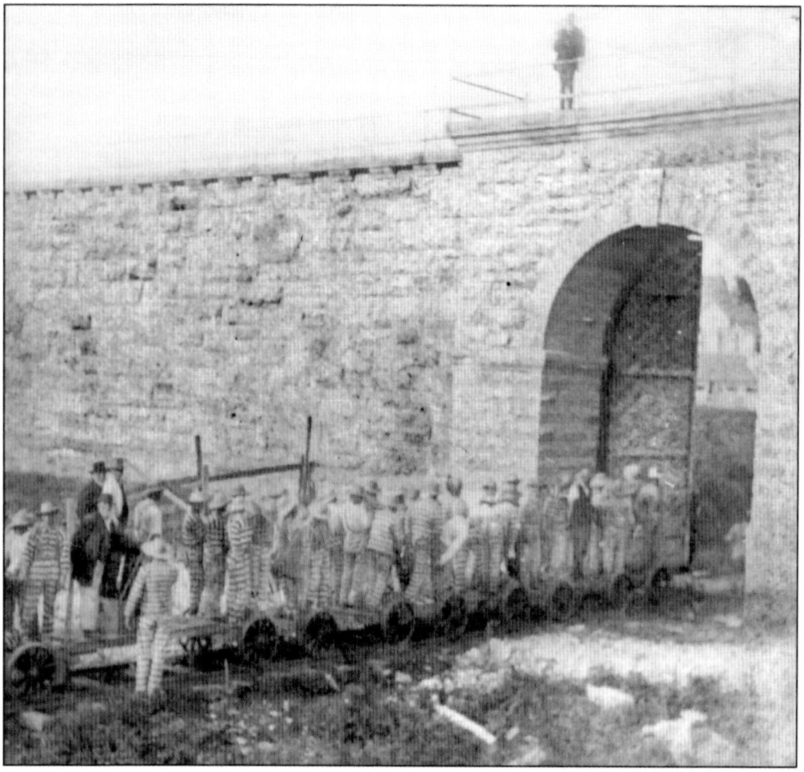

The work crew from the quarry enters the west train gate in this *c.* 1880s image. Over 50 workers went to the quarry and back each day, some by handcars and some walking. The walkers left first so that both groups arrived at their destination at about the same time. (Courtesy Ernie Rairdin.)

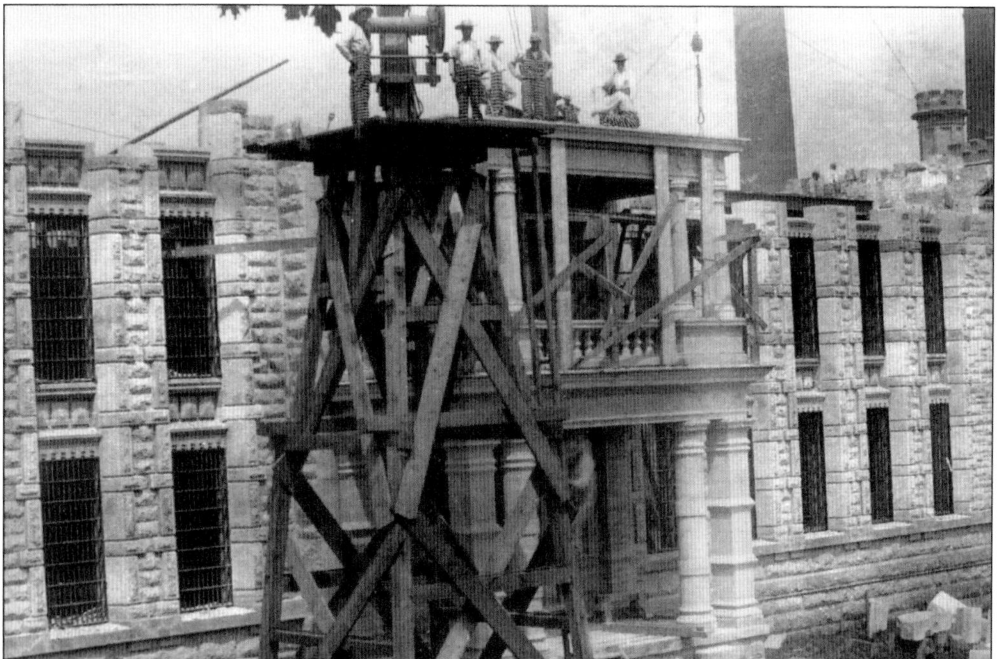

In this photograph, workers have completed the first two floors of the female department building, and by 1891, will have the third floor and the roof finished. Three inmates fell to their deaths while constructing this building. (Courtesy Cecilia Hatcher.)

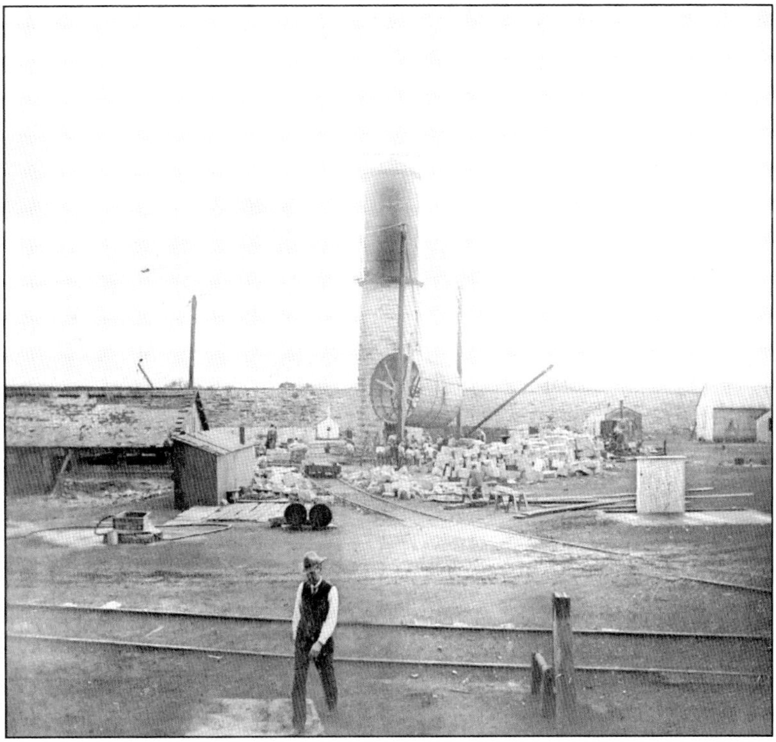

A guard walks across the yard while construction continues in the background. The stone cutting shed is on the left and the west wall stretches across the back. Shop No. 2 is not yet built, which dates this image prior to 1903. Note the water tower in the center of the yard.

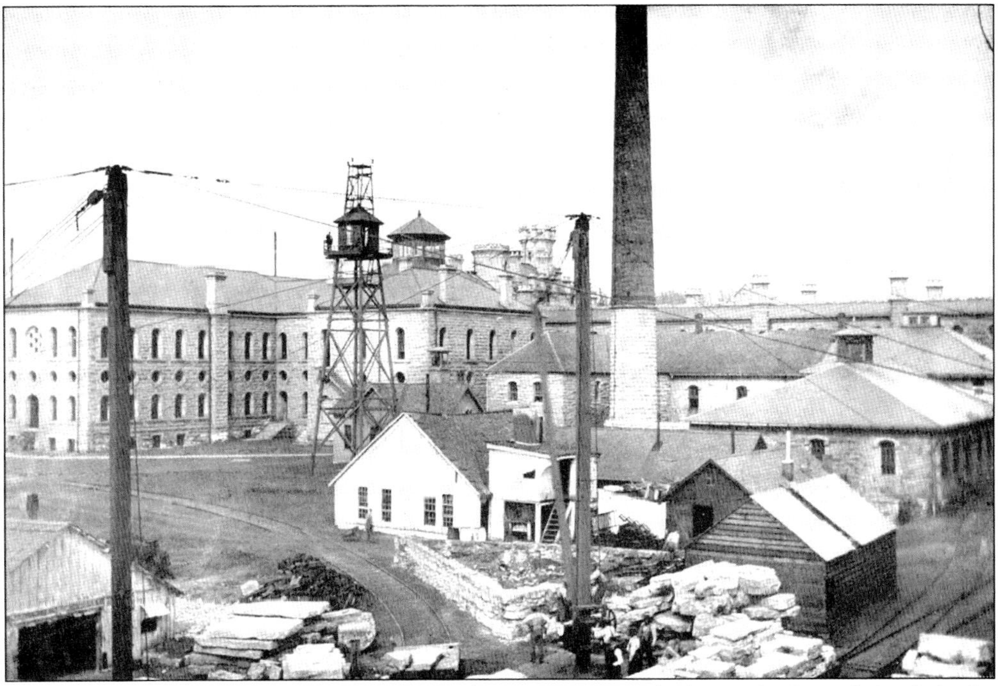

Stone cutting dominated the yard in 1901. The stone cutting shed is at the lower left, while the remaining wooden sheds included the foundry and blacksmith shop. Cables support the gin pole cranes that were used to move blocks of stone. The tall tower at center was occupied by an armed guard when the inmates were out of their cells.

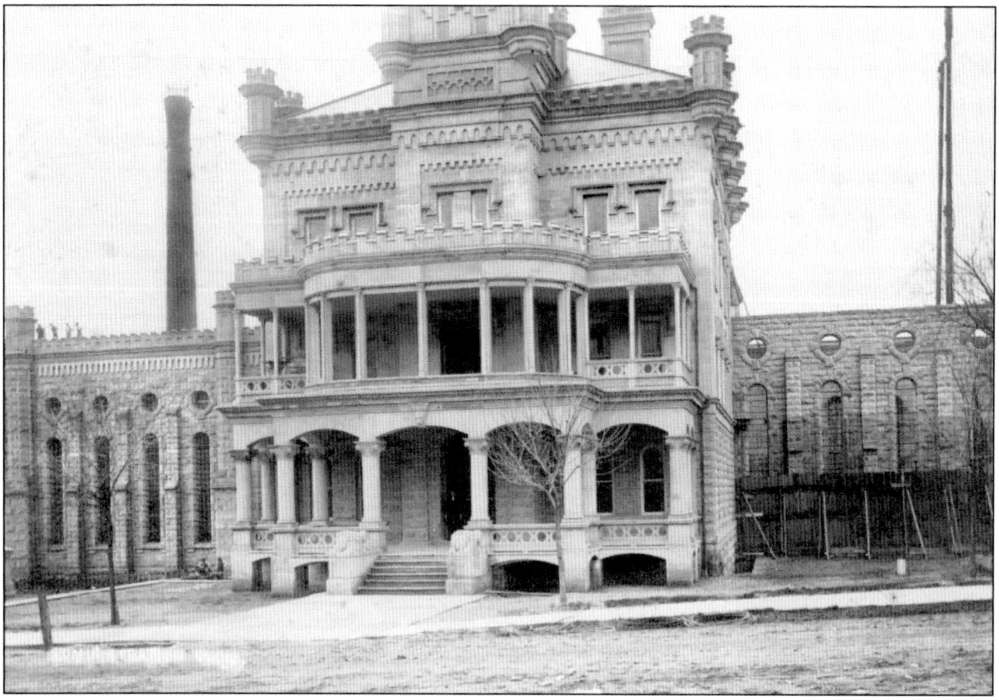

The warden's residence/administration building appears complete. To the right, one can see that the roof is not yet on the north cell house, which dates this image prior to 1904. Note the wooden stockade used to contain the inmate workers.

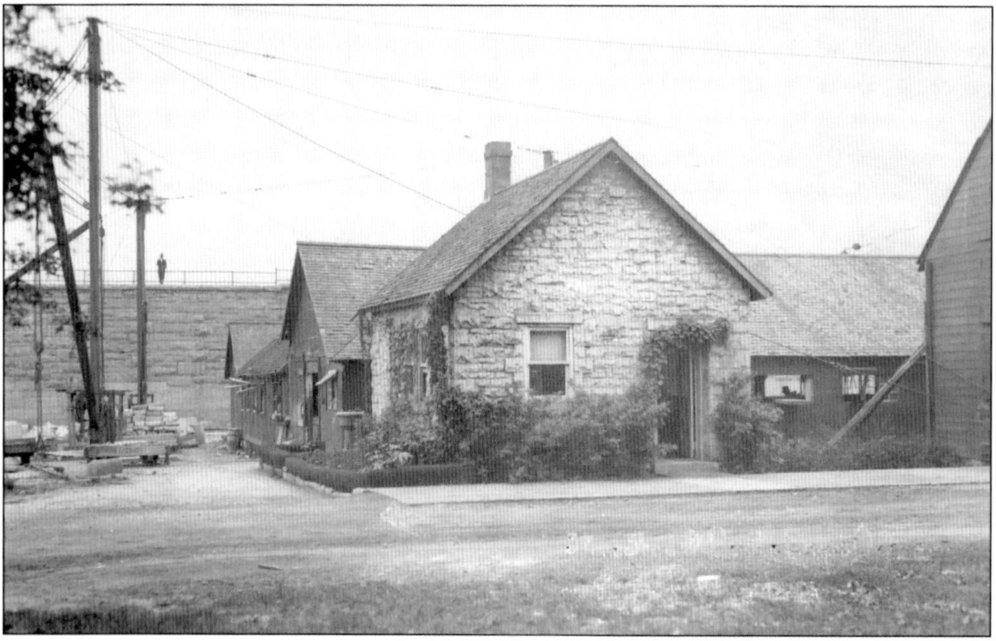

In 1903, stone cutting was moved to the northwest corner of the yard and an effort was made to reduce clutter in the prison. The small stone building was the engineer's office, with the stone cutting shed just behind. To the left are the cranes that lifted the stone and the cables that held them up.

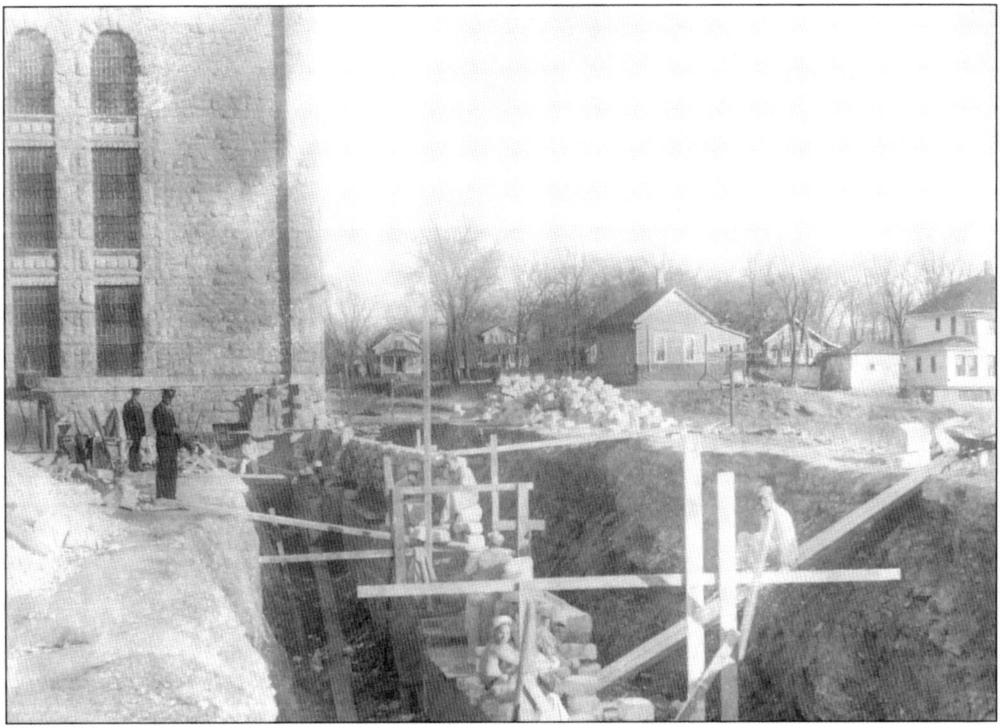

The foundation of the new cell house extends almost 20 feet into the ground and appears to be at least four feet thick in this 1930s image. This would be enough to discourage anyone thinking of tunneling to freedom.

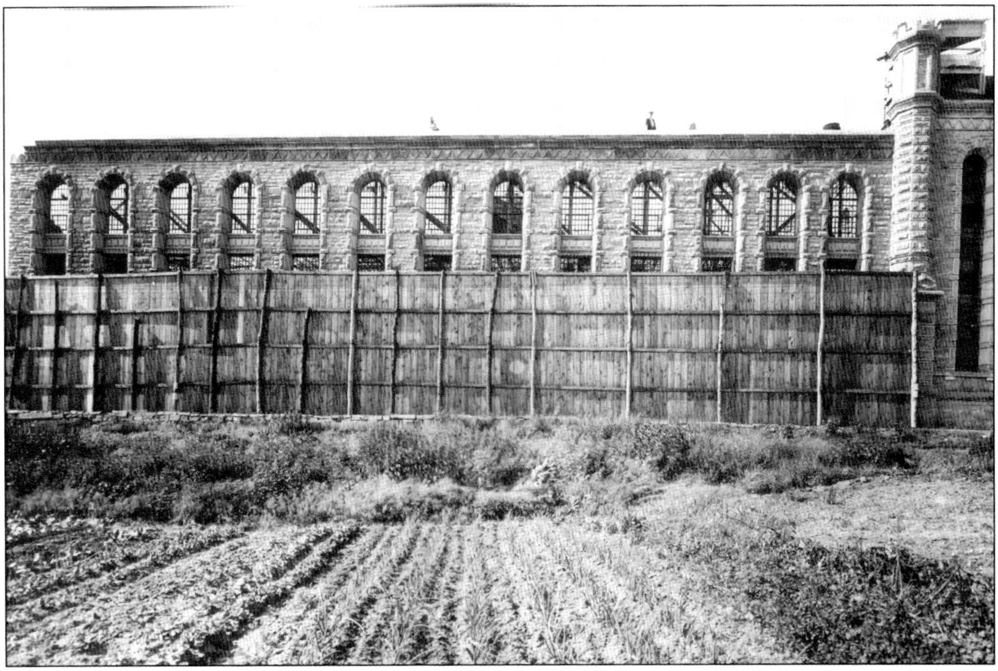

This view from a garden south of the prison shows the cell house before the roof is started. The garden is next to private homes, illustrating how close older prisons often were to residential areas.

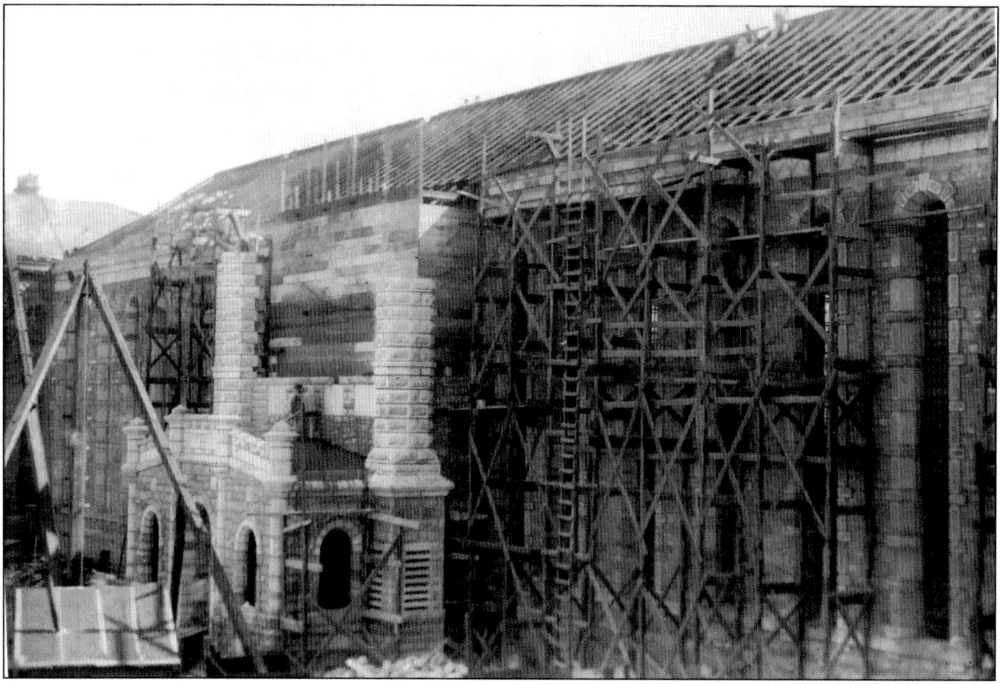

The complexity of building a new cell house is readily apparent in this photograph. The stone used is not just a facing, it is the actual structure of the building.

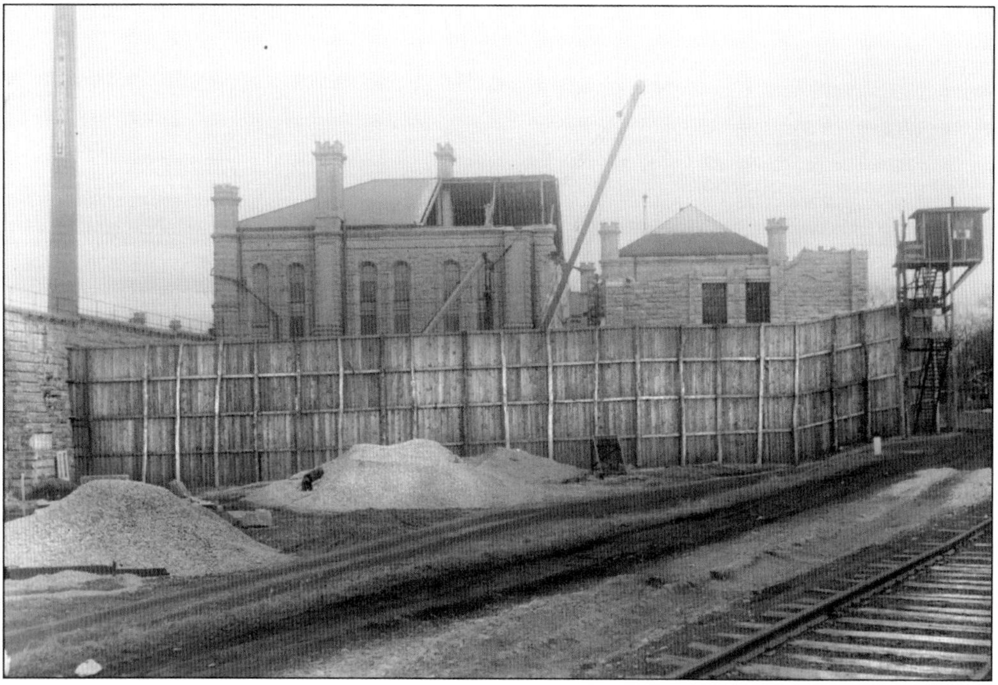

In the late 1930s, the old hospital (on the left) was being dismantled to make room for the new hospital, which is on the right. Mentally ill prisoners were moved to cells in the vacated female department building while construction was completed. Note the 20-foot high stockade and guard tower used to contain the workers.

Two

The Keepers

Criminals and their crimes grab the headlines and our attention, but the ordinary, hardworking men and women who manage the criminals get very little of either. Nonetheless, they are the backbone of any correctional facility. They make sure the food is cooked, the laundry cleaned, and the roof patched. They enforce discipline to ensure a safe environment for everyone. But perhaps one of their most important duties is an intangible one—serving as a role model of law-abiding behavior for the inmates under their authority.

Because of this, prisons have always been interested in hiring staff who display good moral and ethical conduct in their professional and personal lives. An employment application from the late 1880s states that the applicant "is . . . expected to conduct himself when on duty, as well as when off duty, in such a way that he will inspire in the prisoners sentiments of respect for his own moral principles and character."

Until fairly recently, prison work was a man's game. Female employees were few and relegated to lesser roles such as teacher or organist (the exception being the matron who managed the female department—even so, she answered to the warden). Arguably one of the most significant changes in modern prisons has been the dramatic integration of female employees into all facets of institutional operation, including "guards" (now referred to as "correctional officers") and prison administration.

The stress of prison work takes its toll on the individual. Career prison workers have a life expectancy disturbingly shorter than the average American. Yet, contrary to popular opinion, a properly run prison is, physically anyway, a relatively safe place to work. Nonetheless, several Anamosa staff have been murdered in the line of duty over the years, and to these public servants we owe a debt of gratitude.

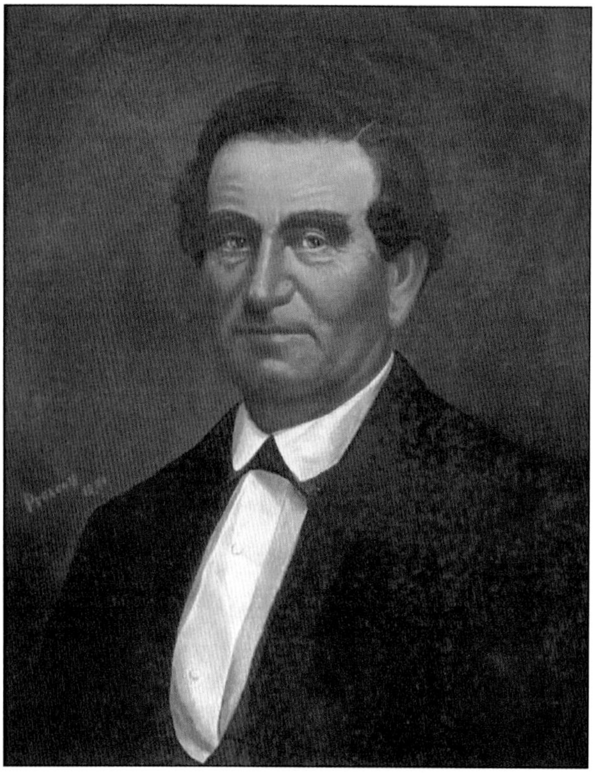

A painting of Martin Heisey, the penitentiary's first warden, is shown here. Before working at Anamosa, he served as warden at the Fort Madison Penitentiary. He was later appointed to the three-member board of commissioners that established the Additional Penitentiary at Anamosa.

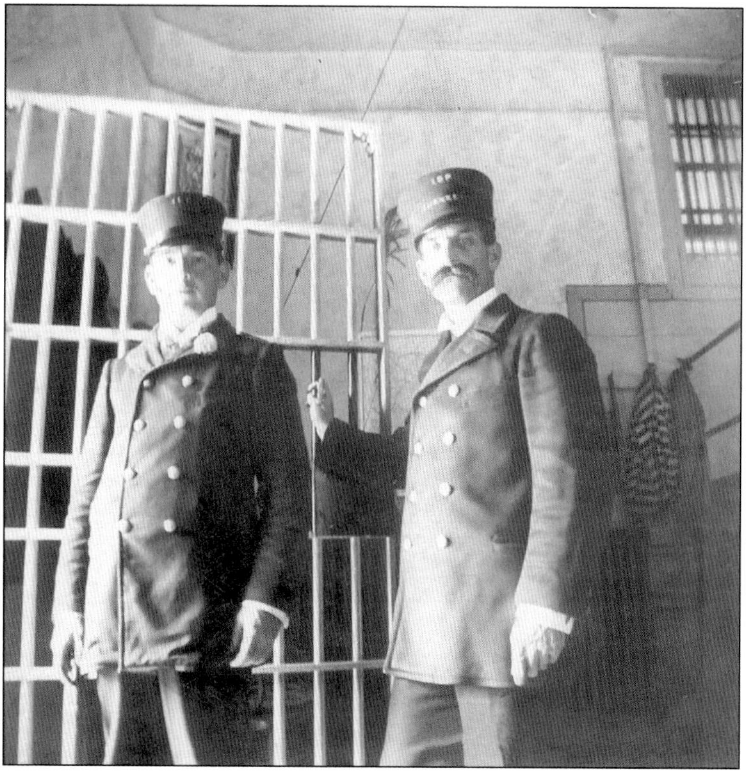

E. M. Cowen (right) was a guard for almost nine years between 1884 and 1893. At the time this photograph was taken, he was the day turnkey at the main entrance of the prison.

Aretus Francis Loomis was a guard at Anamosa from 1896 until 1904. He was a Civil War veteran who served with the New York State Volunteers. He saw action at Gettysburg, was captured at Spotsylvania, and survived four months at the infamous Andersonville Prison. (Courtesy of the Loomis family.)

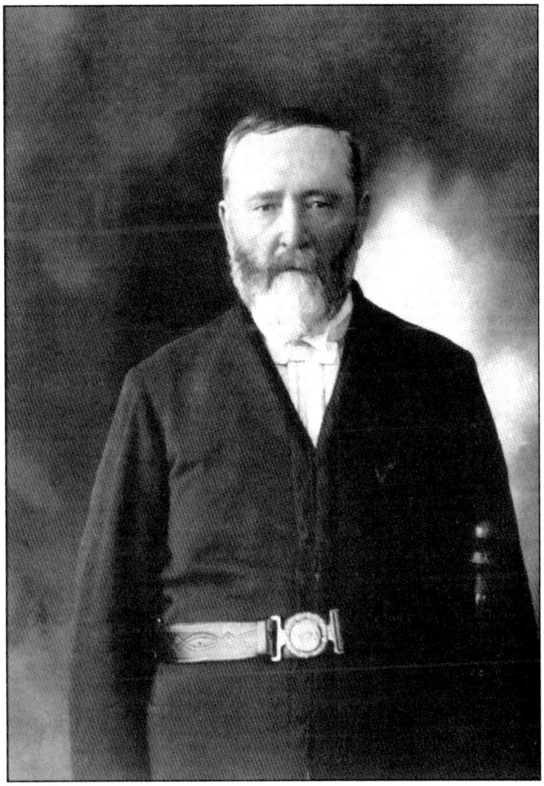

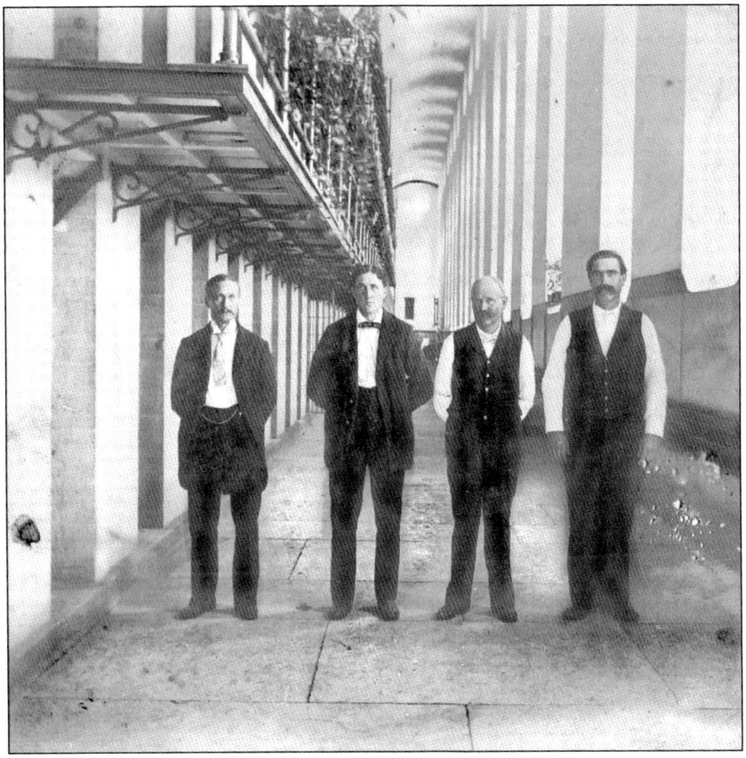

Staff pose in the south cell house, completed in 1881. The large flagstones comprising the floor resulted in the ground floor commonly being referred to as "the Flag." Over a century of foot traffic caused noticeable hollowing of the stone in the most-used areas.

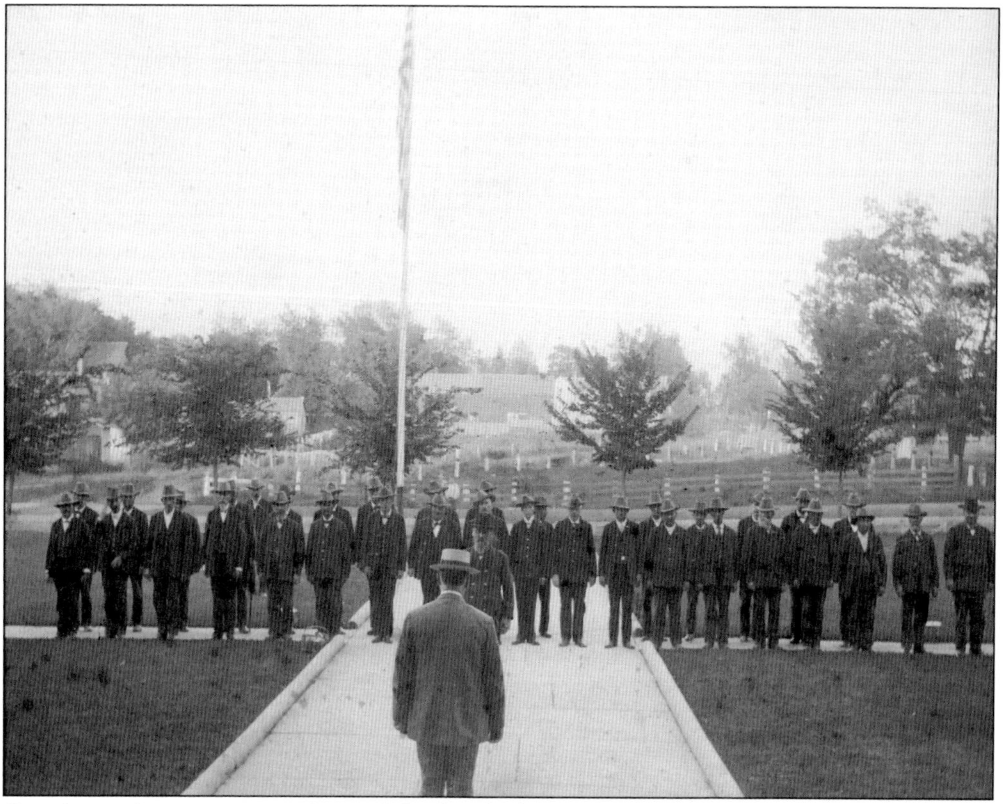

Guards stand at attention in front of the female department building in this 1899 photograph. The man with his back to the camera is likely warden William A. Hunter. For several years the warden's office was located in this building until the warden's residence/administration building was completed in 1903.

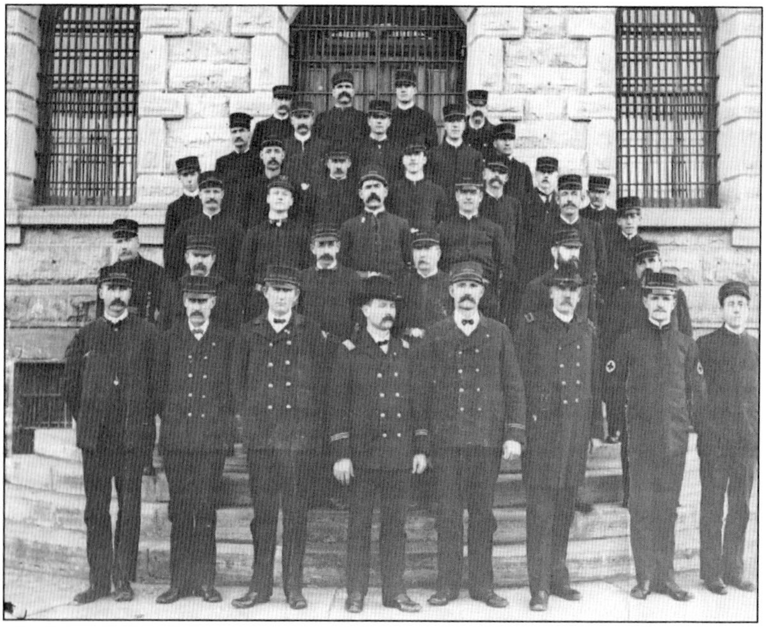

The staff stands outside of the west door of the dining hall in 1903.

William A. Hubbard was employed at Anamosa from 1900 until 1909 and for one year served as the day turnkey, responsible for allowing or denying admittance through the front entrance. His son, Ernest Hubbard, would later hold the same position during his long tenure at the prison. (Courtesy Deb Miller.)

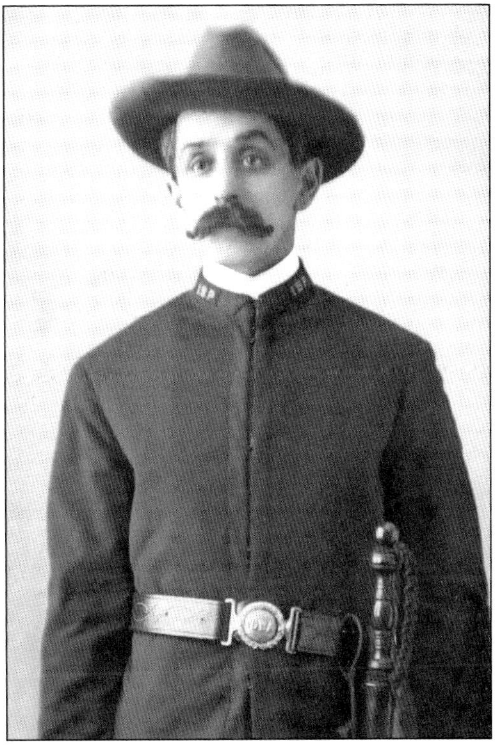

Warden John Baumel interviews an inmate in the 1920s photograph below.

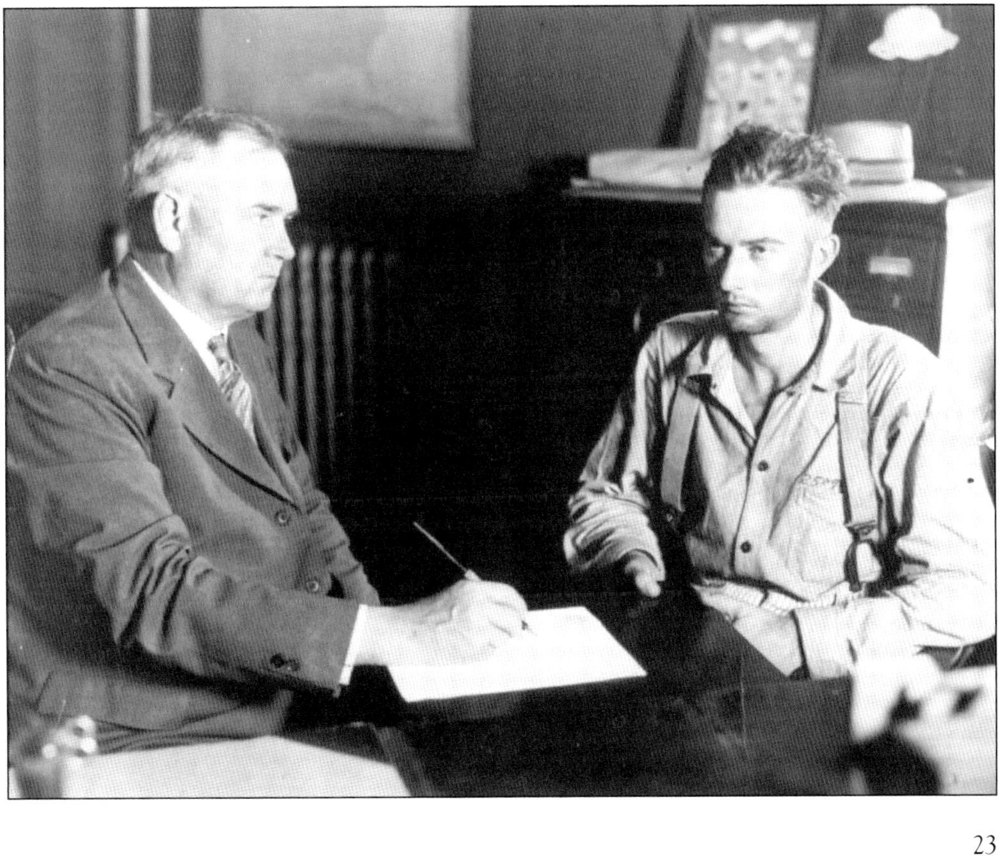

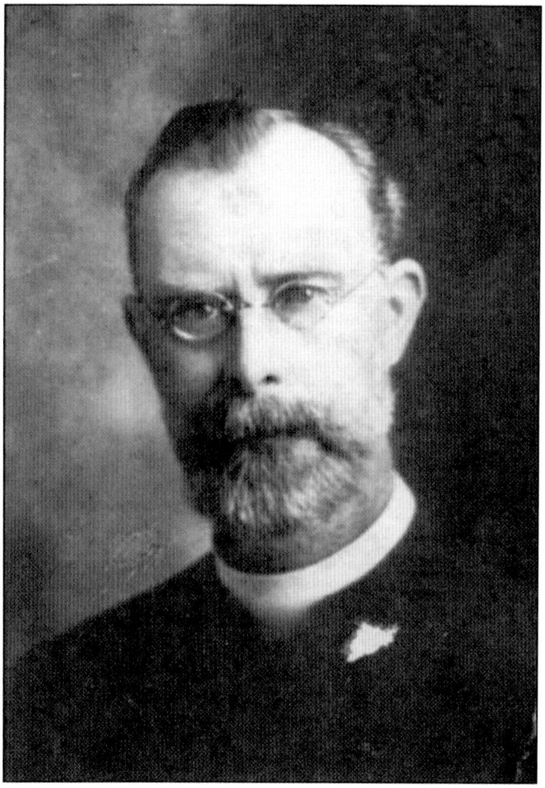

Felix Pickworth was a chaplain from 1901 until 1915. In 1902, the warden reported that, in addition to his religious work, Rev. Pickworth was in charge of the library, the school, the printing office, and the bindery. He also supervised the *Prison Press*, the inmate newspaper started in 1898 by a previous chaplain. The printing shop was first started to print the newspaper and continues to the present as an Iowa Prison Industry shop.

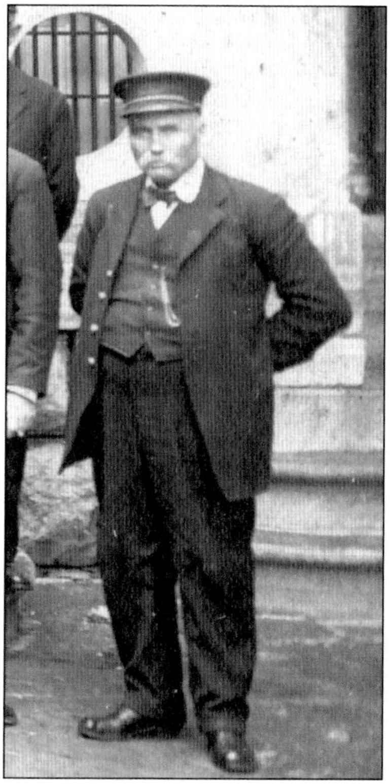

Martin McCarty was probably the longest-serving employee in the history of the Anamosa prison. Most of his career was spent as a gun guard, stationed on the wall where he shot at least two inmates in the line of duty. During his last four years he was the usher, touring visitors through the prison. He broke his hip at age 83 and retired after 49 years of service.

Female employees were rare in 1911 when this photograph was taken. Female department matron Anna Tremon (center) is flanked by night supervisor Mrs. J. D. McCarn (left) and stenographer Rose Fleisher.

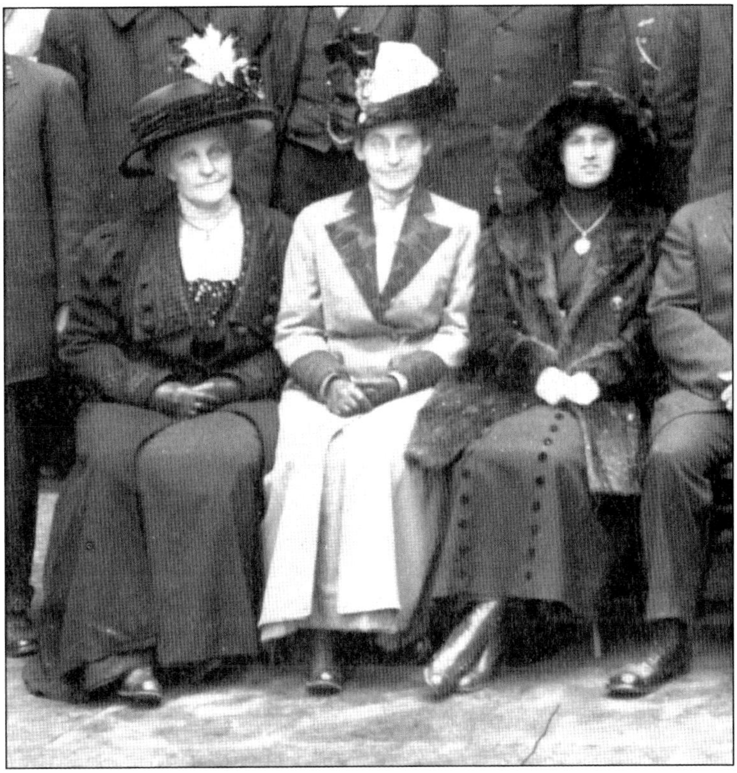

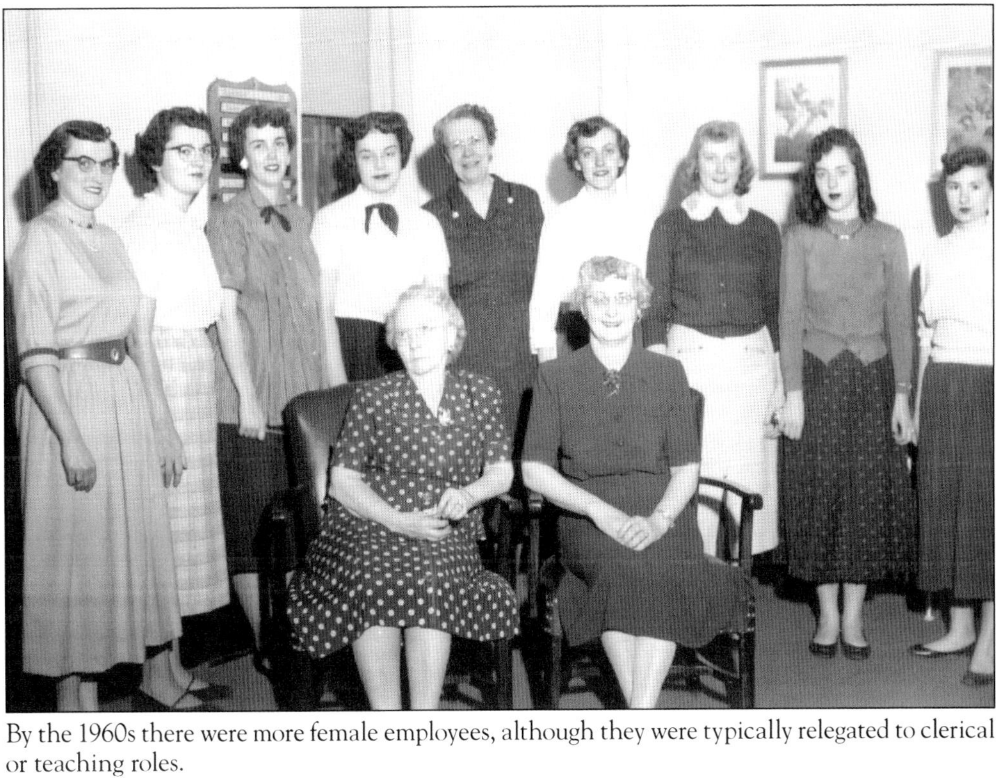

By the 1960s there were more female employees, although they were typically relegated to clerical or teaching roles.

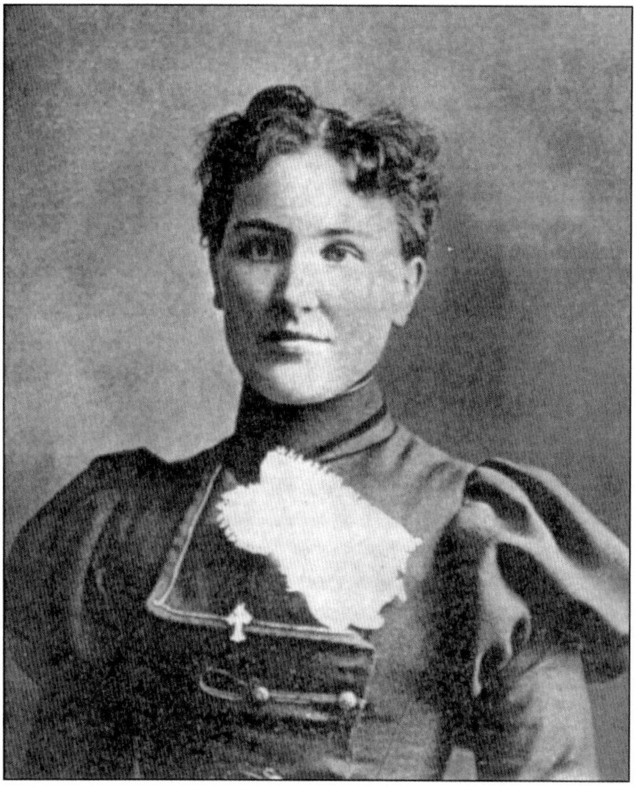

Angie Waterman was matron of the female department from 1898 to 1904. Her philosophy was expressed by the following: "Usually a woman convict is considered one of the lowest of God's creatures—if, in truth, she is supposed to belong to Him at all—for it is a well-known fact that society always considers a fallen woman a thousand times more depraved and contemptible than the self-same character of the masculine gender."

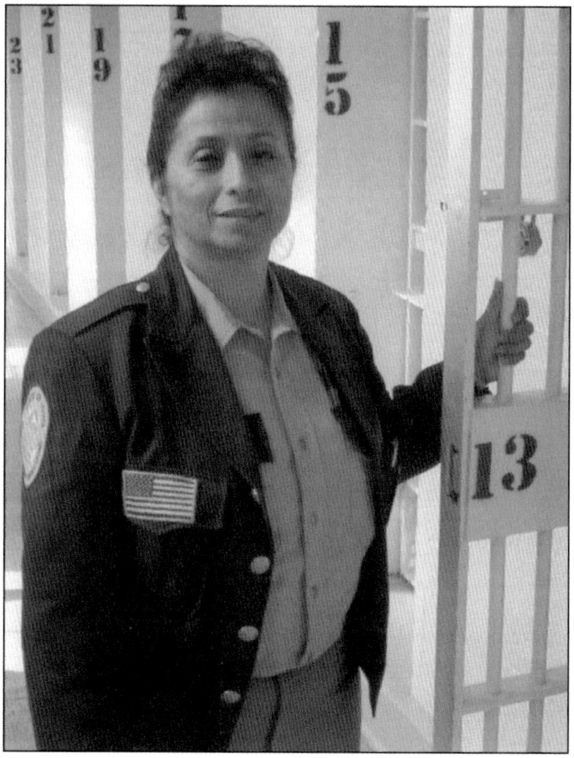

Female correctional officers became more common by the 1990s. Today, women serve in supervisory roles, something unheard of in the early days.

A guards' room located adjacent to the entrance of what is now known as Living Unit B. Completed in about 1932, this is the largest cell house in use at Anamosa.

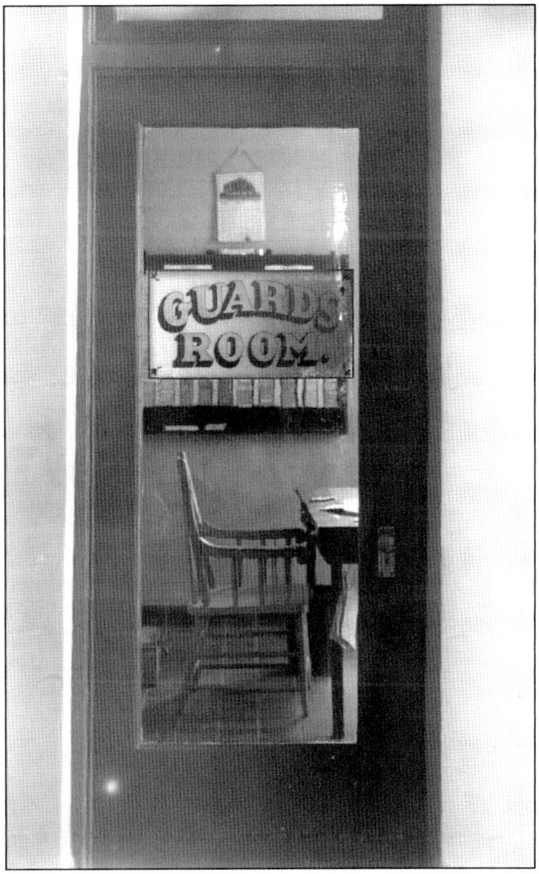

Basking in his young daughter's admiring smile, guard Roy Kellogg (below) is ready to walk to work. Two of his daughters would eventually work at the reformatory, and one is now married to a correctional officer. Kellogg eventually supervised several Prison Industries shops during his 25-year career at the prison. (Courtesy the Kellogg family.)

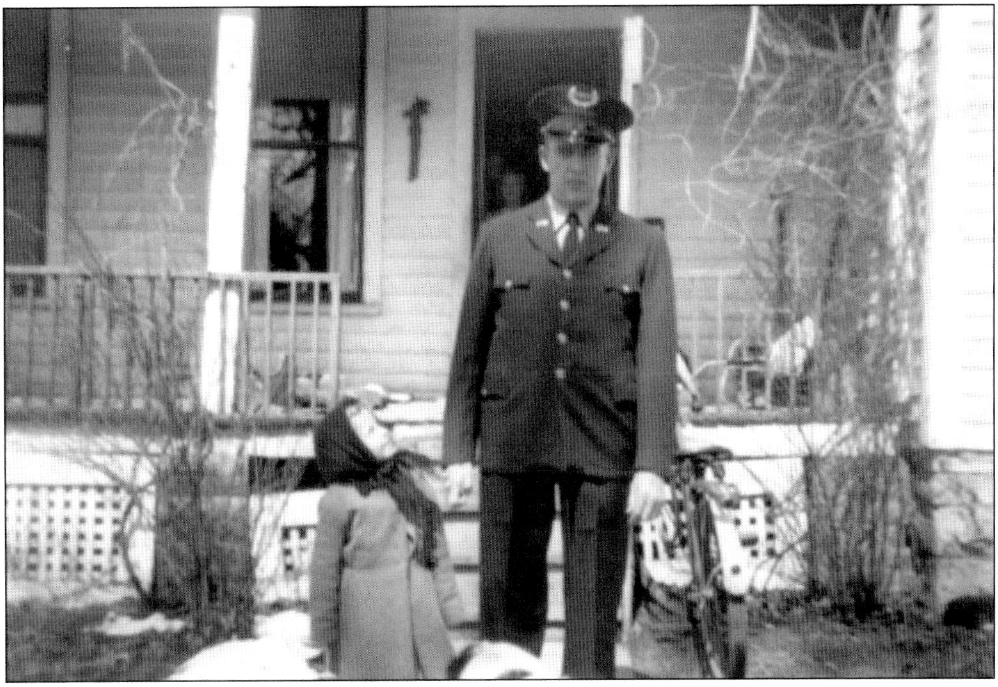

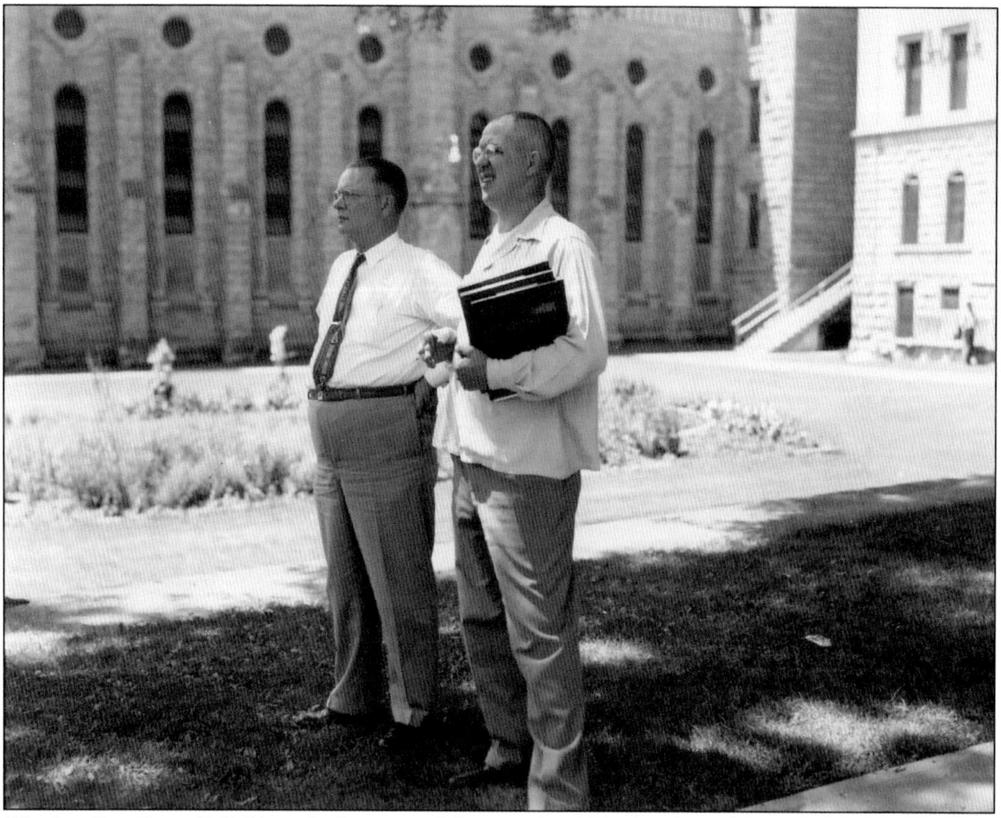

Warden Ray Purcell (left) and educational director Paul Wieler shared an interest in improving the educational programs in the late 1950s. Purcell, a guard who moved up the ranks, and Wieler, a former local public school principal, oversaw the accreditation of the school.

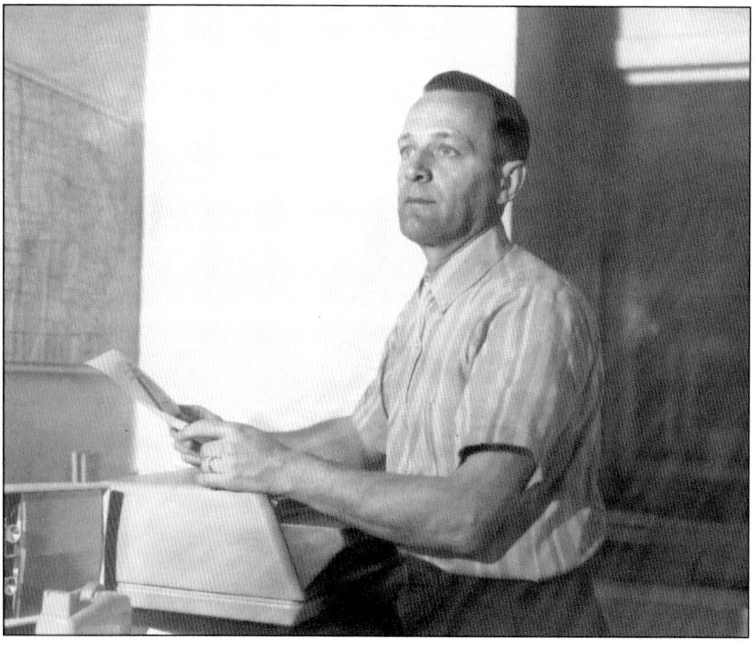

Max Fliehler, left, taught in the local school district until he went to work at the reformatory in 1955. A teacher, administrator, and educational counselor in the prison school, Fliehler was also the staff consultant for the *Hawkeye*, an inmate magazine that was published for many years. Two of his sons followed him into correctional careers. He retired in 1987.

Bill Jensen and Merle Buckner, right, stand at the door of the dining hall in this 1957 picture. It would be several more years before guards would be called correctional officers and they would no longer have to provide their own uniforms.

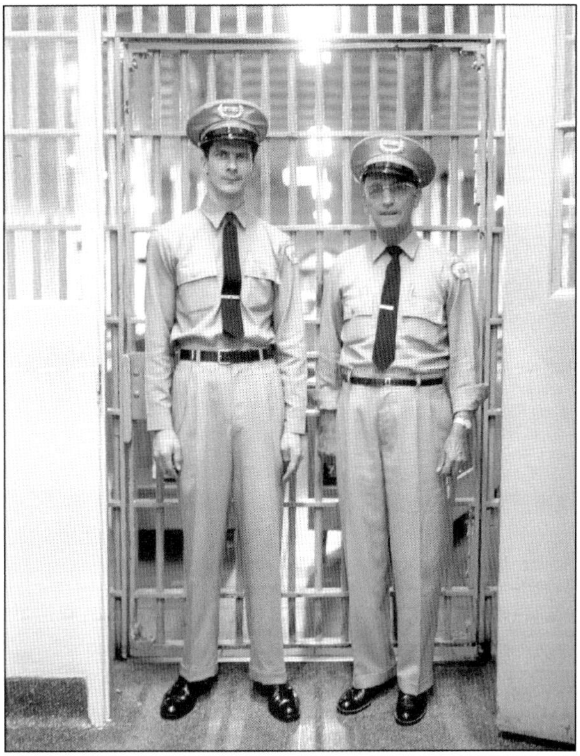

Josephine Rees, below, started teaching basic classes in 1966 after retiring from public school teaching. She worked well with lower functioning students and was a strong advocate for educational programs. When she started at the reformatory, many thought she was the first woman to work with male inmates, but that honor goes to 1880s teacher and chaplain Anna C. Merrill.

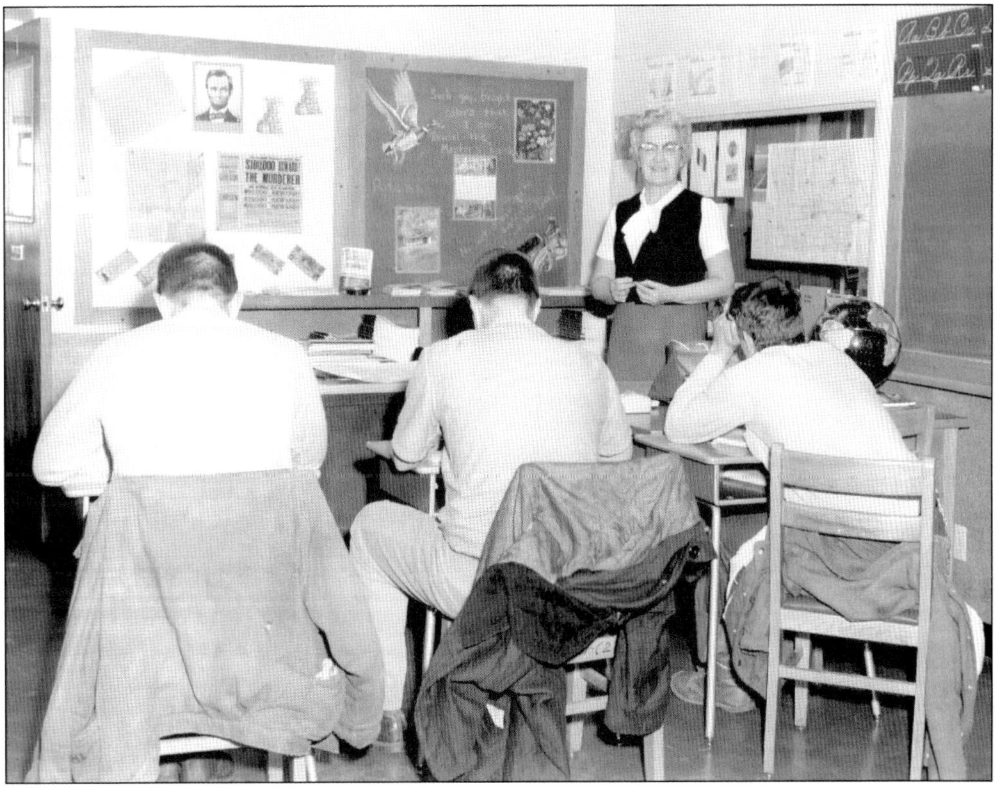

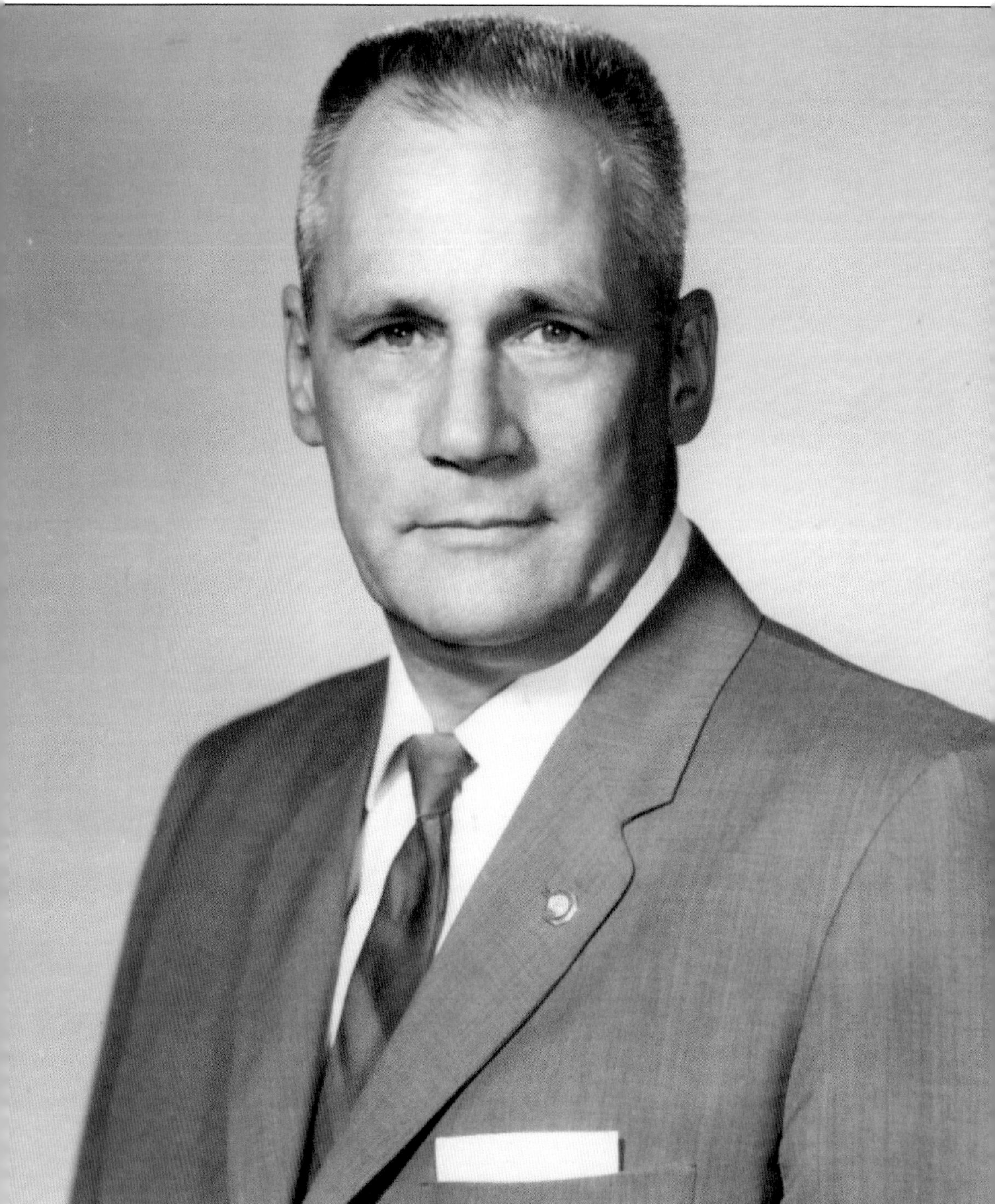

Charles Haugh was appointed warden in 1965. Having retired from a long career in prison security with the Federal Department of Corrections, many expected that a recent emphasis on treatment programs at Anamosa might end. Despite his security background, Warden Haugh introduced some of the most extensive improvements in treatment programming ever seen at Anamosa.

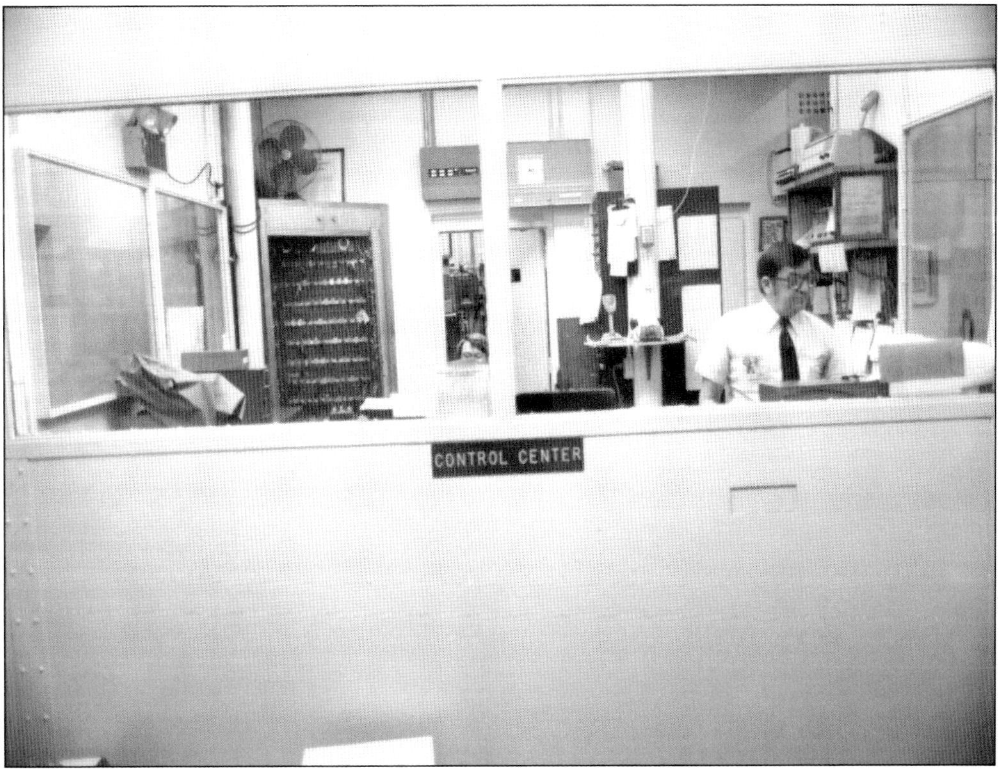

Above, correctional officer Robert Fulwider works in the control center in this undated photograph. The control center operates the pedestrian entrance to the prison, issues keys, operates the switchboard, and monitors security equipment. In past years, before the county sheriff's office operated on a 24-hour schedule, the control center also dispatched local police, fire, and ambulance services as well as monitored local burglar alarms.

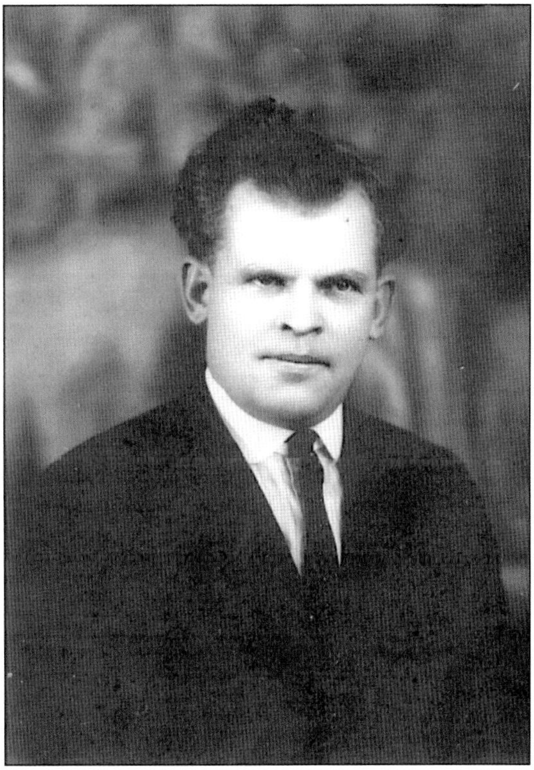

J. August Pearson, right, oversaw prison construction from 1920 until 1943, working under the supervision of the Iowa state architect. Pearson also supervised convict work crews in the construction of stone arch bridges that still remain in the Wapsipinicon State Park located adjacent to the city of Anamosa. During his tenure, several shop buildings, a large hospital, and a large cell house were constructed.

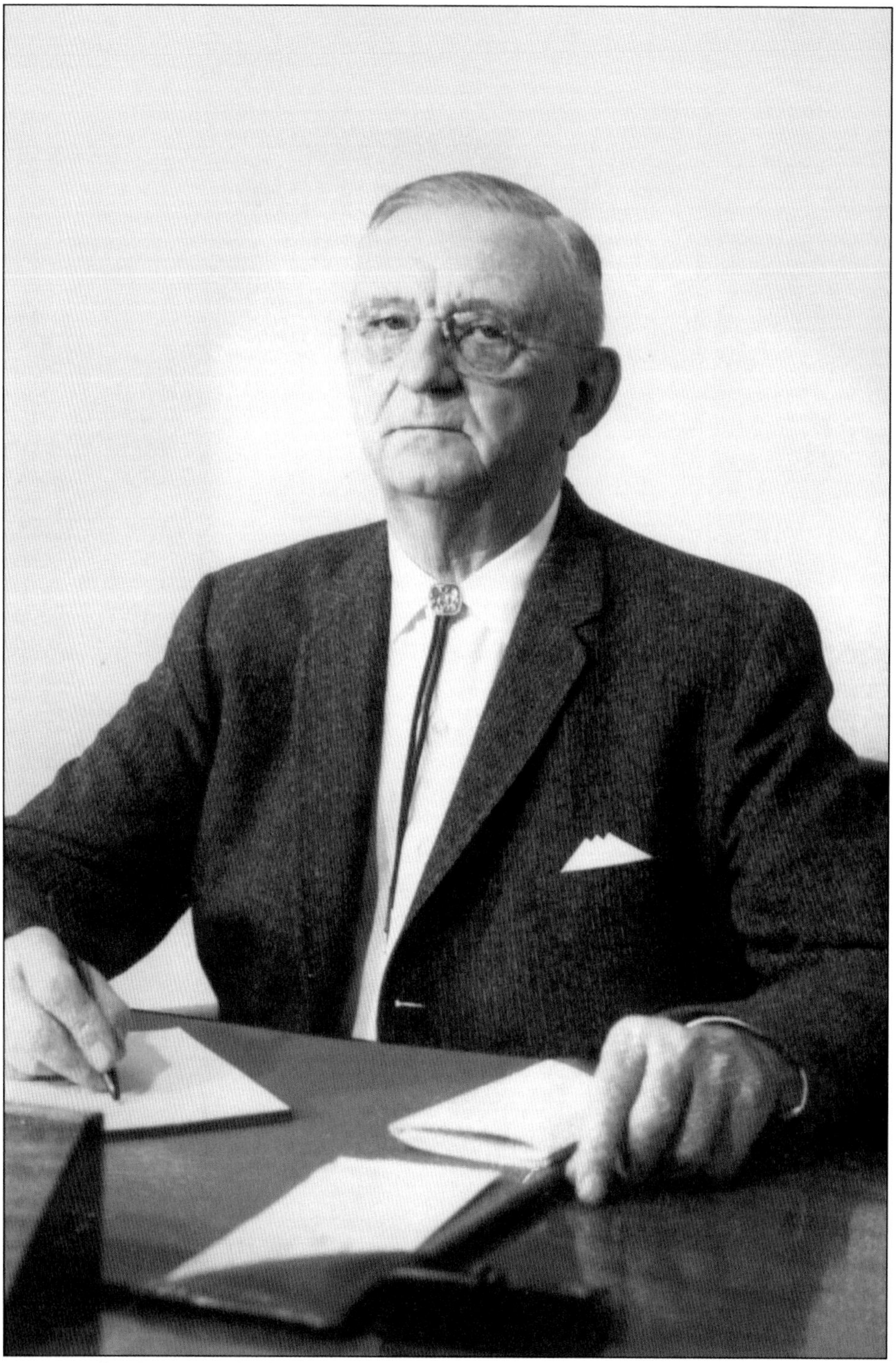

Deputy warden Roy Smith (known as "Pappy" behind his back) started as a guard in 1917. He progressed through the ranks, eventually serving as deputy warden his last 12 years before retiring in 1964. He was a stern disciplinarian who almost never missed work and rarely delegated authority.

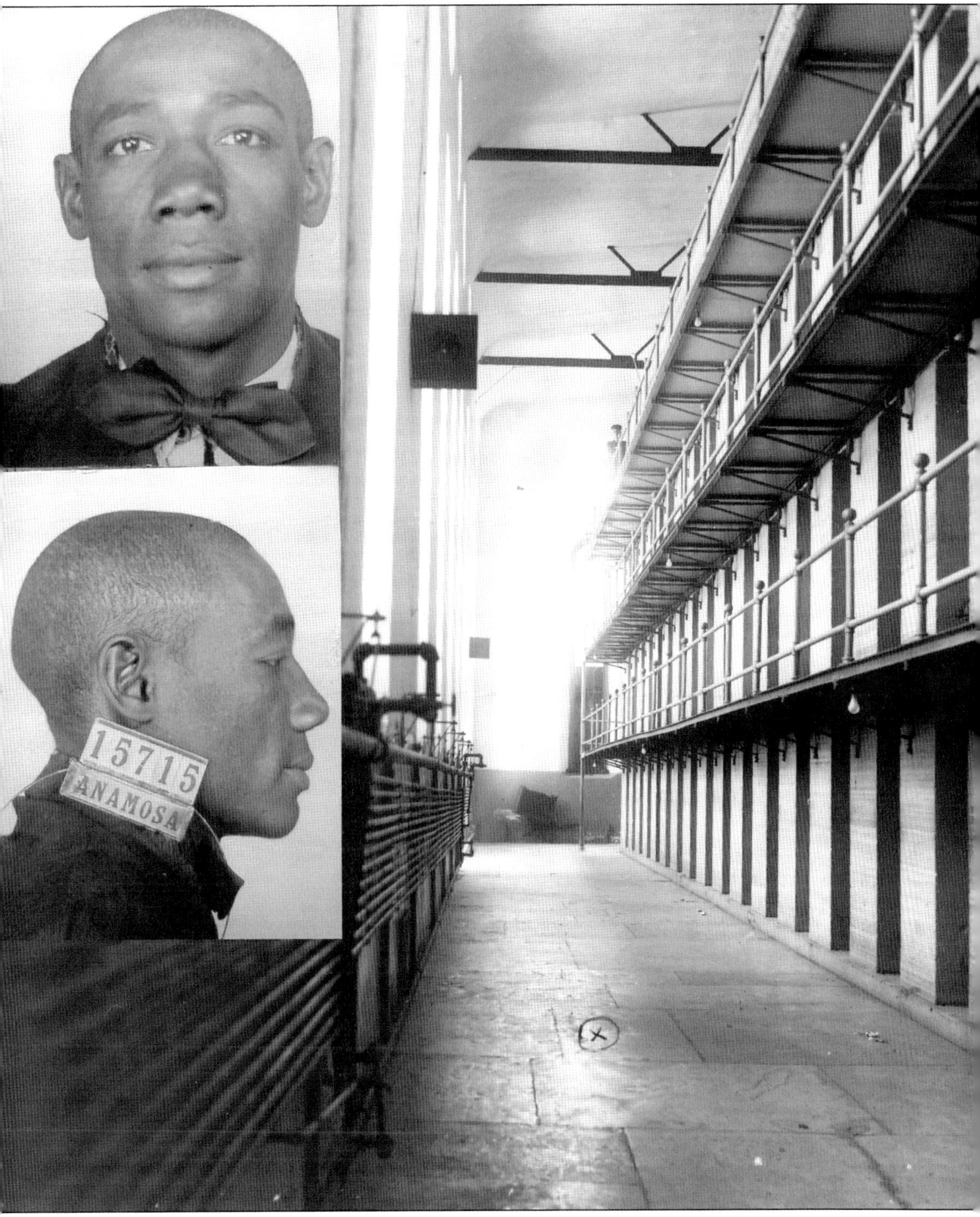

In January 1936, veteran guard Charles E. Strickel was removing inmate Richard Renicks from a cell in the south cell house when Renicks struck the officer and threw him over the gallery railing to his death. This photograph dates from the incident, with a mark showing where the officer landed on The Flag. Renicks, well-behaved prior to the attack, is pictured on the left.

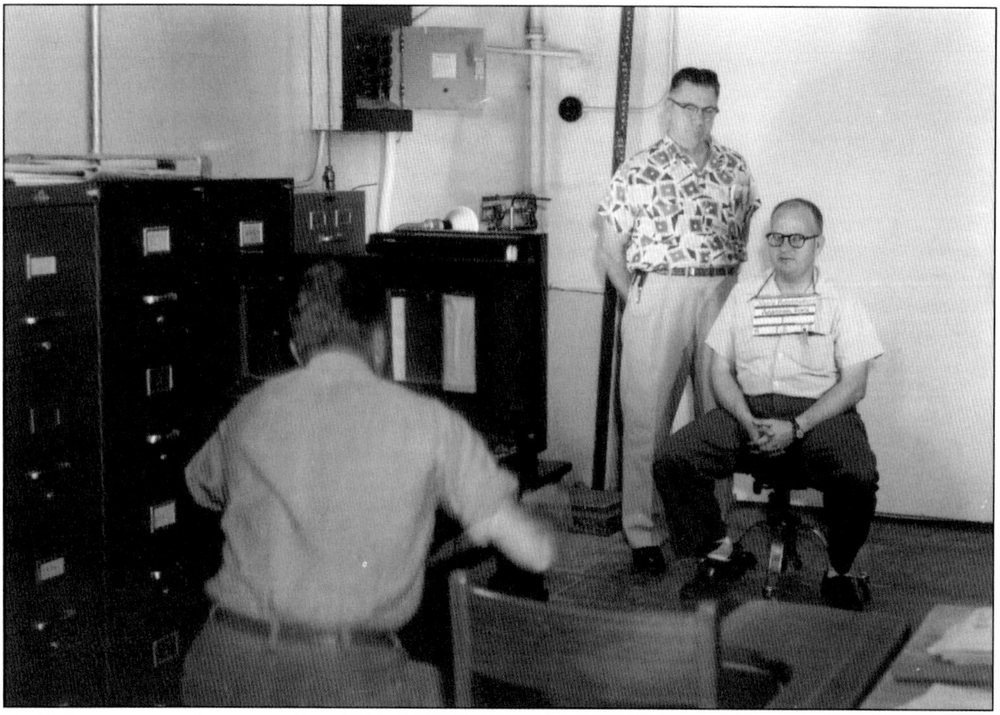

A. B. Corne started as a guard in 1949. After stints in several shops, he was placed in charge of the records office. He supervised several inmates who photographed and fingerprinted new arrivals and managed the inmate records. Here he stands next to a man being photographed. Eventually, employees replaced the inmate clerical help. Corne retired in 1976 at the age of 70.

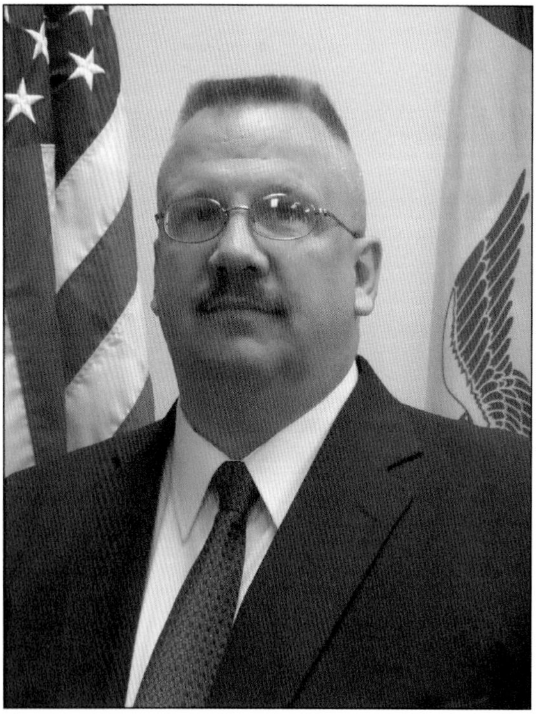

John Fayram was appointed the current warden of the Anamosa State Penitentiary in March 2009 at the age of 49. Born in the local hospital only a block from the prison, he grew up in the town of Anamosa and first worked as a correctional officer at the penitentiary while in college.

Three

The Kept

Every inmate ever confined at Anamosa can recall their reaction when they first laid eyes on this forbidding-looking fortress that would soon be their home. Its 19th-century prison designers tried to strike a balance between form, function, and a deterrent effect. The intimidating structure was intended to be a silent warning to would-be lawbreakers. In fact, most inmates who come to Anamosa once never return. Most who come through the prison gates are ordinary as far as criminals go. Iowa has always had its fair share of burglars, thieves, robbers, and murderers. At the time of this writing, over 200 men are doing "all day" at Anamosa, prison parlance for a life sentence.

However, a few of Anamosa's prisoners have earned lasting notoriety. Serial killers John Wayne Gacy and Robert Hansen each did a stretch at Anamosa before beginning their depredations. Youthful murderers John Wesley Elkins, Charles Cornwell, and Lester Smith were sentenced to Anamosa at extremely young ages, creating a management headache for their respective wardens. Jewel thief Frank Hohimer's career was made into a Hollywood movie. Harry Hortman's journey included a date with the hangman's noose and a trip to the World Series. The list includes women as well—Margaret Hossack was convicted of ax-murdering her abusive husband; her story was later transformed into the award-winning short story "A Jury Of Her Peers" by Susan Glaspell.

Thousands of souls have lived and died at Anamosa. Here are a few of their stories.

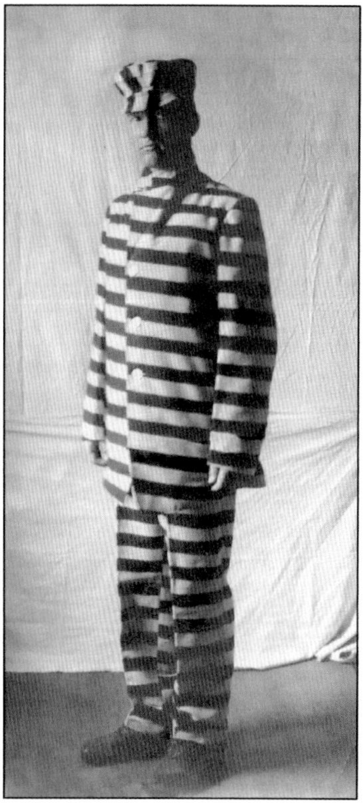

In the early years, striped garb was the standard for all inmates. By 1900, the grade system was implemented, and only the less cooperative had to wear the dreaded stripes.

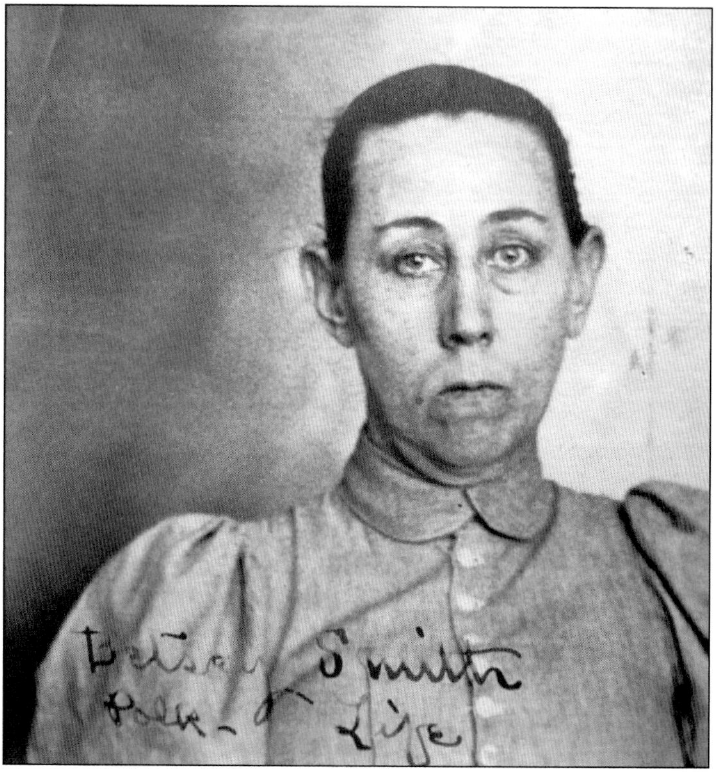

Betsey Smith and her daughter Cora McCamley became cellmates at Anamosa in the 1890s after feeding Smith's husband rat poison. Both received life sentences. Ironically, young Cora committed suicide while in prison by ingesting a poisonous cleaning powder. Some two dozen black spiders were found in her handkerchief, leading to speculation that she intended to poison herself with them if the cleaning powder had failed.

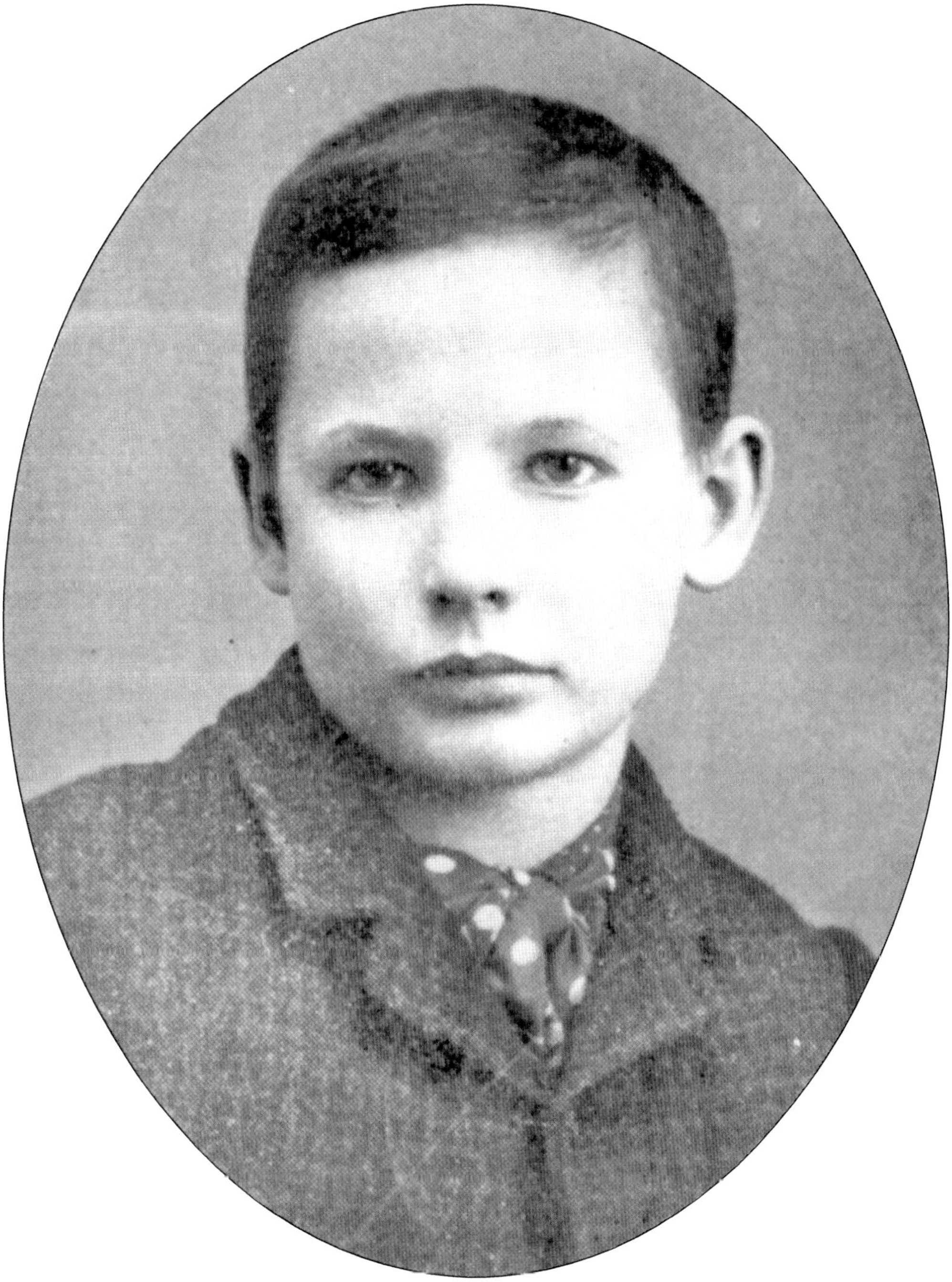

John Wesley Elkins may be the youngest lifer ever. At the age of 11, he shot and killed his father, then beat his stepmother to death. In 1890, after arriving at Anamosa, he told the warden that his parents beat him unmercifully. First an errand boy in the warden's office, he later educated himself by working in the prison library. He eventually took up correspondence with influential contacts outside of the prison who were willing to work for his release. Following a well-publicized debate in the Iowa legislature, the governor ordered a conditional release in 1902. (Courtesy of Cornell College Archives.)

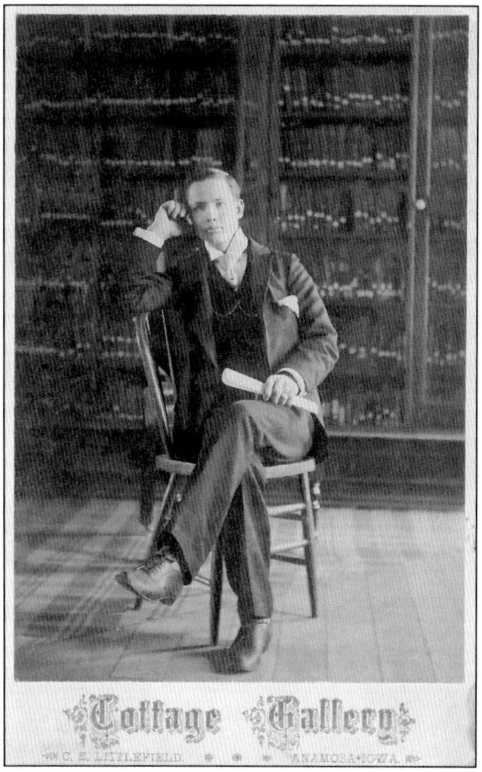

This photograph of Elkins is thought to have been taken at the time of his parole, perhaps with his release papers in his hand. He first attended the Cornell College Academy for two years before moving to St. Paul, where he was a clerk for a railroad. He eventually married and moved to California, where he and his wife raised poultry. He died in 1961. There was no indication he was ever again in trouble with the law.

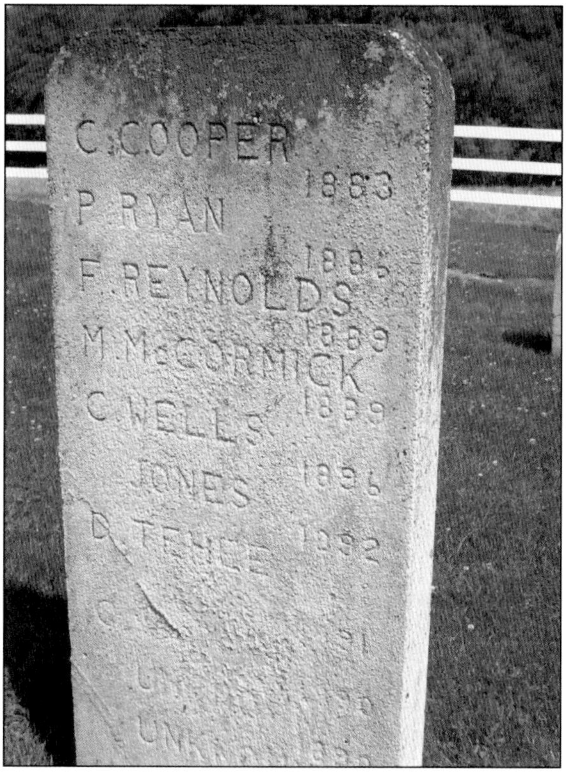

Although Wild West outlaw Charles "Polk" Wells is listed on this gravestone, he is not buried in the prison cemetery. His body was shipped to his home area of St. Joseph, Missouri. The best explanation for this "grave" mistake was a clerical error. In his autobiography, Wells claims to have rubbed shoulders with the likes of Jesse James, Kit Carson, and Wild Bill Hickock.

John Hossack, a well-respected and successful Iowa farmer, was axed to death in his bed on December 2, 1900. His wife, Margaret Hossack (right), was accused of the murder. She was convicted in April 1901 but later won a new trial that resulted in a hung jury. Hossack was freed, never tried again, and died of old age, maintaining her innocence to the end.

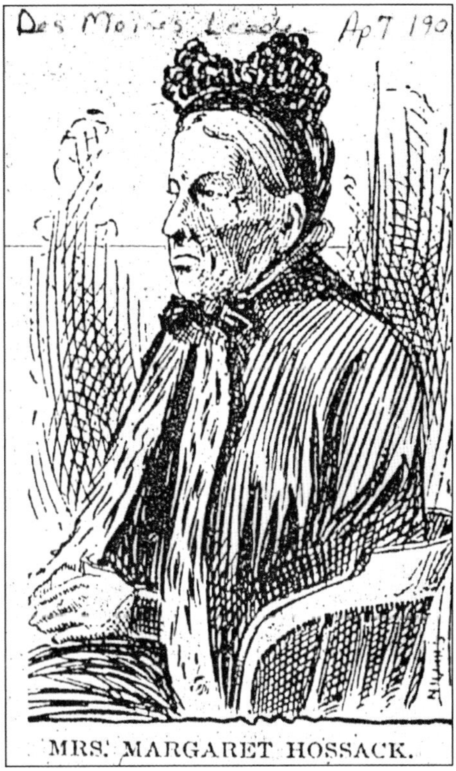

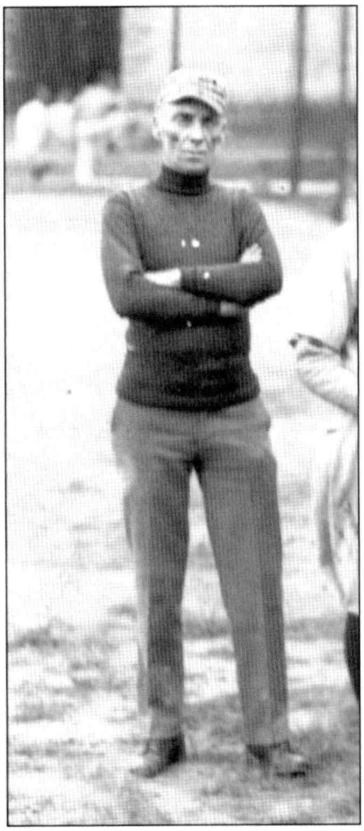

Originally sentenced to death for killing his girlfriend, Harry "Snap" Hortman was later resentenced to a life term. His love of baseball led to a long reign as manager of the prison baseball teams. In 1932, Warden Ireland, an avid Chicago Cubs fan like Hortman, took him with him to see a World Series game in Chicago, leading to considerable public controversy.

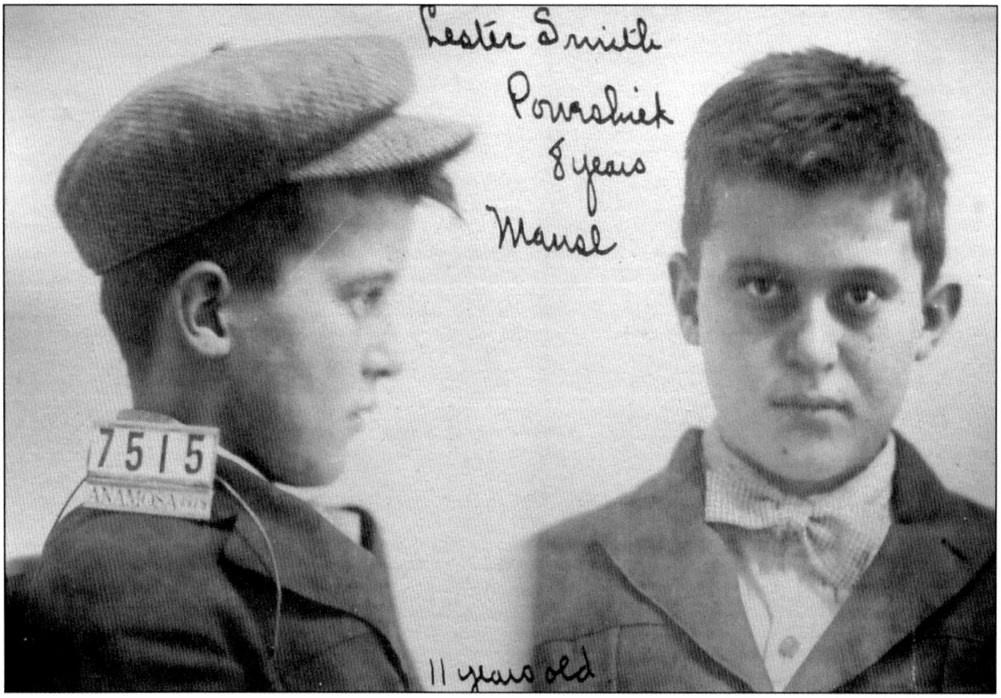

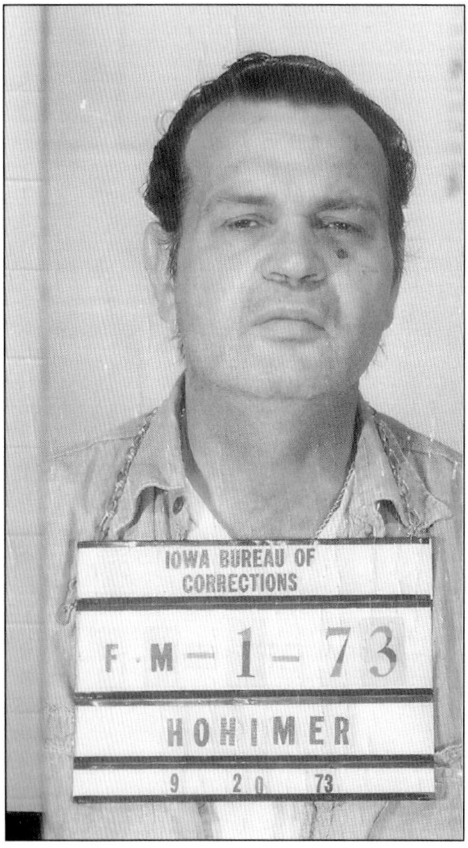

Lester Smith, pictured above, may be the youngest inmate admitted to Anamosa. He was 11 years old when he arrived in November 1914 to serve an eight-year sentence for manslaughter. Lester was attempting to shoot his abusive father when a brother stepped in the line of fire and was killed. Records listed his occupation as "schoolboy." He received his final discharge in August 1921.

Frank Hohimer served time at Anamosa during the mid-1970s. He was a federal inmate and was moved from prison to prison for his protection. He was a professional jewel thief and plied his trade against the very wealthy in many areas across the country. While at Anamosa, Hohimer worked on his book, *The Home Invaders: Confessions of a Cat Burglar*. The 1981 movie *Thief*, starring James Caan, was based on the book.

Charlie Cornwell was 14 when he arrived at Anamosa in 1924 to serve a life sentence for killing a 4-year-old boy. Thought to be mentally deficient, the judge did not want to send him to prison but could see no other option. The prison baseball team made him their batboy, and he apparently adjusted well to prison.

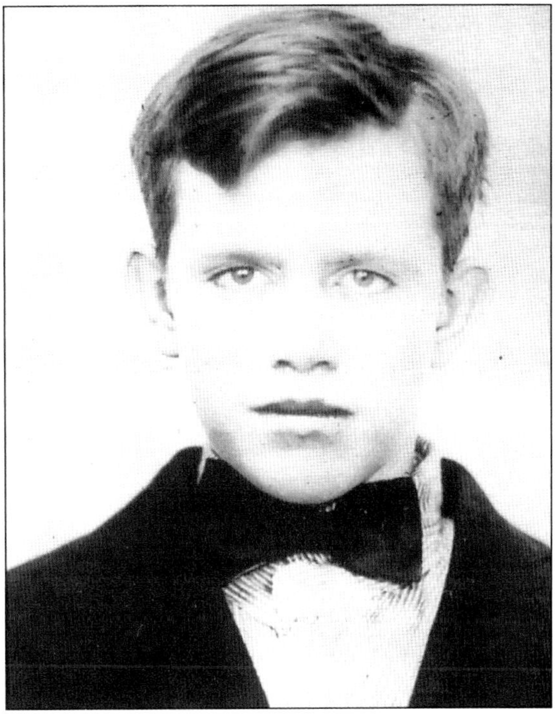

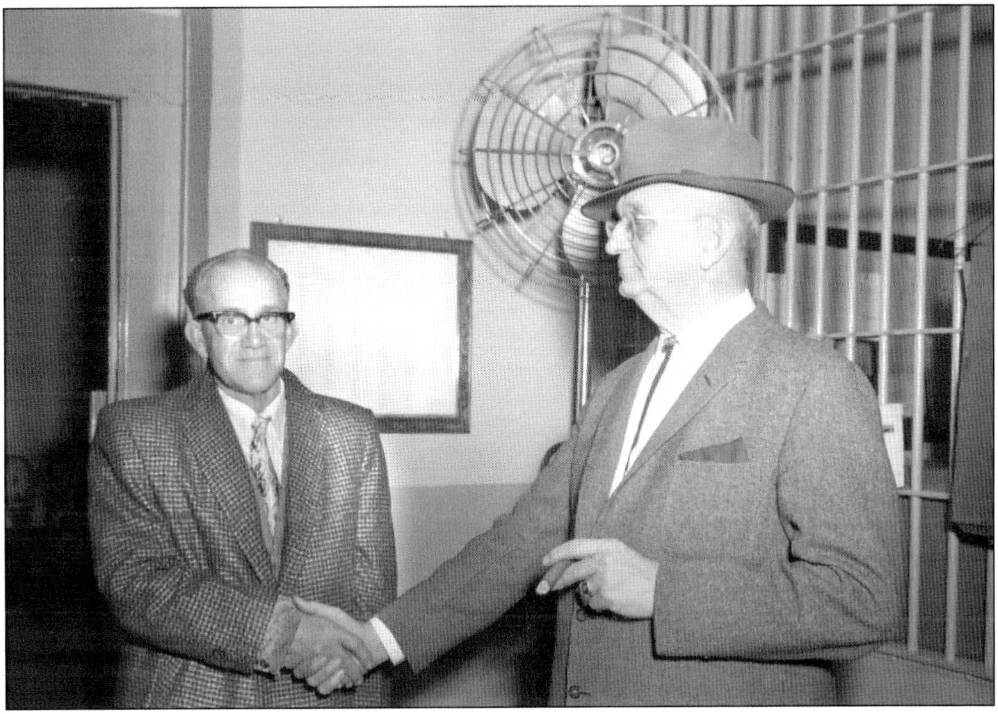

Two long-timers say goodbye at the prison gate: deputy warden Roy Smith (right) shakes the hand of Charlie Cornwell as the inmate is paroled after serving 36 years at Anamosa. Cornwell eventually returned to his hometown, where he was well received. Supported in part by odd jobs and picking up beverage cans, he died at the age of 79, having finally found his place in life.

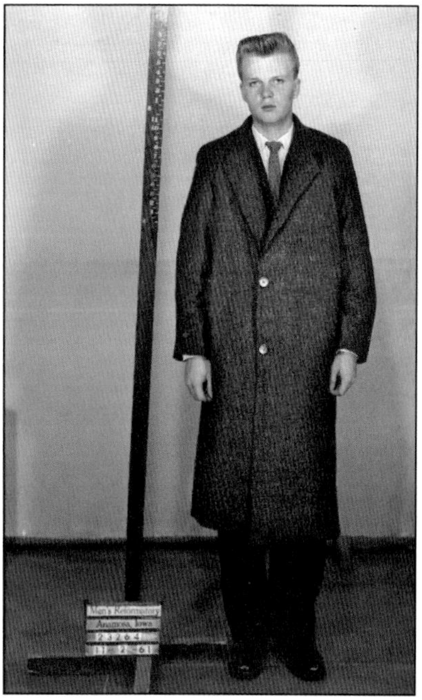

Having a tailor shop on the premises helped, as inmates generally received a set of clothes when they discharged.

Robert Hansen, below, served 20 months for arson in the early 1960s. He later moved to Alaska, where, from 1971 to 1983, he murdered at least 17 women and raped many more. A licensed pilot and expert marksman, Hansen would fly his victims to remote locations. After sexually assaulting them, he would set them free in the freezing wilderness and hunt them down with his high-powered hunting rifle.

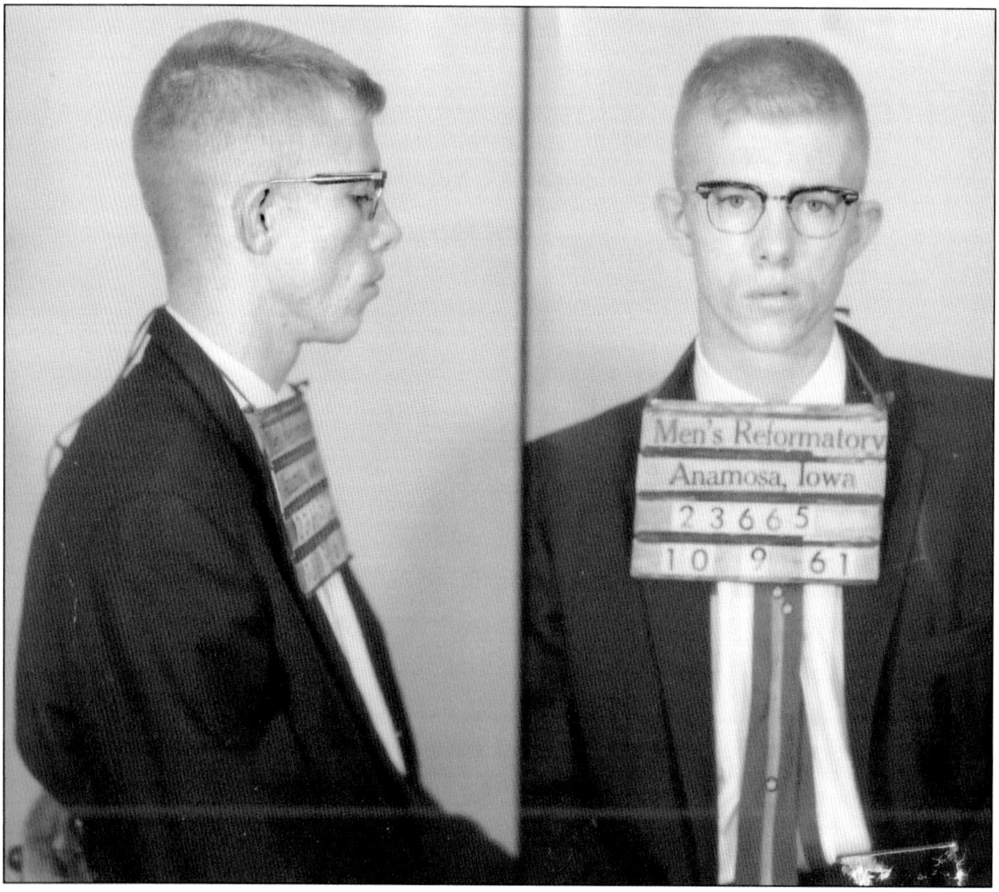

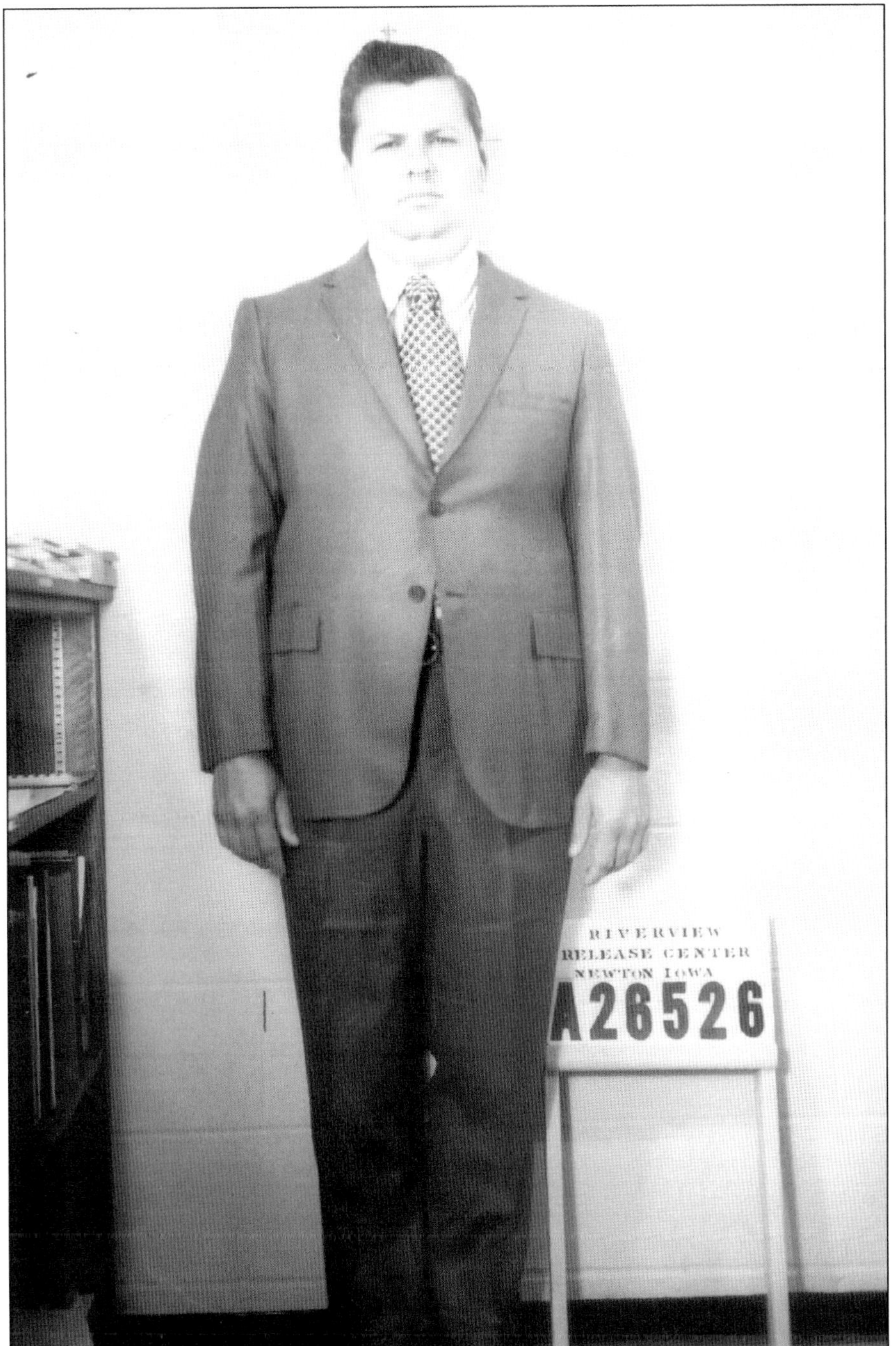

John Wayne Gacy entered Anamosa in December 1968, serving a 10-year sodomy sentence for a case involving a teenage boy. While in Anamosa, he was active in the reformatory Jaycees, worked as the lead inmate cook, and adjusted well. In the spring of 1970, he was paroled to the Chicago area where his mother lived. In 1980, he was tried and convicted of killing 33 young men and burying them in the crawl space under his house, thus becoming one of the most prolific serial killers in American history. In 1994, he was executed in Illinois by lethal injection.

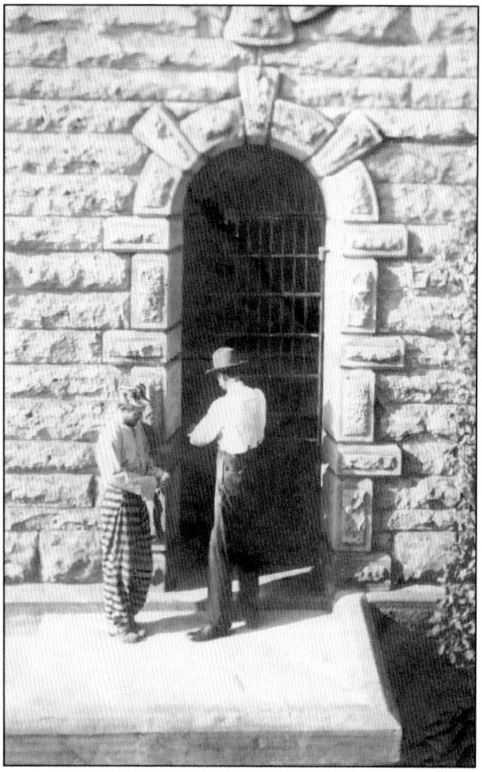

Where there are prisons, there are rules and rule breakers. This early-1900s inmate is being escorted to solitary confinement as punishment for some infraction of prison rules. In the early days, his diet would have consisted of bread and water during his stretch in "The Hole."

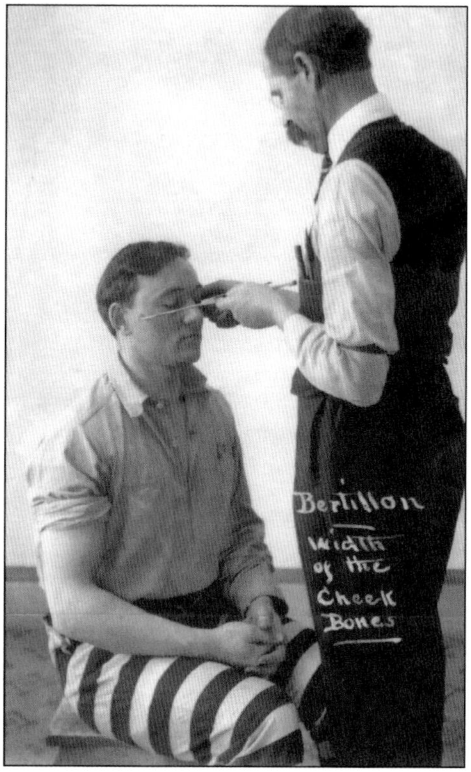

The Bertillon system of identification involved recording many measurements of the body to create a "descriptive photograph" that could be used to make a positive identification. These measurements were taken at Anamosa for many years, but the system was discredited by the early 1900s, and fingerprints soon replaced Bertillon numbers. Anamosa's old measurements and the equipment used to obtain them have disappeared over the years.

Four

WORK

The old saw "idle hands are the devil's workshop" has never been truer than in a prison facility. Keeping the mind and body productively occupied has always been a priority for prison administrators. In the early days of Anamosa's construction, this task was not difficult, as there was plenty of hard physical labor to go around. Stone had to be quarried, shaped, and placed, and the prison grounds had to be graded. The old prison cliché of inmates breaking rocks was a reality then. In addition, someone had to perform the daily cooking, cleaning, and other routine duties the prison required. After all, the judge had sentenced the inmates to hard labor.

As the population grew and construction work waned, it became necessary to find other work for the convicts to do. Some of the early industries that contracted with the prison included making aprons, butter tubs, and cob pipes. However, these efforts were criticized because they competed unfairly with private enterprise. Laws were passed mandating that prison factories could only sell to other tax-supported agencies. In essence, the state became its own best customer. Thus Iowa Prison Industries was born, and continues to the present day, making everything from license plates and highway signs to custom furniture. It also provides crucial opportunities for inmates to learn good work skills and habits.

Until the program was de-emphasized in the 1970s, Anamosa's farm operation needed inmate workers. Work crews were needed at the granite quarries in Lyon County and the state farm at Clive. During World War II, the prison kept everyone busy fulfilling government contracts for soap powder and tailored goods. Job opportunities for inmates came and went over the years. Gainful employment for inmates remains a continuing challenge for prison managers everywhere.

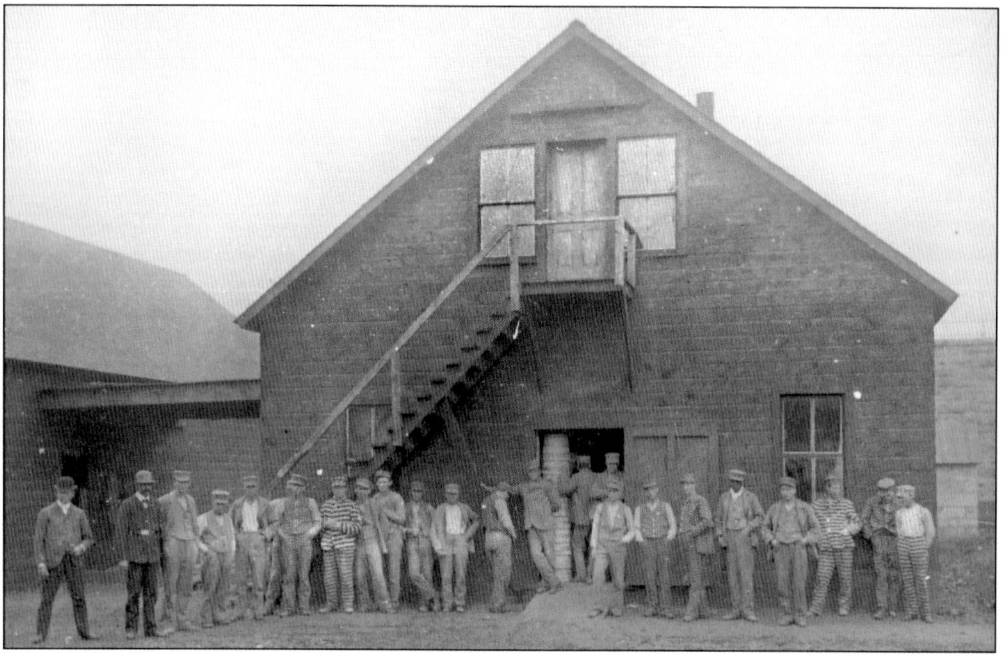

The American Cooperage Company was formed in 1899 by a group of Anamosa businessmen. By 1900, they had signed the prison's first inmate labor contract to employ 25 inmates in the manufacture of wooden butter tubs. A stack of butter tubs can be seen in the doorway. This building burned in 1902, with a total loss estimated at $16,000.

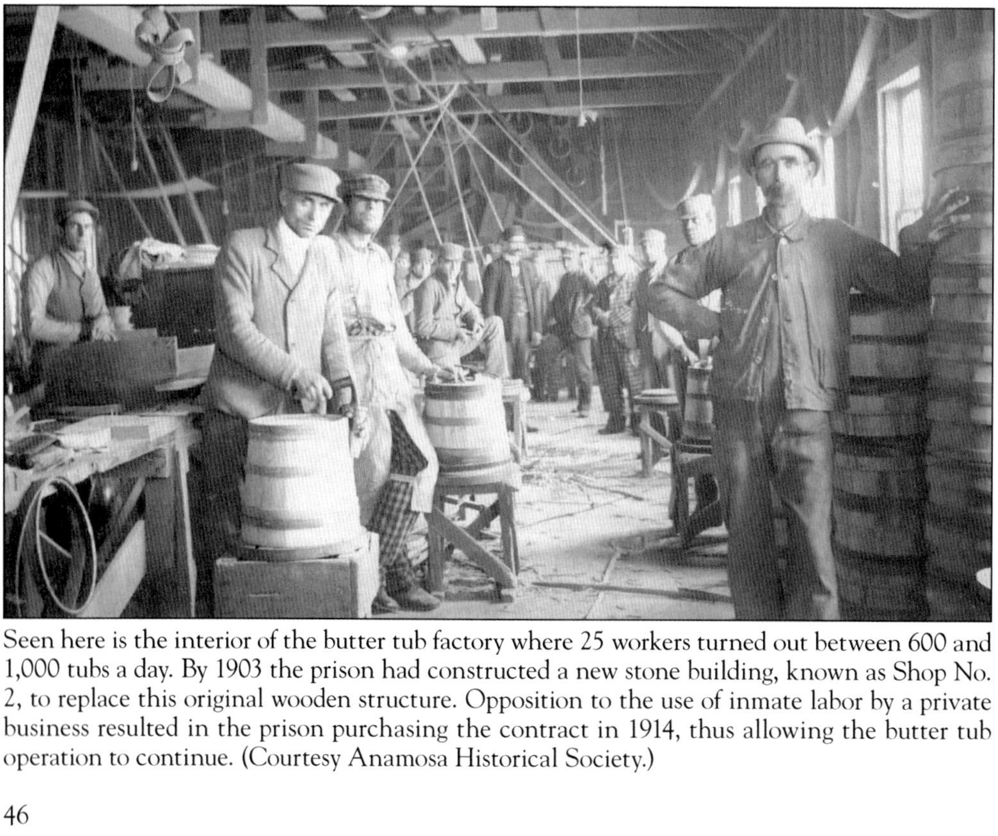

Seen here is the interior of the butter tub factory where 25 workers turned out between 600 and 1,000 tubs a day. By 1903 the prison had constructed a new stone building, known as Shop No. 2, to replace this original wooden structure. Opposition to the use of inmate labor by a private business resulted in the prison purchasing the contract in 1914, thus allowing the butter tub operation to continue. (Courtesy Anamosa Historical Society.)

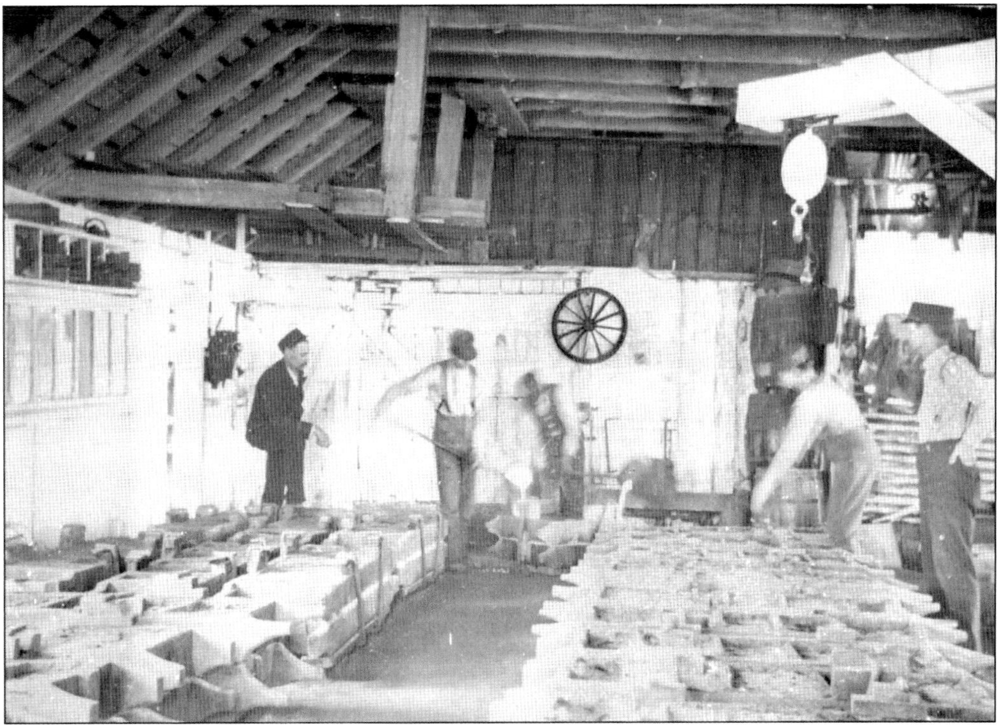

The foundry was located just west of Shop No. 1 and adjacent to the blacksmith's shop. Here the workers are pouring molten iron into a mold under the watchful eyes of two guards. Products made included stair banisters, tools, and iron fittings used in the construction of the prison.

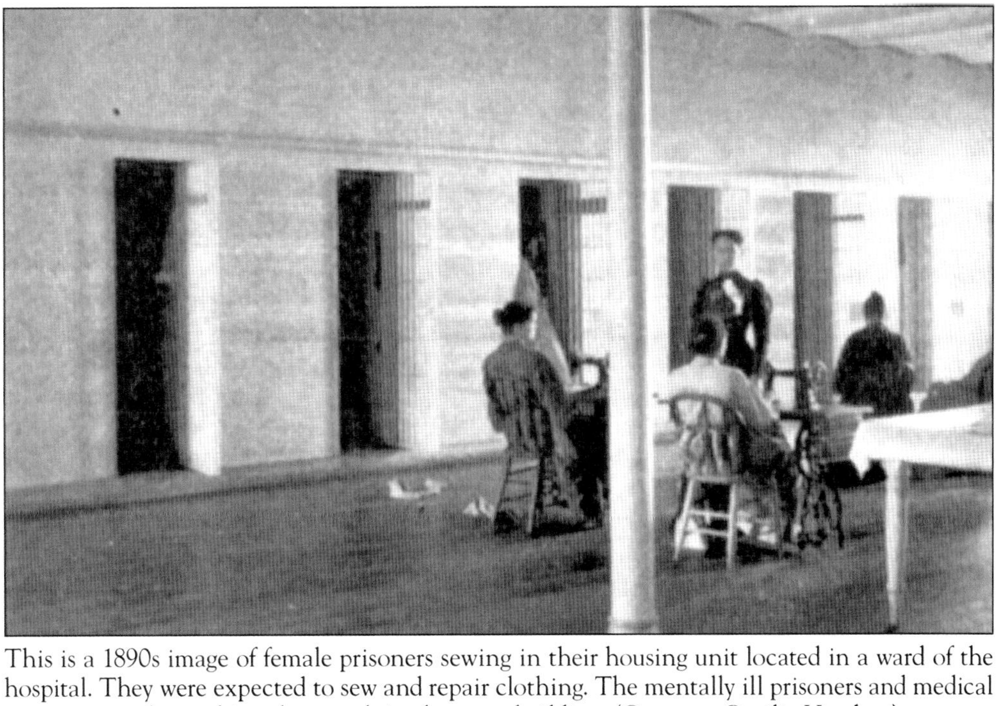

This is a 1890s image of female prisoners sewing in their housing unit located in a ward of the hospital. They were expected to sew and repair clothing. The mentally ill prisoners and medical patients were located in other wards in the same building. (Courtesy Cecilia Hatcher.)

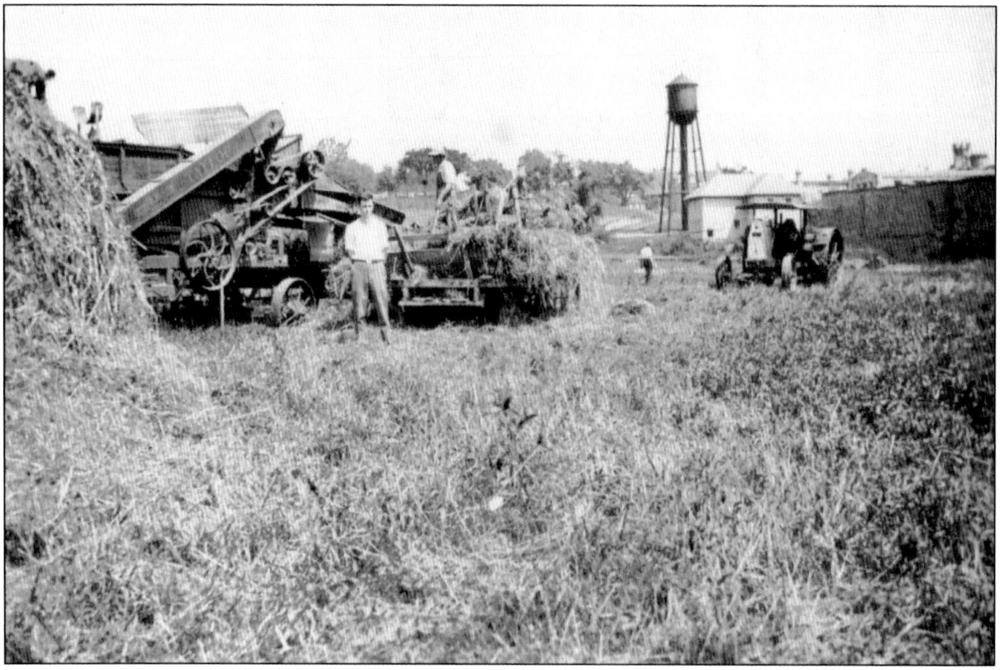

Farm workers are threshing just north of the prison during the 1920s. The old water tower and the cheese factory can be seen adjacent to the north wall. (Courtesy Cecilia Hatcher.)

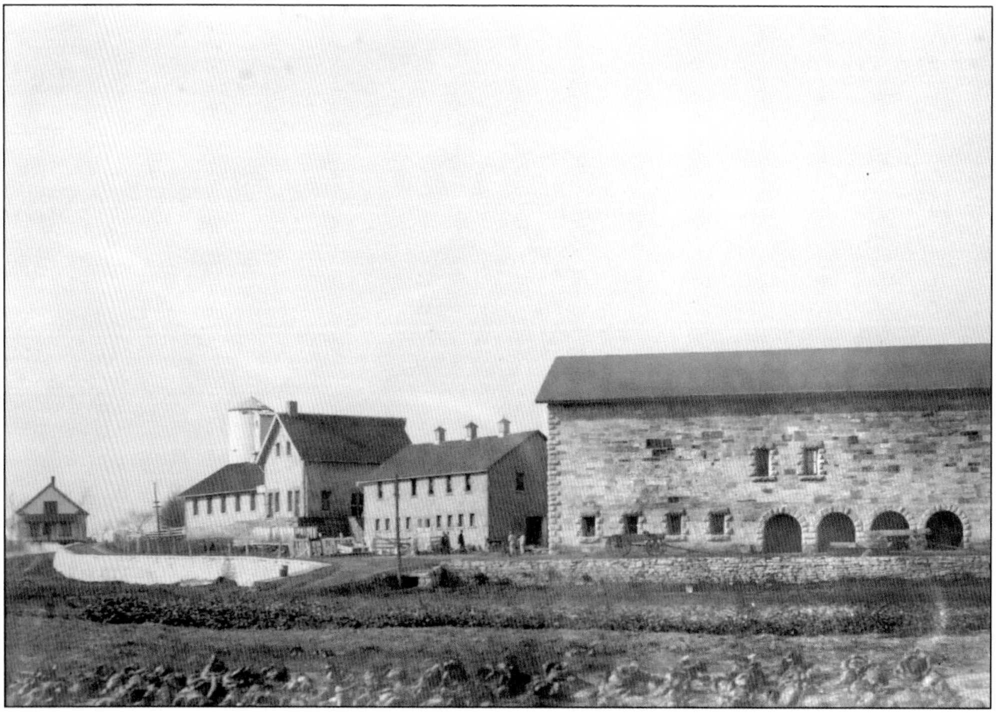

Farm No. 1 is appropriately named. It is close to the institution and the buildings are the most striking of the seven state farms located around Anamosa.

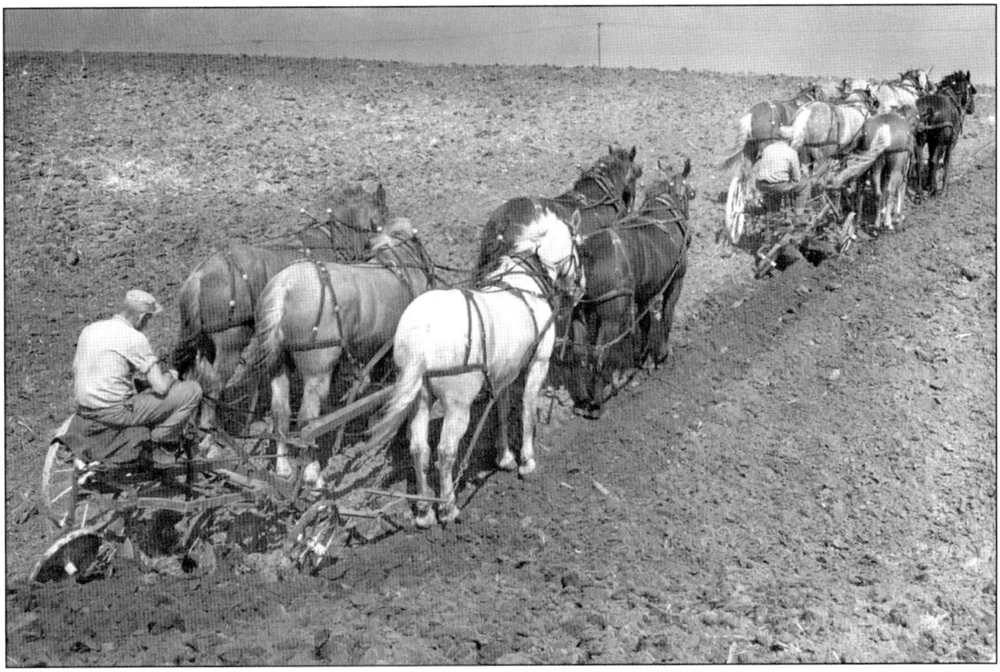

The prison plowed with horses and mules much later than many Iowa farmers. This image's date is unknown, but the power line in the distance suggests it was after rural Iowa electrification.

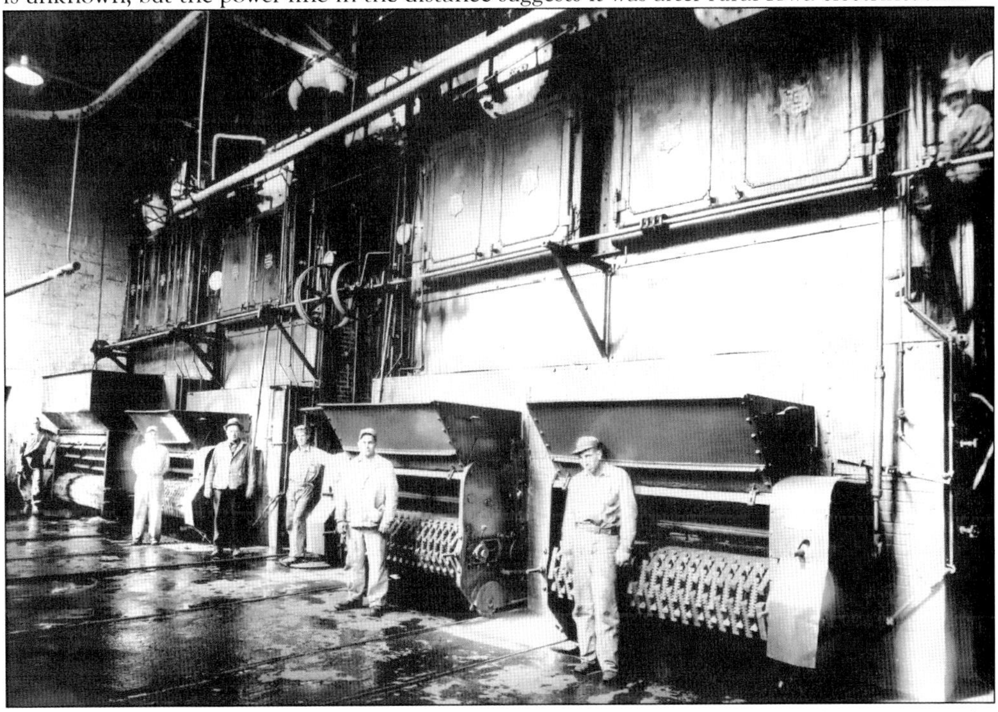

In the 1930s, these boilers produced steam to power the institution's electrical generators. The large rollers behind the inmate workers fed coal into the firebox. Located in the rebuilt Shop No. 1, this power plant was used until a new plant was completed in the late 1950s. The old boiler room was then remodeled into a gymnasium, which is still in use today.

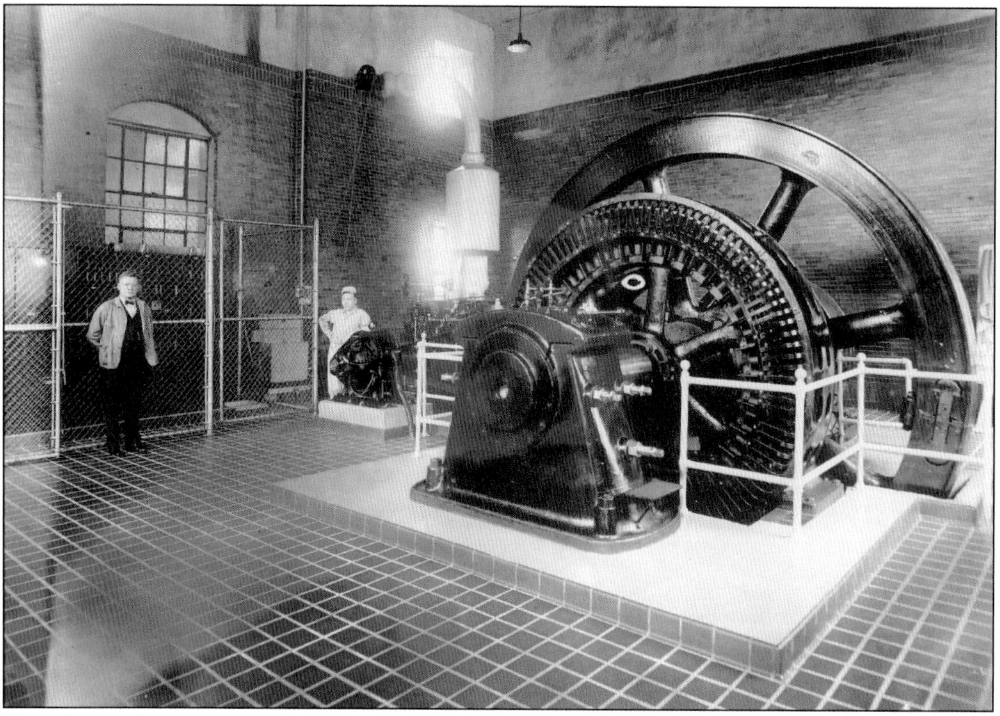

This electrical generator produced power for the institution. Located in what is now the maintenance shop, it was adjacent to the boiler room where the gym is now located.

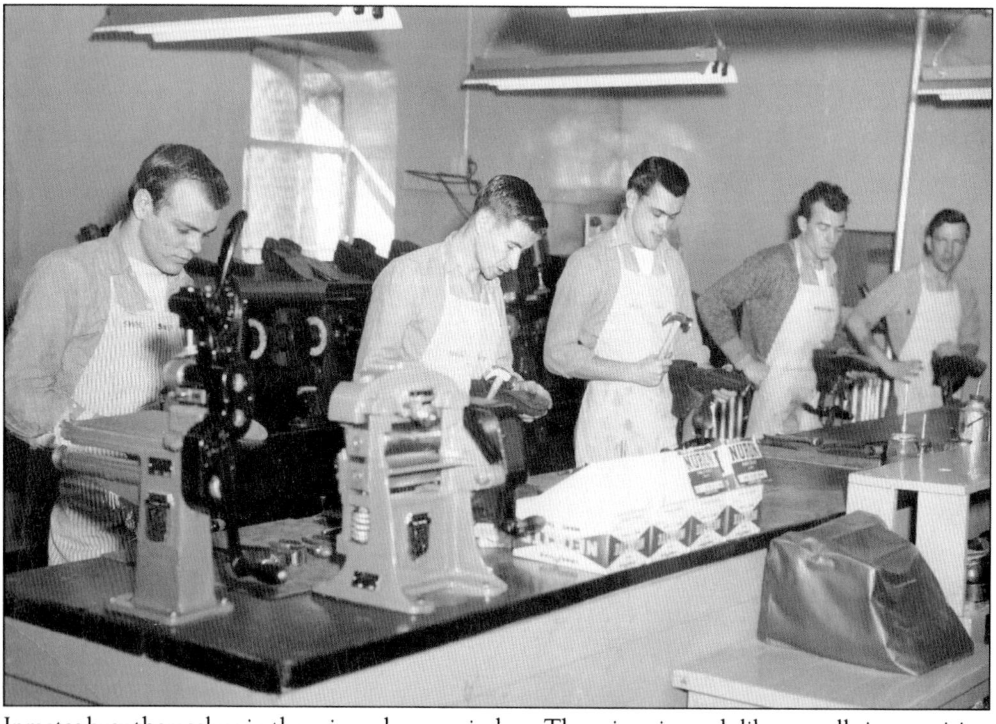

Inmates busy themselves in the prison shoe repair shop. The prison is much like a small city, requiring services such as a laundry, barbershop, and tailor. (Courtesy Anamosa Historical Society.)

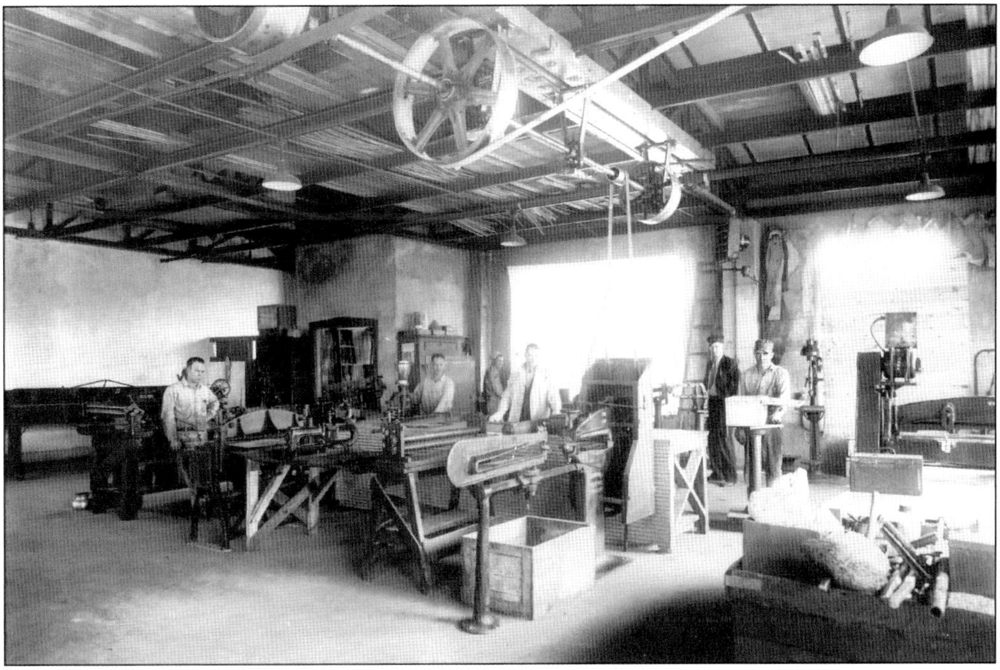

Over the years, different shops came and went as demands changed. Some of these shops included the apron factory, screwdriver factory, butter tub factory, and tobacco factory. The metal shop, above, made metal bushel baskets and corrugated culverts. (Courtesy Anamosa Historical Society.)

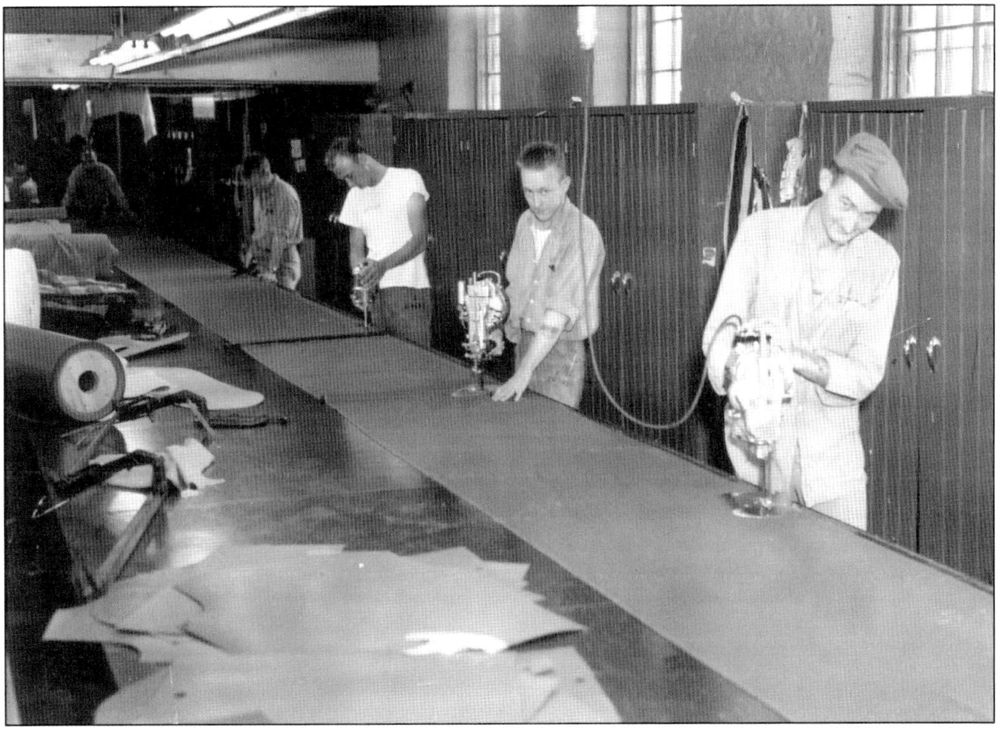

Workers cut cloth in the tailor shop. Damaged by fire in the 1963 riot, this shop was never reopened. Instead, discharging inmates were taken to a local clothing store to purchase release clothing.

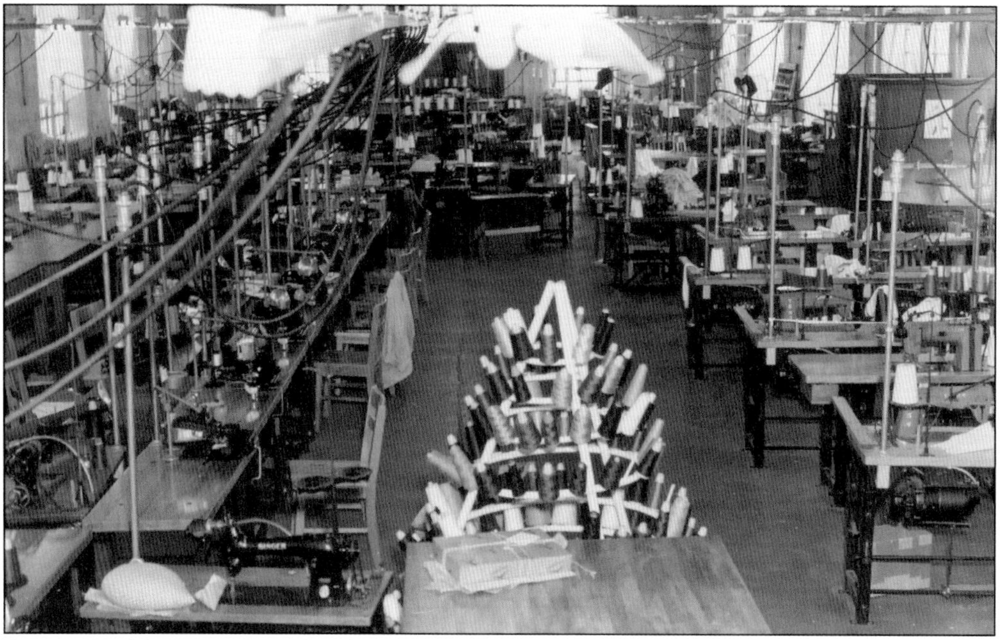

During World War II, the tailor shop contracted to make 25,000 pairs of work suits for the U.S. Navy, sometimes at the rate of 960 pairs a week. Few men complained about the overtime work this required, seeing it their contribution to the war effort. (Courtesy Anamosa Historical Society.)

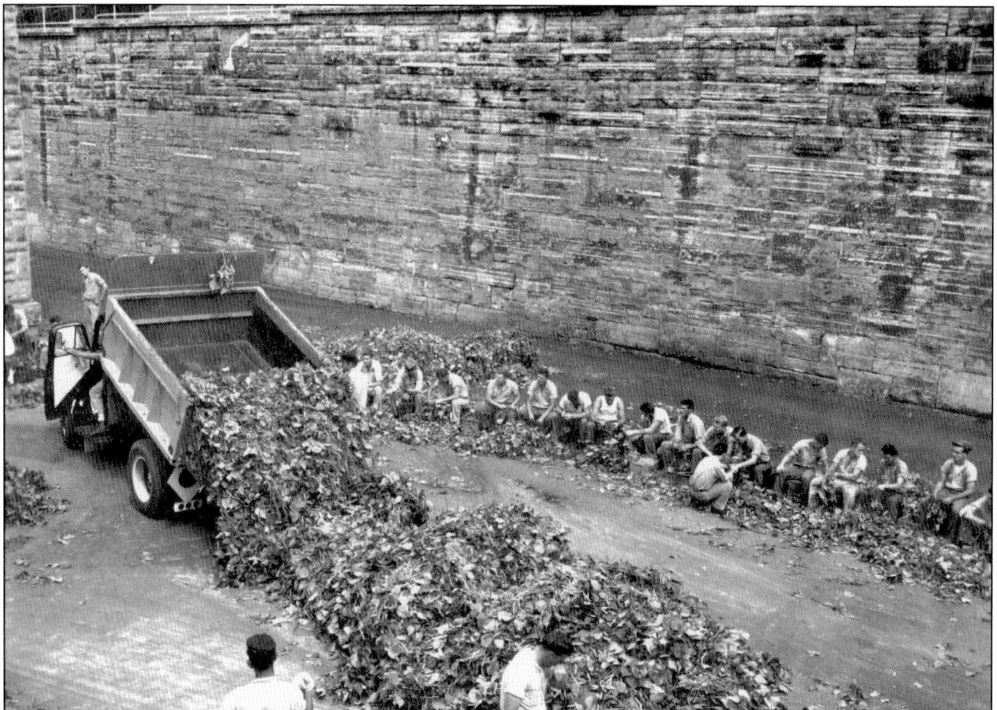

A work crew husks corn behind the cannery. Founded in 1934, the factory canned prison-grown vegetables and sold them to other institutions. Between 1940 and 1942, the prison sold over $70,000 in canned goods. The cannery was damaged by fire during the 1963 riot and never reopened.

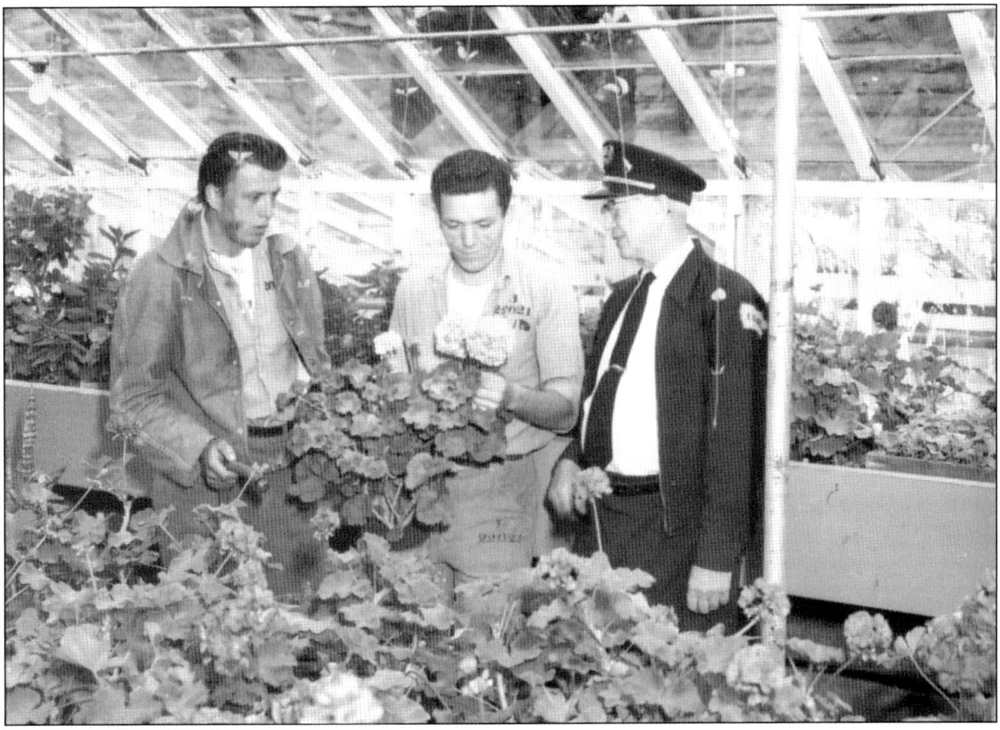

Yard captain Ernest Hubbard visits with two greenhouse workers.

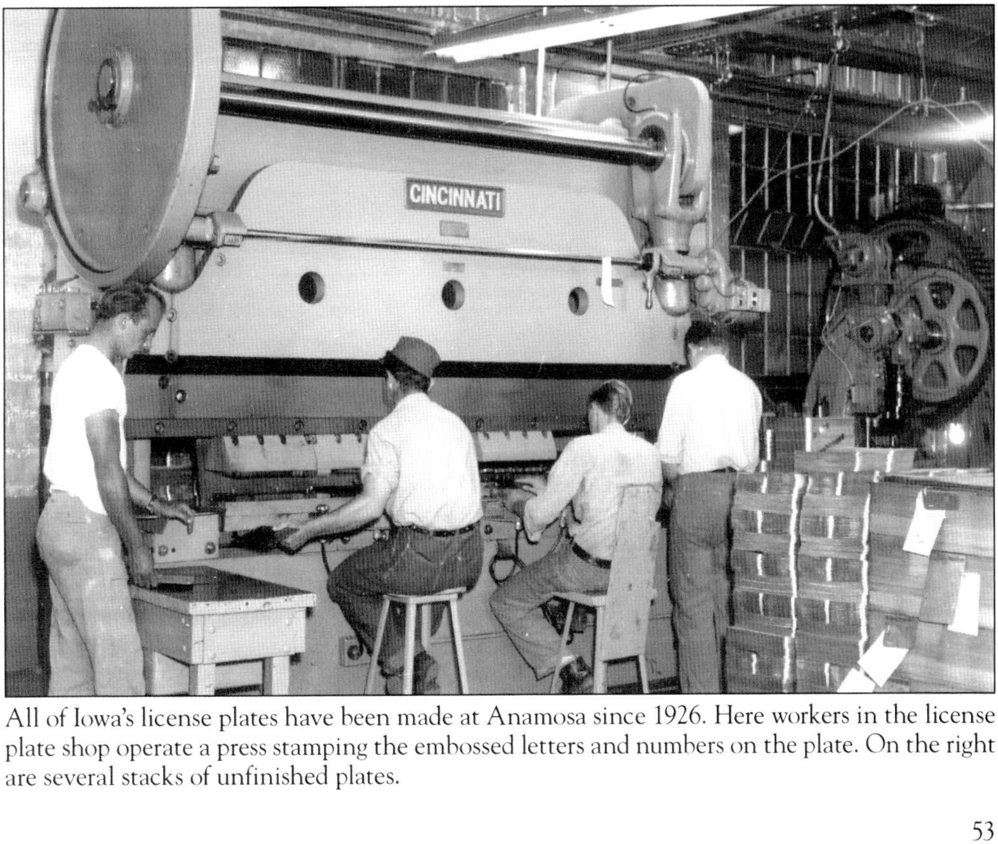

All of Iowa's license plates have been made at Anamosa since 1926. Here workers in the license plate shop operate a press stamping the embossed letters and numbers on the plate. On the right are several stacks of unfinished plates.

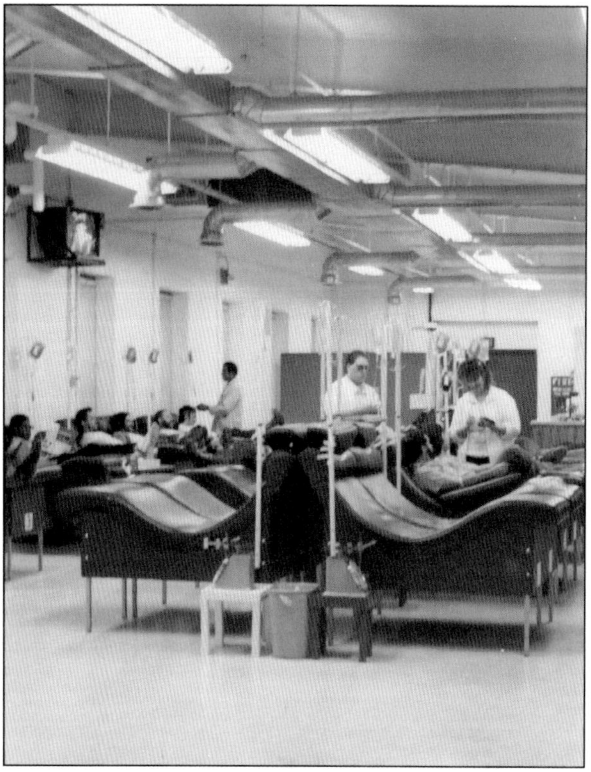

The plasma center paid inmates to donate and was a popular way of gaining extra spending money during the 1980s. Increased concern about blood-borne diseases, especially among prison populations, ended the practice nationwide after a few years.

In the 1880s, a small child watches from the curb as two inmates break up rocks in the street in front of the new prison. The frame house was the first warden's office and would later be moved inside the walls to serve as the yard captain's office.

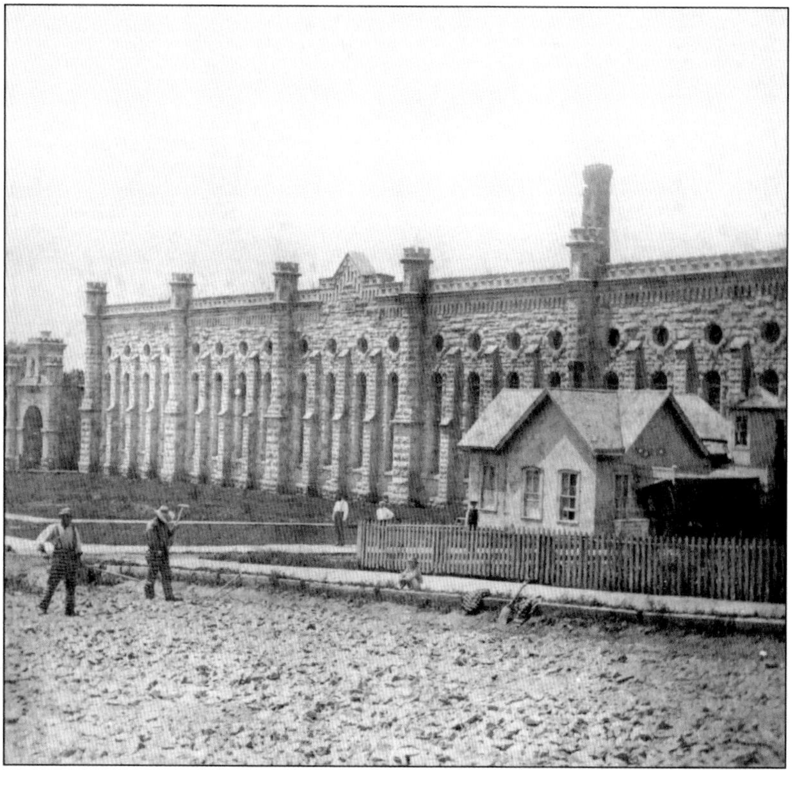

Five

PLAY

Recreational activities help the inmates pass the time and also help to reduce problems in the yard. Consequently, the prison has long made provisions for prisoners' athletic, artistic, and creative expression.

Sports of all types have been encouraged. Baseball, which reached its peak of popularity in the 1930s, has an especially long and storied history inside the walls. Inmate teams not only played each other, but outside teams as well. In fact, the 1932 prison team was a legendary one, going 23-1. The games were well attended and the cause of great anticipation, excitement, and probably more than a few side bets. Football, basketball, and even boxing also took their turns in the popularity parade.

For the more artistically inclined, the prison has almost always promoted some type of craft area where painting, woodcraft, pottery, leatherwork, drawing, and other types of expression could be pursued. Some inmates possess remarkable artistic skill, perhaps a testament to all those years in a cell with little more than pencil and paper. The prison allows them to sell their completed work to help supplement their often-meager income.

In the early years, inmates were allowed to have a wide variety of tools in their cells for their various hobbies, which Warden Hunter perhaps felt was too much of a good thing. When he assumed command in 1898, he ordered the cell house searched and cleared of all such items, resulting in the removal of 12 wagonloads of grindstones, saws, chisels, files, vises, anvils, shells, and hammers.

Self-help organizations and special-interest clubs have come and gone over the years. A model-car racing club, prison newspaper, and a local radio station all proved transitory. Alcoholics Anonymous, however, has stood the test of time and has been a mainstay at the institution for over 50 years.

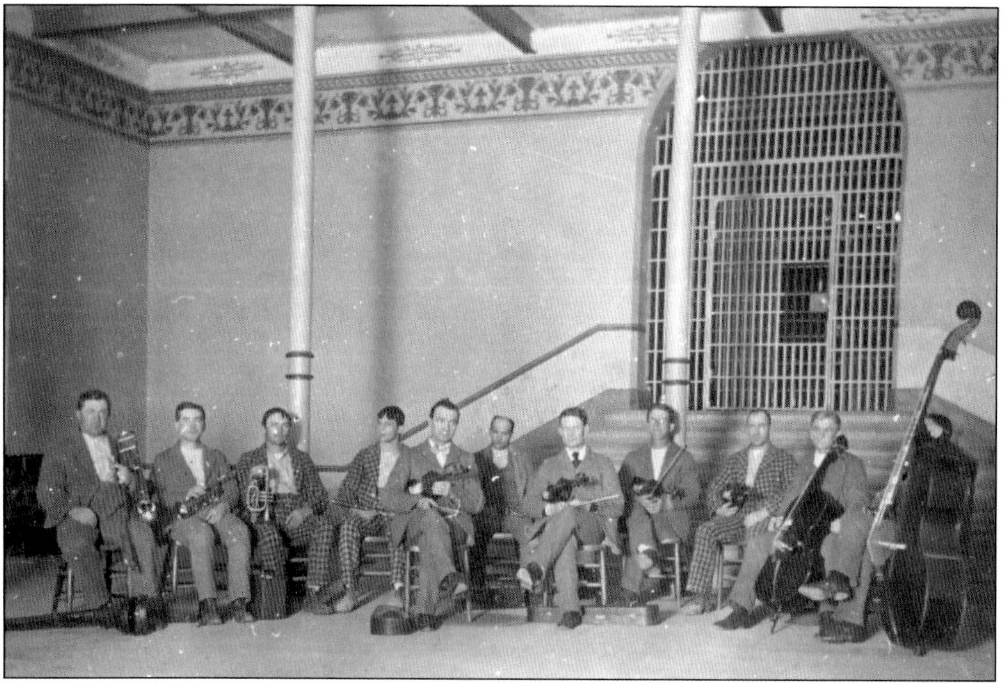

The prison orchestra gathers in the rotunda in this *c.* 1900 picture. Behind the barred door is the office of the turnkey, who controlled access to the prison. After coming down the steps, one could look up four stories to the dome and cupola at the top. By the 1950s, the floor was raised to the level of the door, and the current control center was built in the left corner of the rotunda.

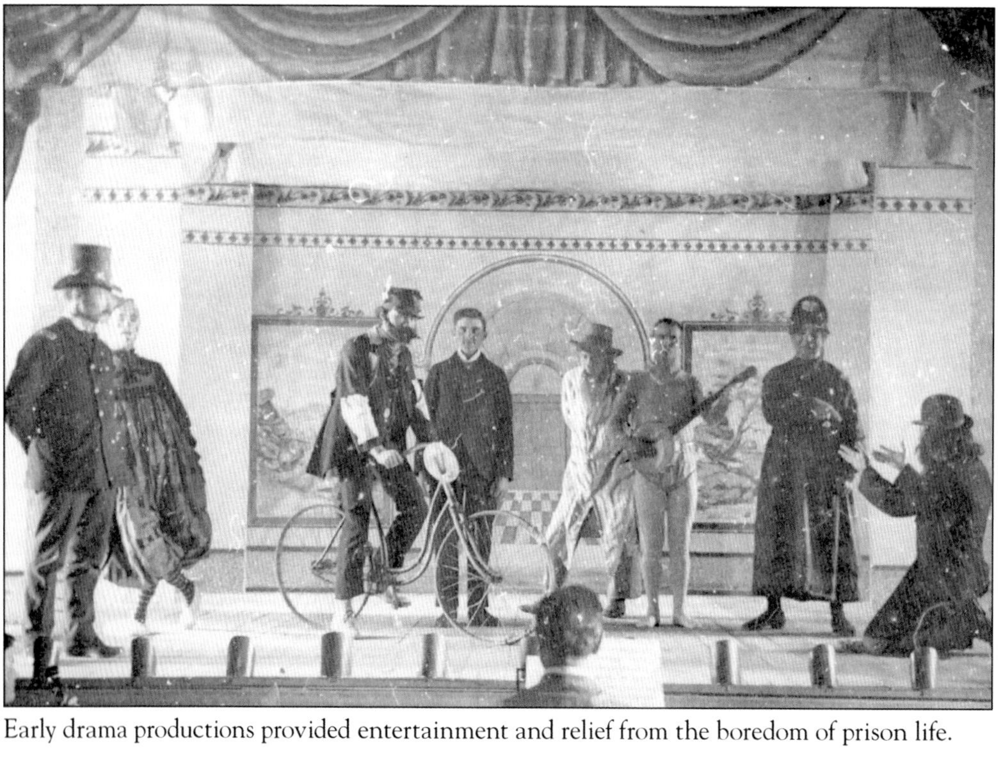

Early drama productions provided entertainment and relief from the boredom of prison life.

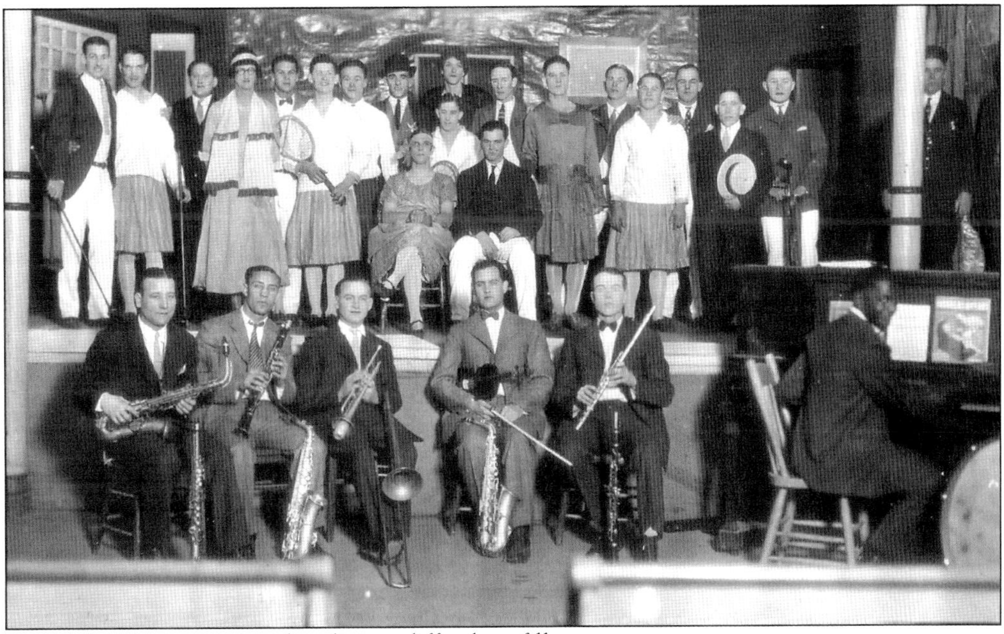

In an all-male prison, female roles are difficult to fill.

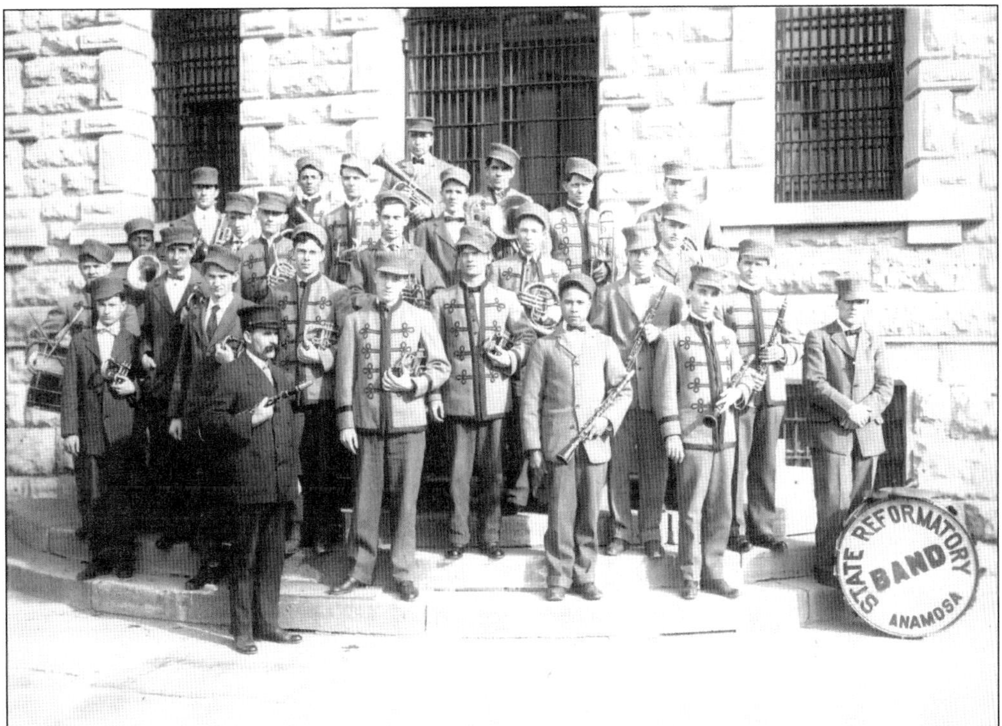

Musical groups entertained other prisoners and even performed in the local community. For many years, the prison band held weekly summer concerts in the nearby state park.

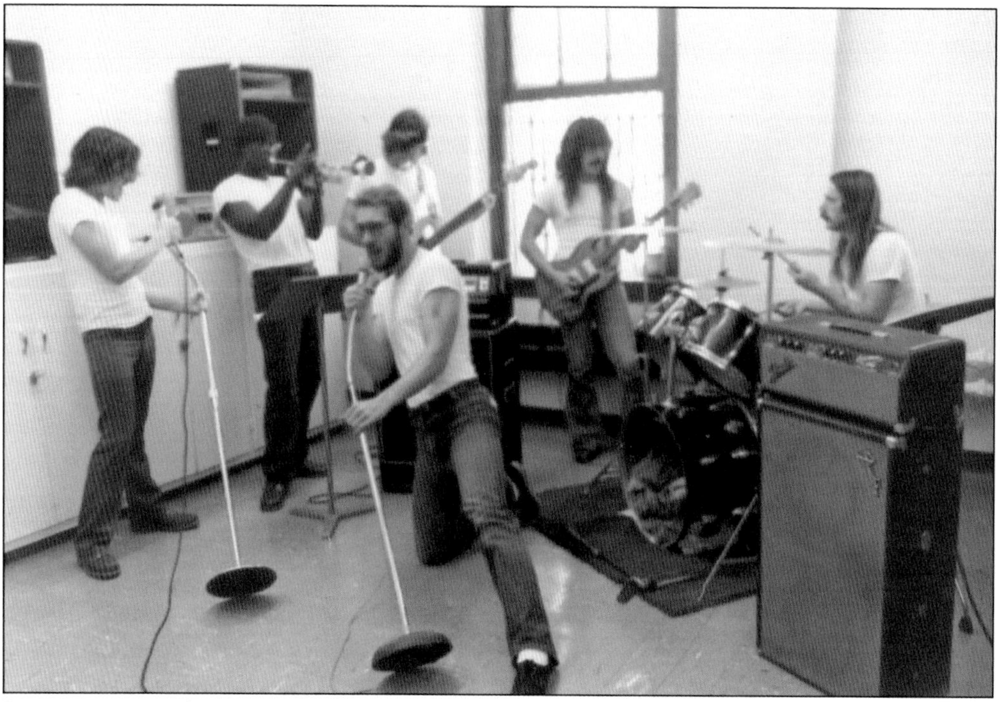

Prisoners jam in the music room in the 1970s.

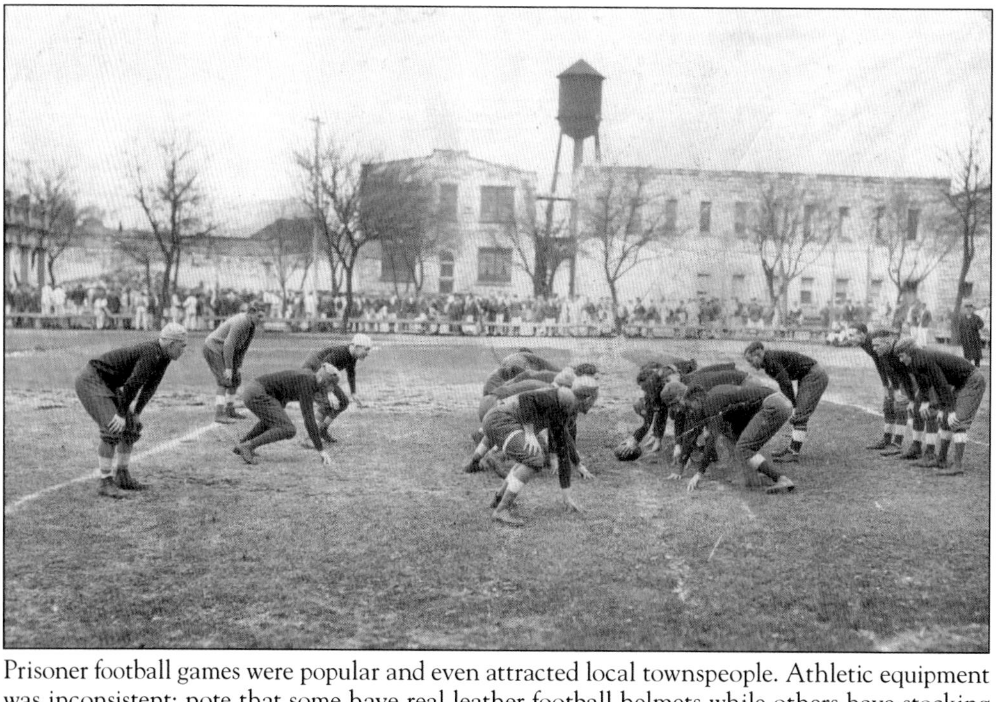

Prisoner football games were popular and even attracted local townspeople. Athletic equipment was inconsistent; note that some have real leather football helmets while others have stocking caps or no headgear at all. The photograph dates back to the early 1920s.

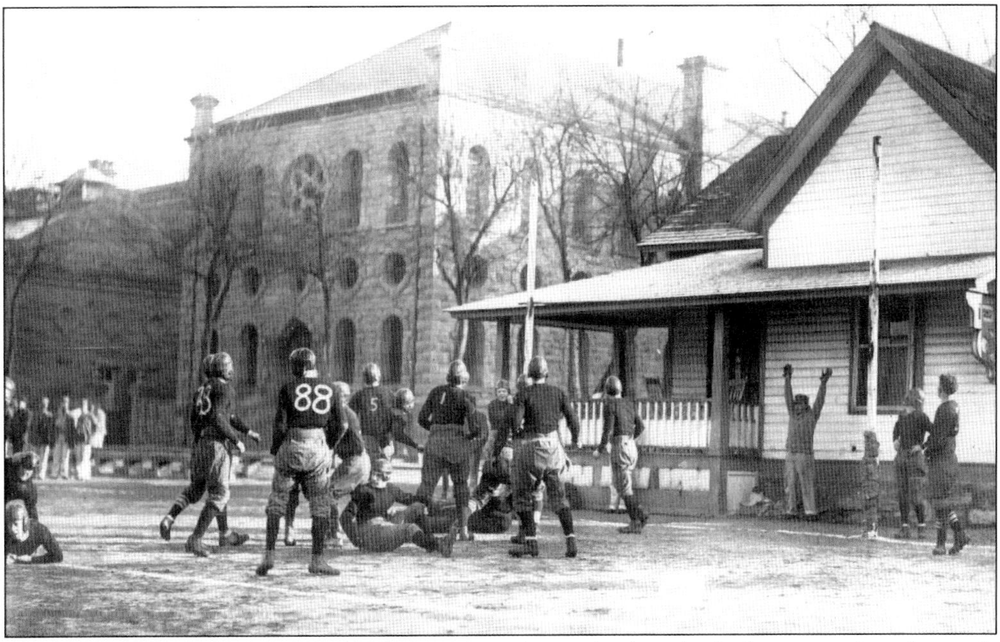

A spectator raises his arms to offer his opinion about whether the kick was good in this early football game. The uprights are attached to the yard captain's office porch.

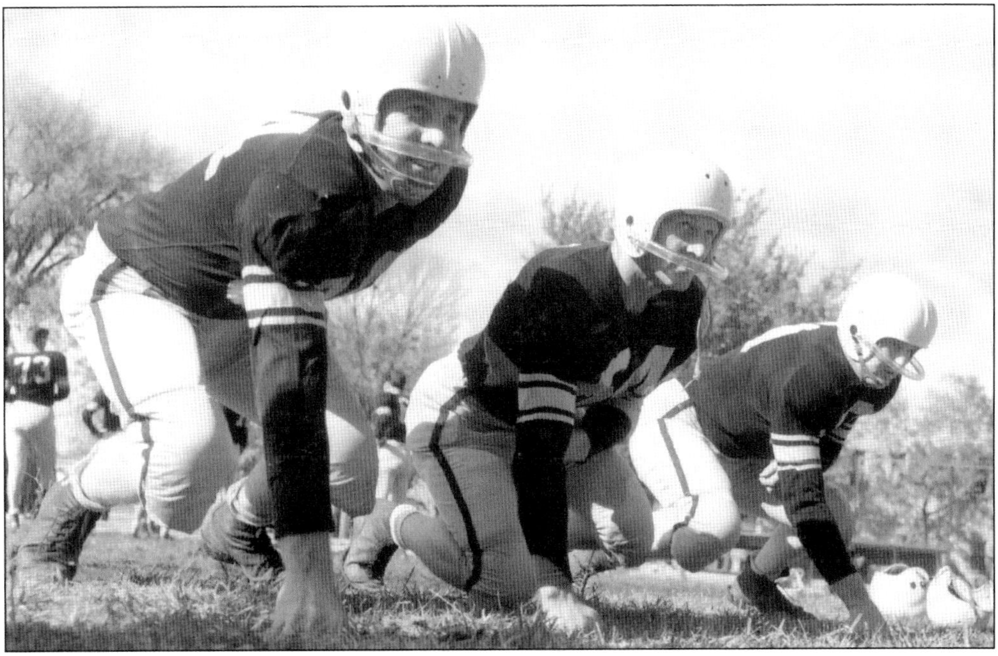

During the 1960s, Anamosa played in an eight-team semipro football league comprised of town teams in eastern Iowa and Illinois. Away games with Illinois teams were held in Davenport, since the prisoners could not leave the state. Some of the uniforms were old practice uniforms donated by the University of Iowa.

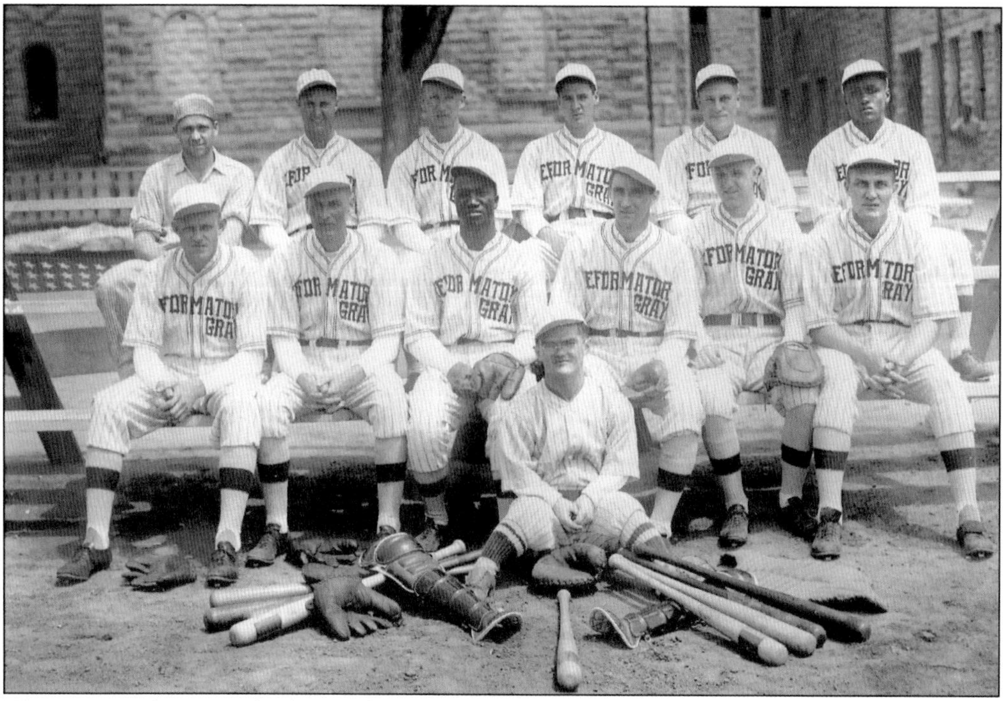

The natty uniforms are further evidence that baseball reigned supreme in the 1930s. The batboy may be Charlie Cornwell (see page 41). The team is racially integrated, long before Jackie Robinson broke baseball's color barrier in 1947.

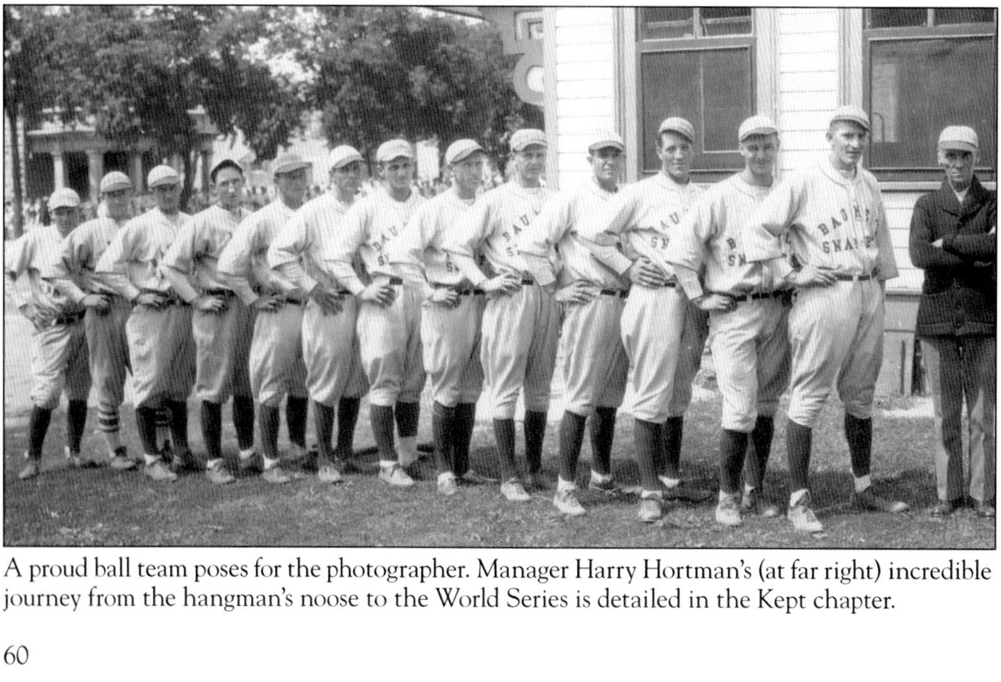

A proud ball team poses for the photographer. Manager Harry Hortman's (at far right) incredible journey from the hangman's noose to the World Series is detailed in the Kept chapter.

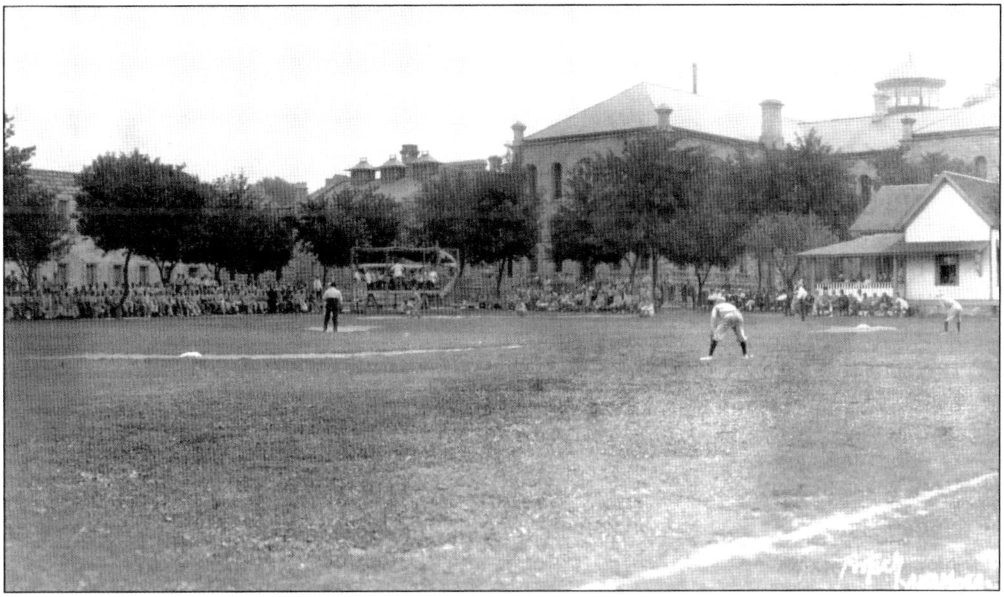

Sporting events drew large crowds. Note the pep band behind home plate

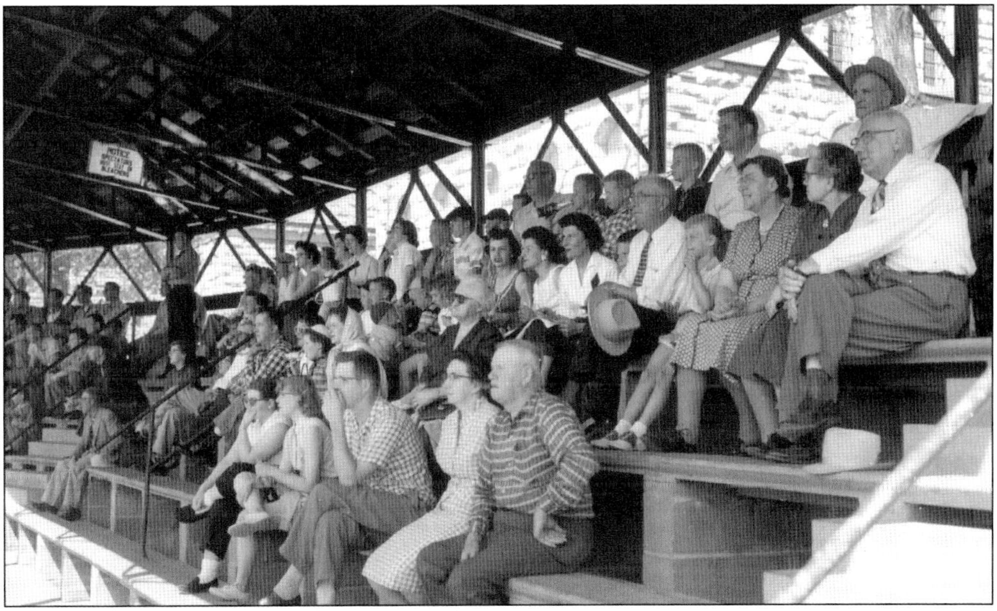

During the reformatory years, local town teams would play the prison team and spectators would be allowed in to watch. Most of these fans are from the nearby town of Solon, cheering on their favorite team in this 1955 photograph.

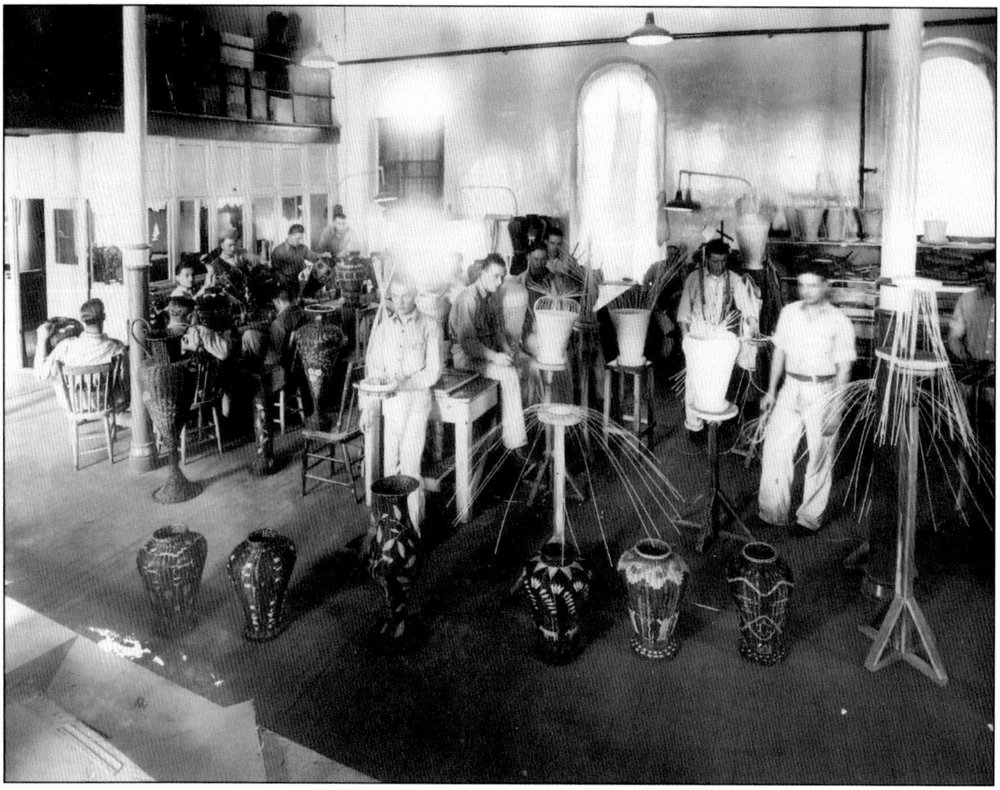

Basket weaving became a popular hobby around 1930. This work area appears to be in the back of the auditorium. Few details are known, but local lore is that the skill was introduced by Native American prisoners who were held at Anamosa for the federal government. Their influence included the presence of a large totem pole in the city park that was adjacent to the prison.

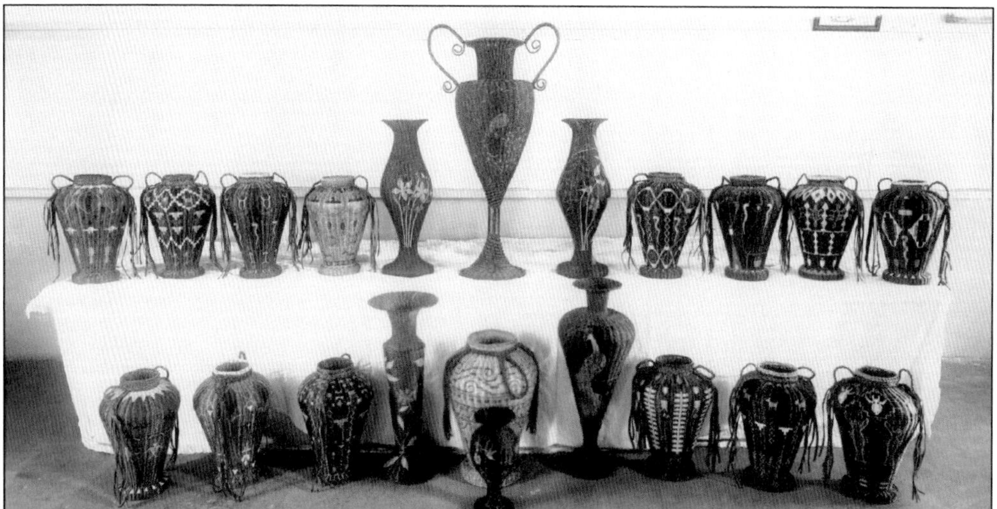

These inmate-produced baskets have a unique style that includes hand-painted decorations. They occasionally appear on Internet auctions, where they create some interest.

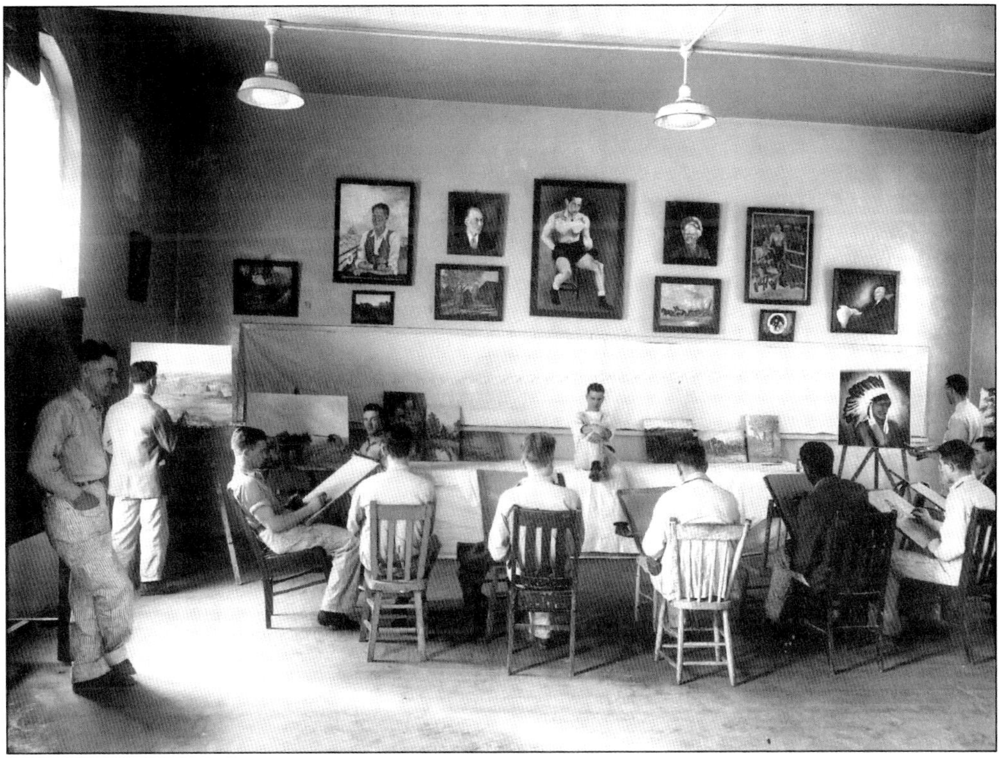

Art and hobby craft activities have been common throughout the institution's long history. Some of the more talented artists have even been able to sell items, while others send them home to family members.

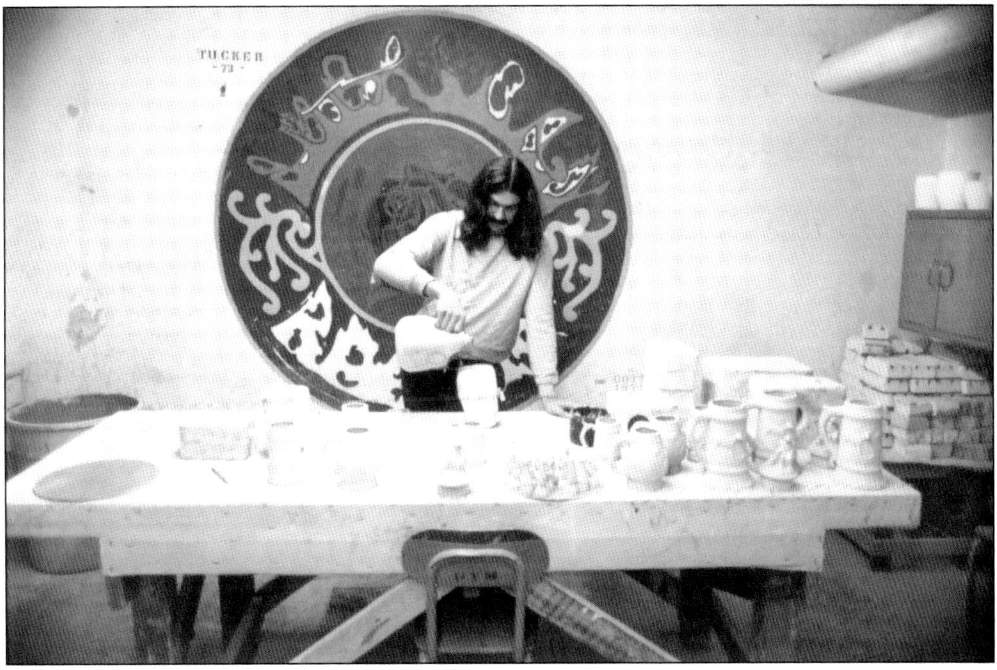

Ceramics in the hobby craft area is pictured in the 1970s.

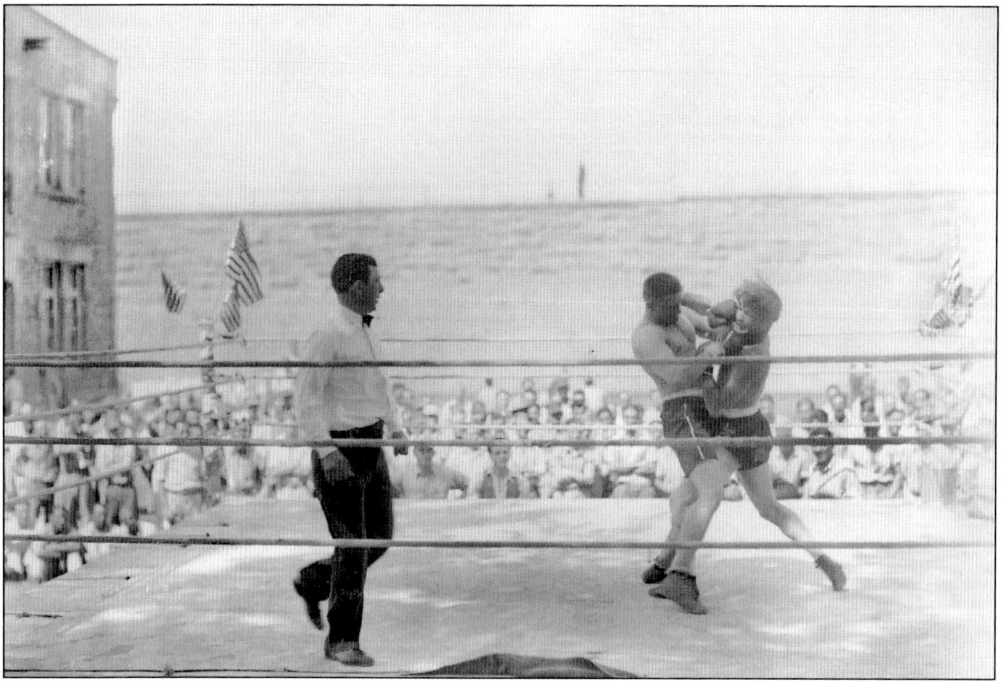

Boxing was a popular sport, with bouts often held on holidays. Boxing was also allowed to settle grudges among the inmates. Shop supervisors had access to gloves, and an impromptu ring would be set up to facilitate the grudge fight. This practice was ended in the early 1960s after an inmate at the Fort Madison Penitentiary died from injuries sustained during a fight.

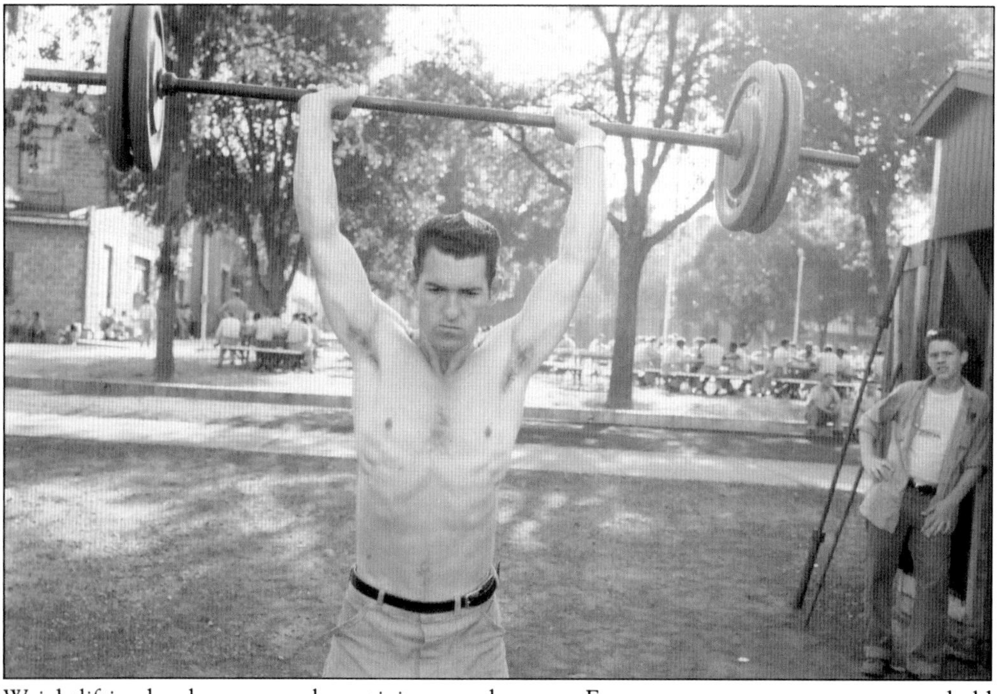

Weightlifting has been a popular activity over the years. For many years, tournaments were held between correctional institutions, with lifts compared by telephone to determine the winners.

Pickup games have long been popular in the prison yard.

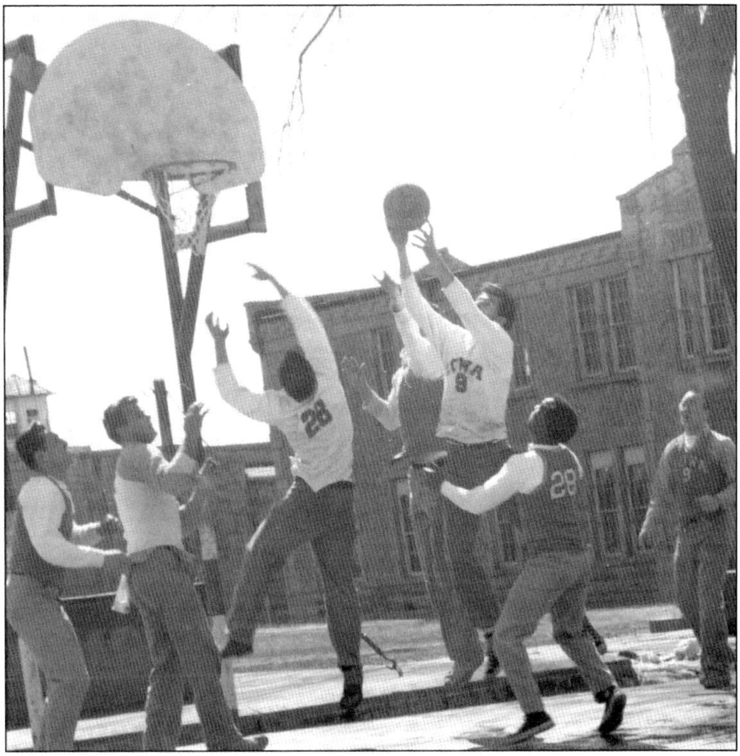

During the reformatory years, the inmate officials below refereed the prison league games that pitted shop teams against each other. The zebra stripe shirts were ironic in a prison setting.

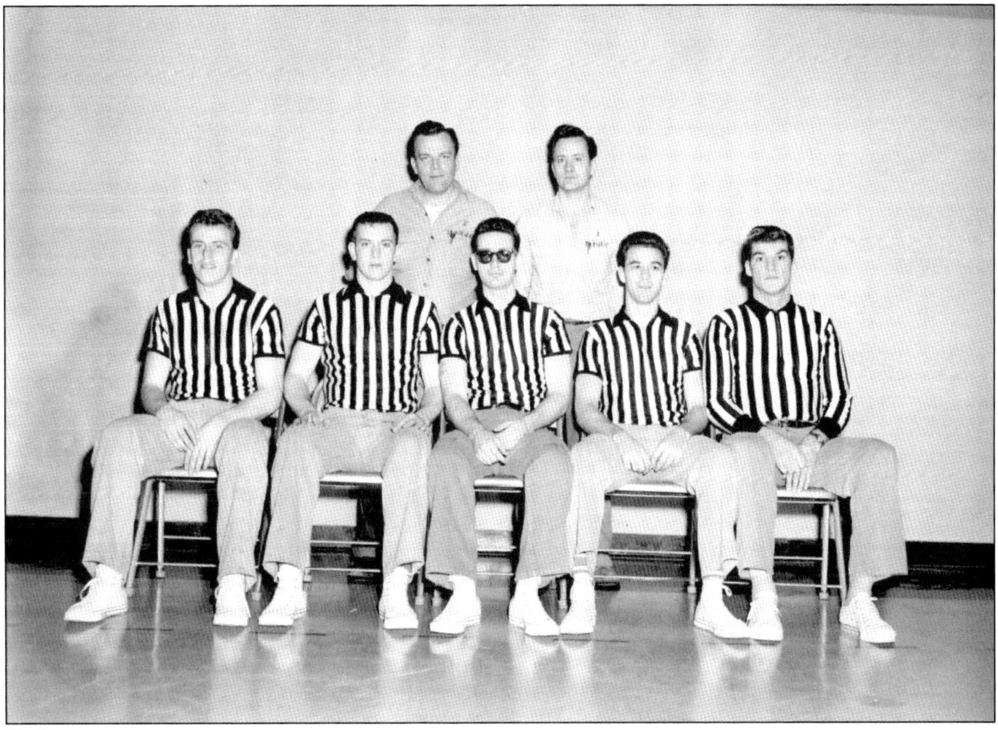

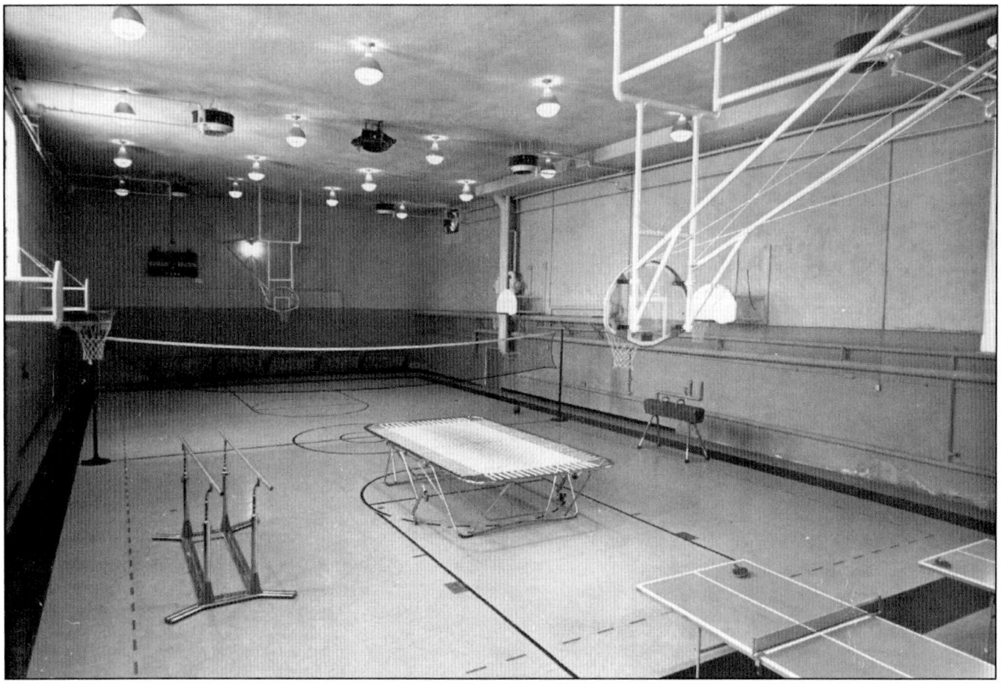

This was originally the boiler room in Shop No. 1. After the new power plant was built in the late 1950s, the area was remodeled for the gym.

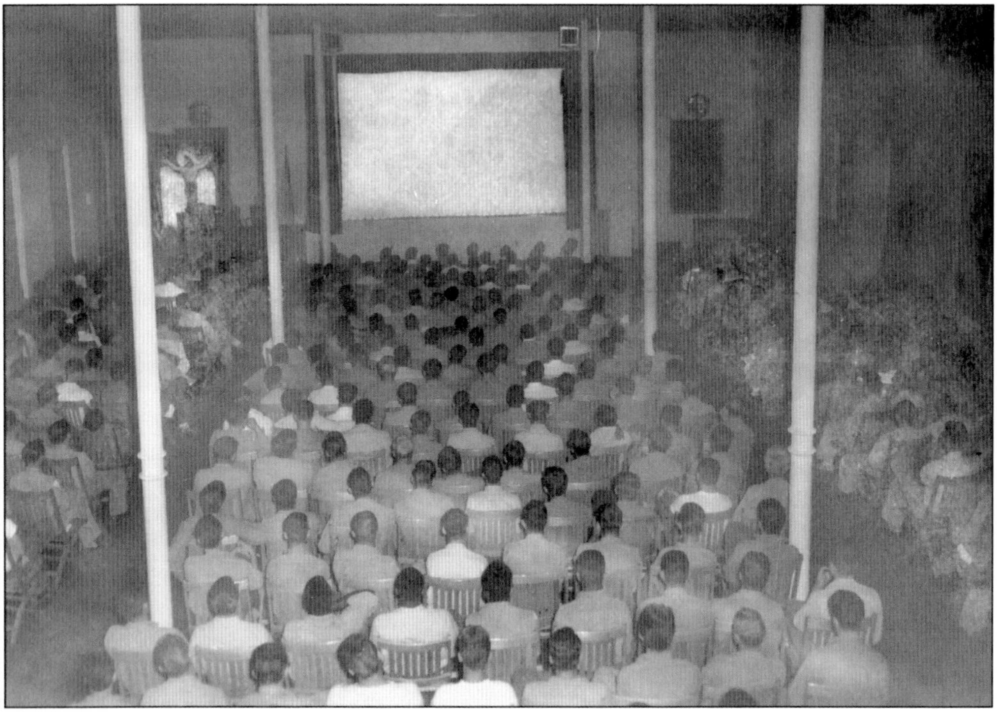

When the former chapel became an auditorium, it was used for theater and music programs. Later it was used to show a weekly movie, until the changing population brought about increased security concerns. Movies are now shown over the television system; inmates watch in their cells.

Six

Hearts and Minds

It may seem as though inmate rehabilitation is a fairly new concept, but it is actually very old. The root of the word penitentiary means "to feel regret." By design, prisons were intended not only to be places of punishment, but of reflection and change. When the prison was first established in Anamosa, local townsfolk quickly "adopted" the inmates, calling them "our prisoners" and showing intense interest in their care and welfare. They donated books and magazines and helped arrange for Sunday school. They delighted in the story of one young inmate who actually requested to stay after his sentence ended, so that he could finish learning the stonecutting trade. The story was evidence that positive things were happening inside the walls.

During the early years, treatment programs were an afterthought compared with the more practical issues of prison security and discipline. This was true in prisons everywhere. Prisons were, after all, supposed to be hard places, and treatment seemed soft. During the 1960s, however, the wisdom of discarding this punitive mindset and embracing the possibilities of treatment and change became gradually adopted into the mainstream of corrections nationwide. At Anamosa, warden Charles Haugh presided over this pivotal event, overseeing the broad expansion of education, vocational training, recreation, and counseling services. Although society's support for prison treatment tends to wax and wane, it seems clear that treatment is here to stay. Broadly defined, treatment involves healing the body, mind, and spirit. What follows are images from these efforts over Anamosa's long history.

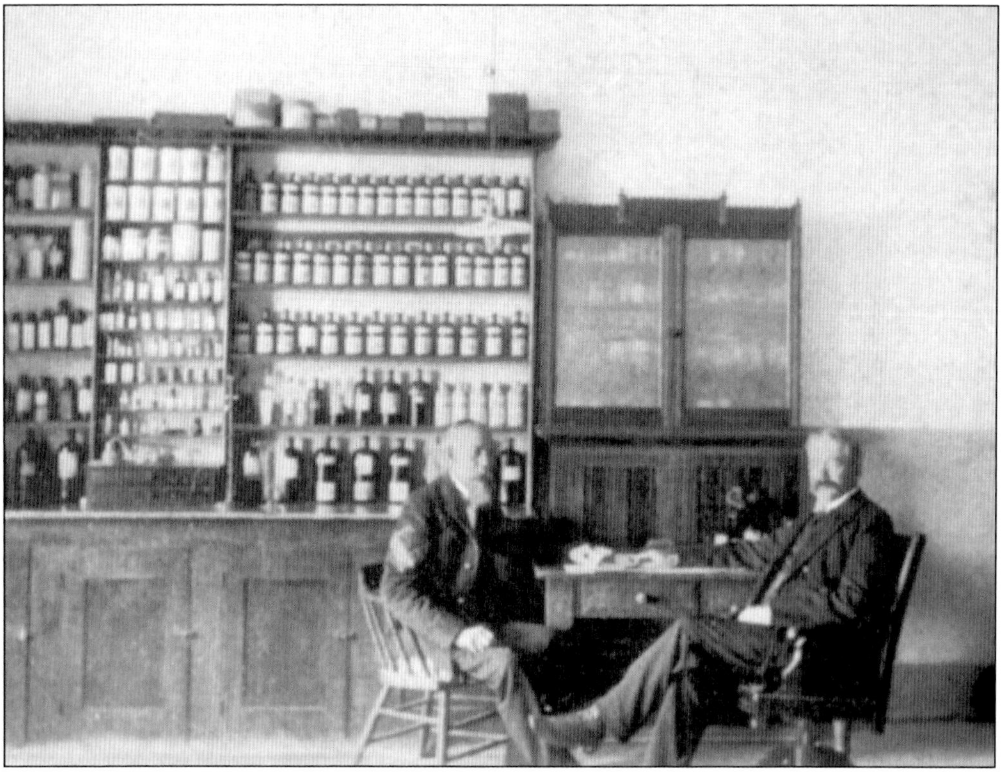

This early photograph shows the doctor's office and pharmacy. (Courtesy Cecilia Hatcher.)

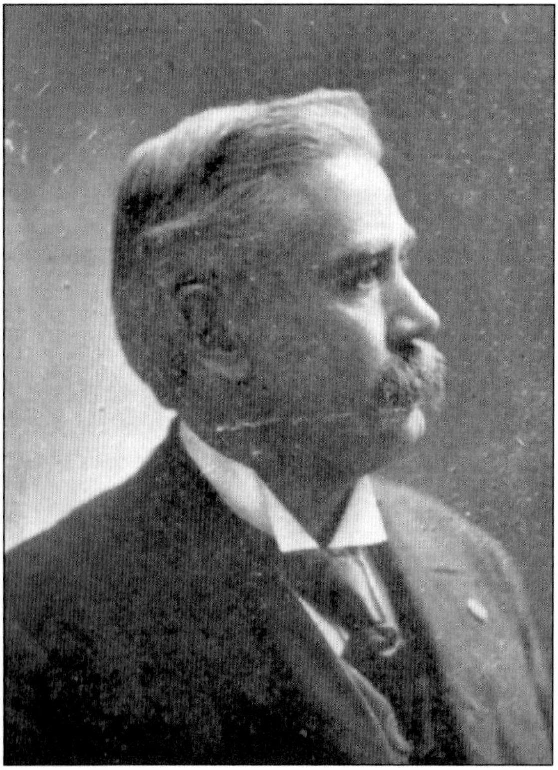

Samuel Druet was the institutional physician from 1898 until 1910. Medical care was often provided by a local practitioner who divided his time between the prison and his private office.

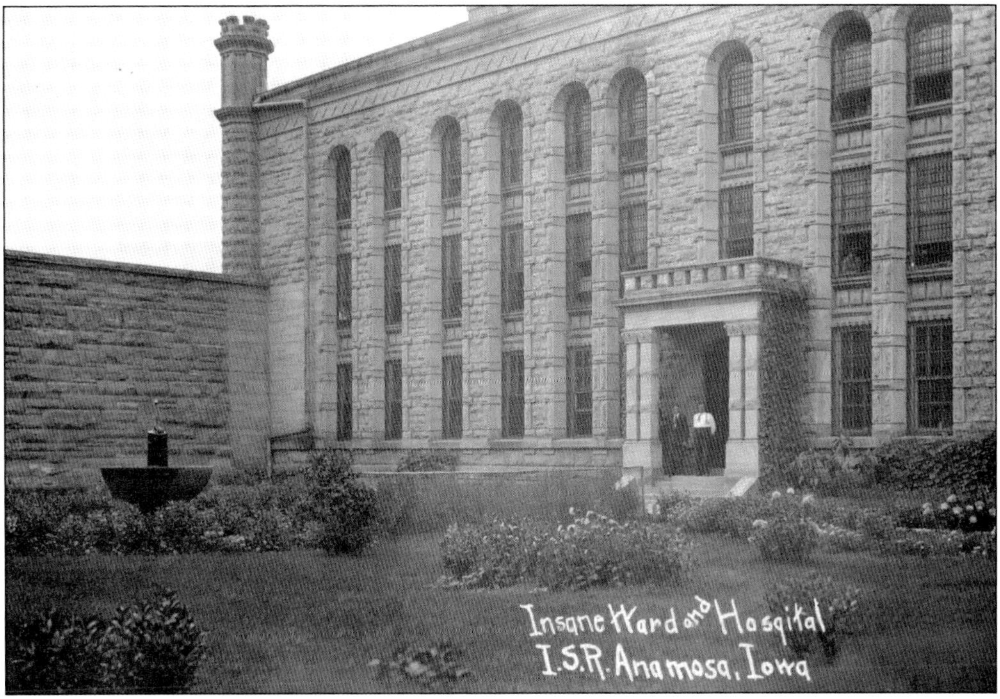

Beginning in 1889, the building above housed Iowa's criminally insane prisoners. Each of the three floors had two wards. Female inmates lived in one of the wards before the female department building opened in 1902. The prison hospital ward was also here. Located outside of the south wall, the building had its own courtyard. It was dismantled in the 1930s to make room for a new hospital.

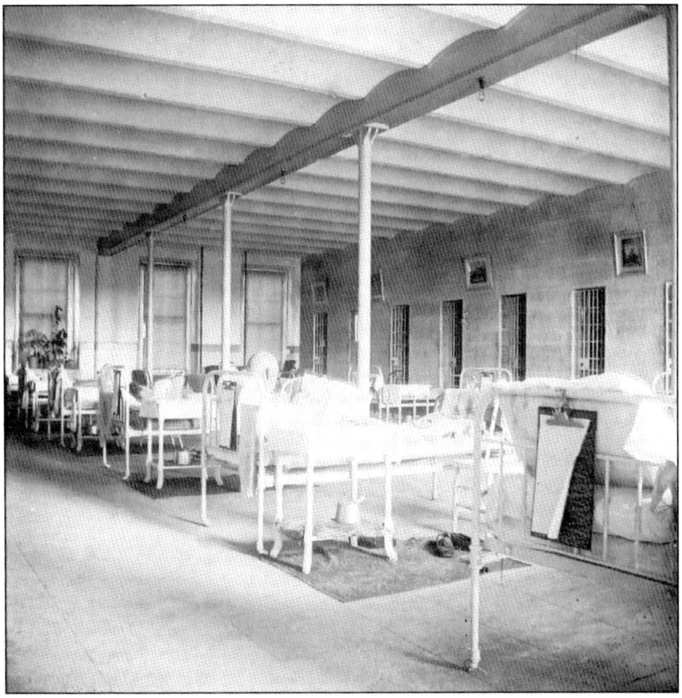

This medical ward, right, was located in one of the six wards in the hospital/insane ward building.

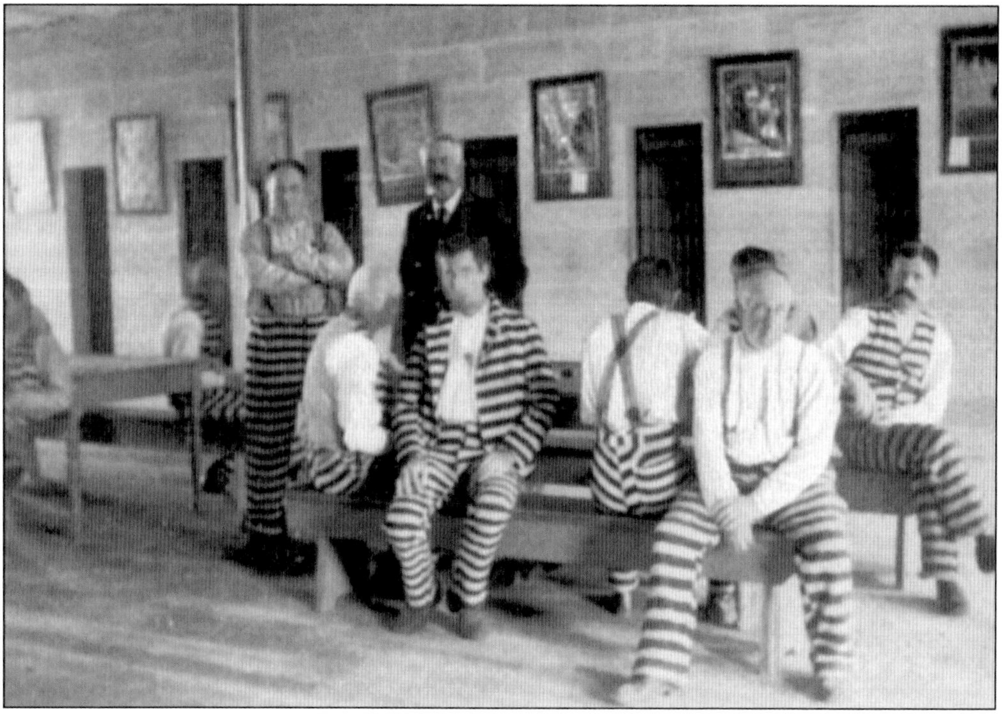

Inmates lounge in the insane ward in the late 1800s. Despite the pictures hanging next to each cell door, the ward is a rather barren environment.

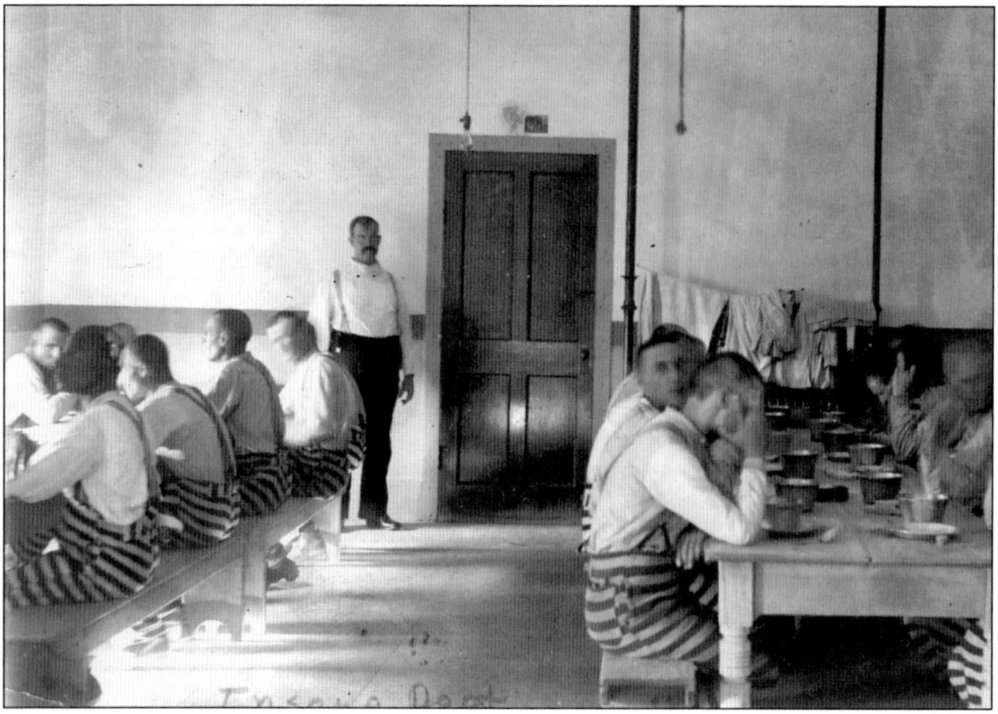

Since the criminally insane were kept separate from the regular prisoners, they ate in their own dining room. This picture was taken in the late 1800s.

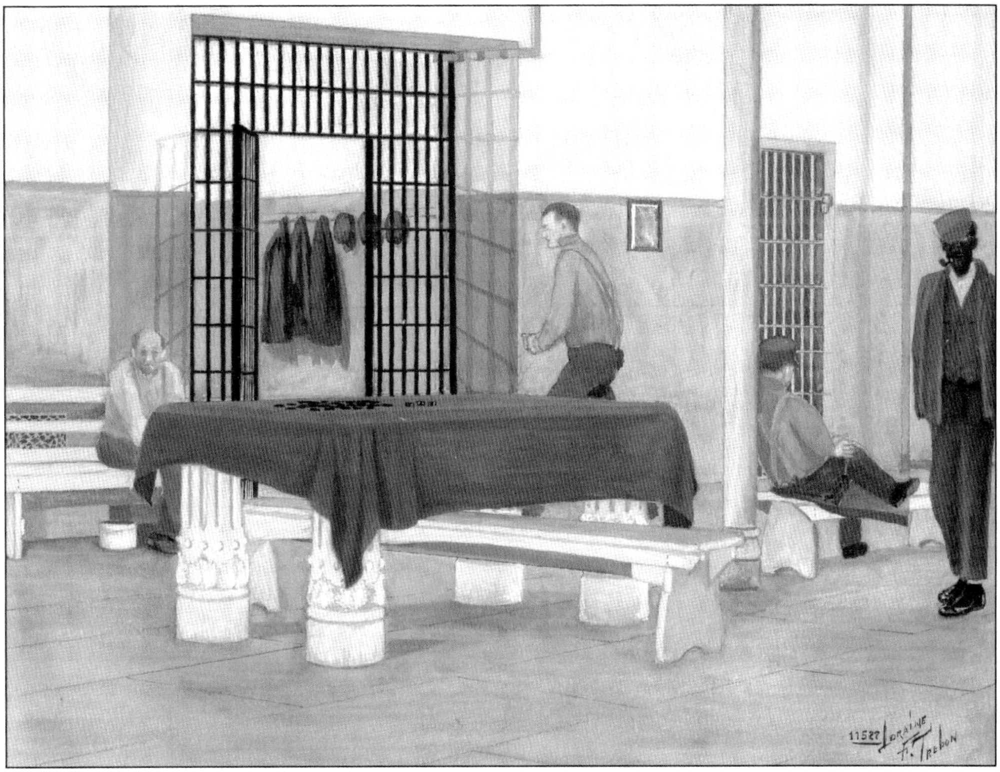

A longtime resident of the Criminally Insane Ward painted this picture of the ward and presented it to warden Charles Ireland in the early 1930s.

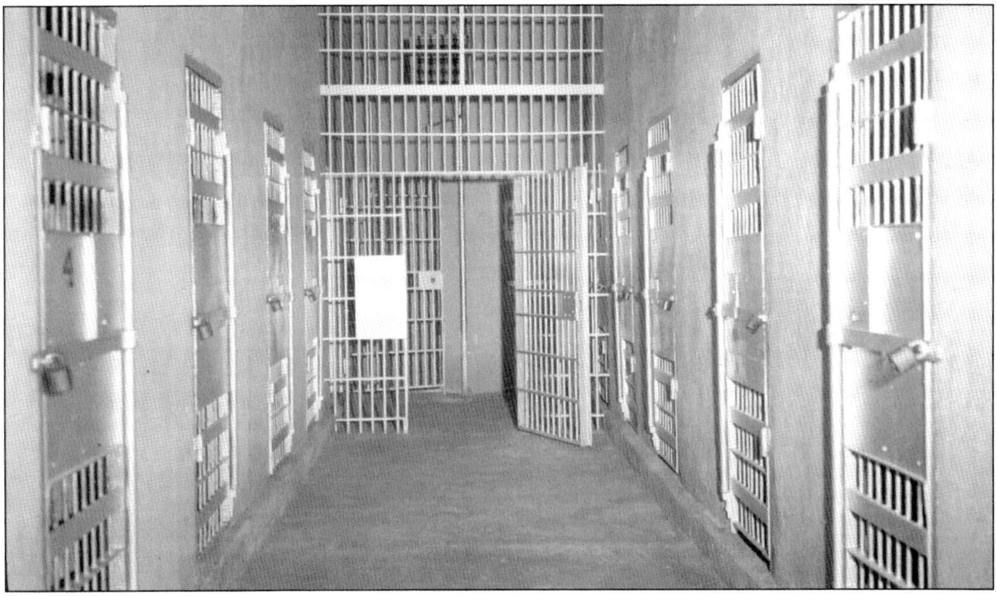

These security cells were in Anamosa's second hospital for the criminally insane. By the 1950s, Iowa was one of the last states to house the criminally insane in a penal institution; state mental health institutions provided psychiatric services at Anamosa for only a few hours per year. In the late 1960s, a separate psychiatric institution was established near Iowa City.

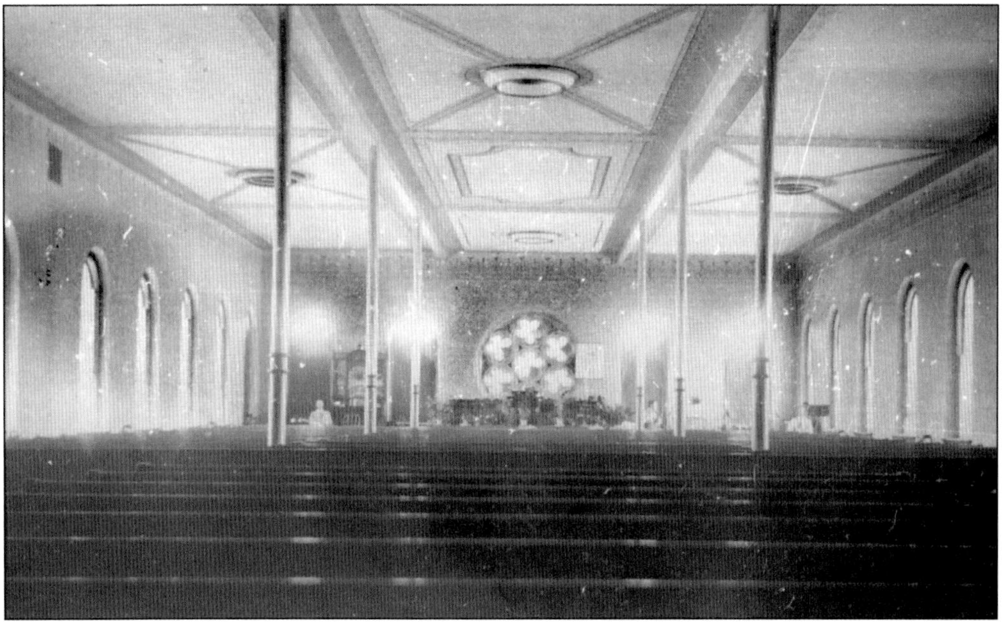

The chapel seated over 800 men for Sunday services. A balcony in the back was used by female prisoners and the local citizens who occasionally attended. After church attendance was no longer mandatory, a smaller chapel area was sufficient and the old chapel became an auditorium used for theater and music programs.

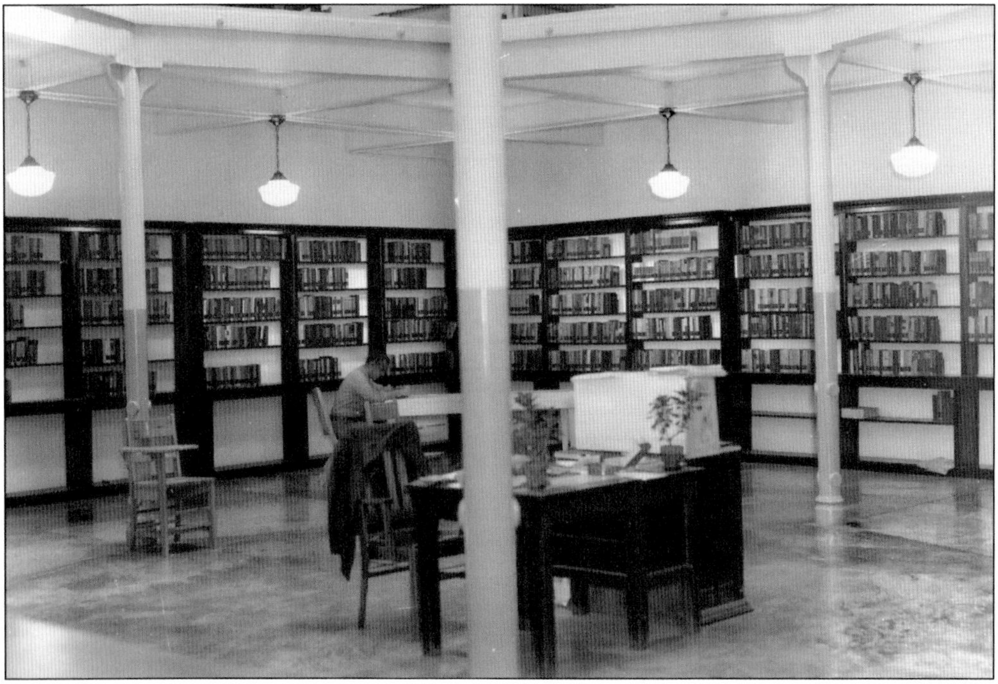

The library was located on the rotunda's second floor for many years. When the rotunda floor was filled in, the library remained. Note the location of the pillars and the place where the railings had been attached. This area was later used for the visiting room and, by the 1980s, the record office.

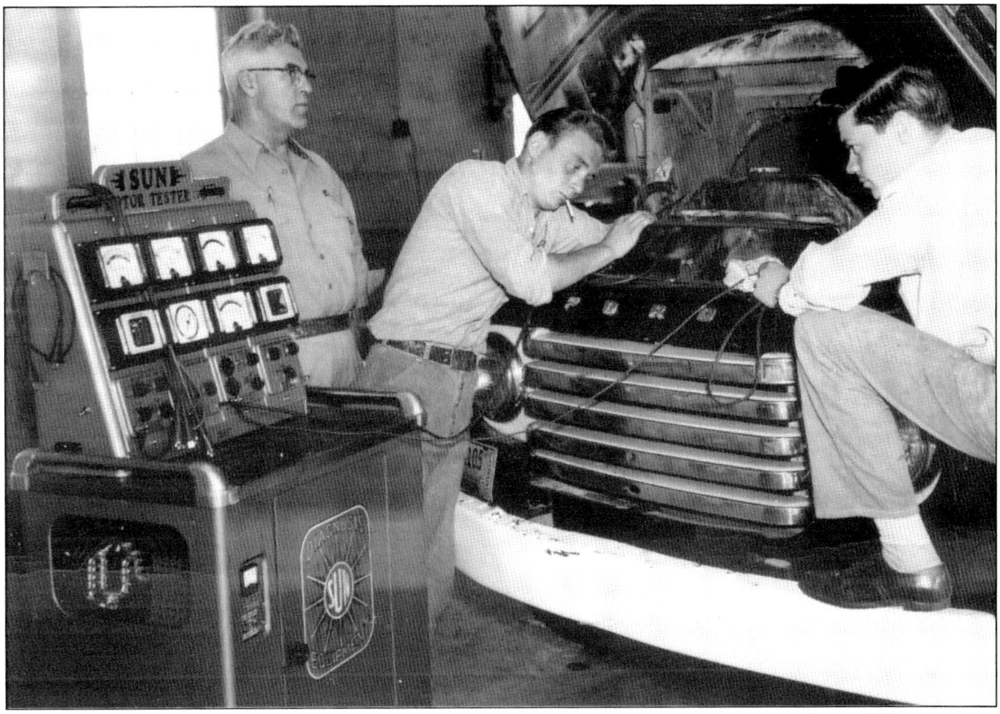

Motor school instructor Howard Fisher supervises two inmate mechanics in this 1950s image.

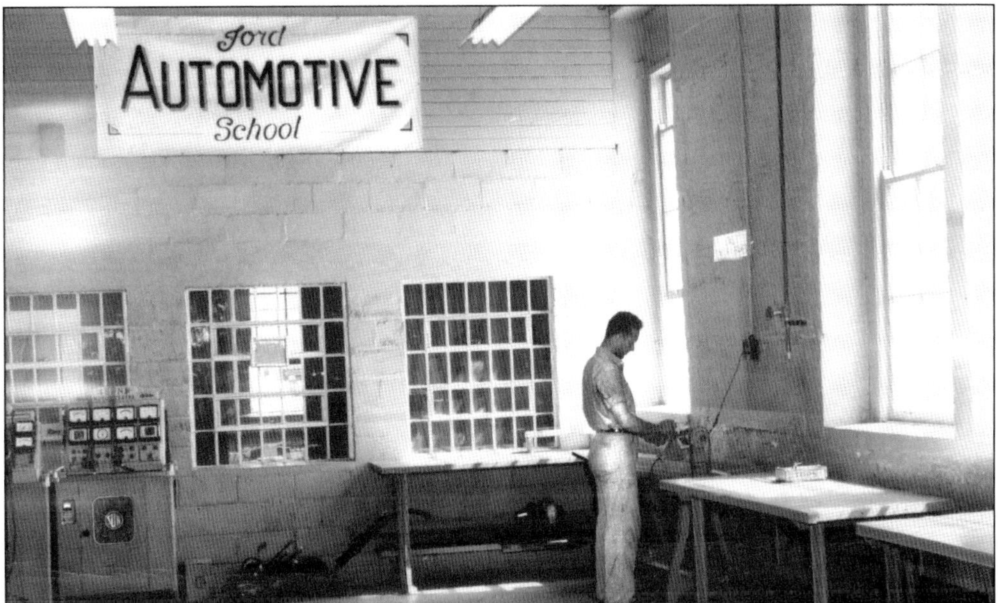

In 1953, the Ford Motor Company donated equipment to help start a training school in automotive repair. First located in Shop No. 2, the program expanded and was eventually moved to its own building. In 1969, Kirkwood Community College contracted to supply all academic and vocational programs, including the automotive school and an auto body repair program. As financial constraints increased, both programs were eliminated.

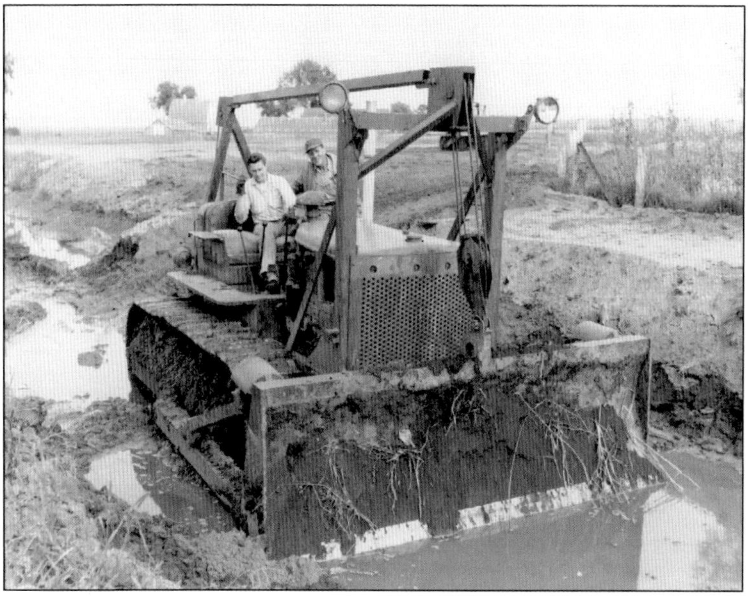

Starting in 1958, the reformatory offered vocational training in heavy equipment operation. While the subject was popular, the machinery was outdated military surplus, and the program was eventually terminated.

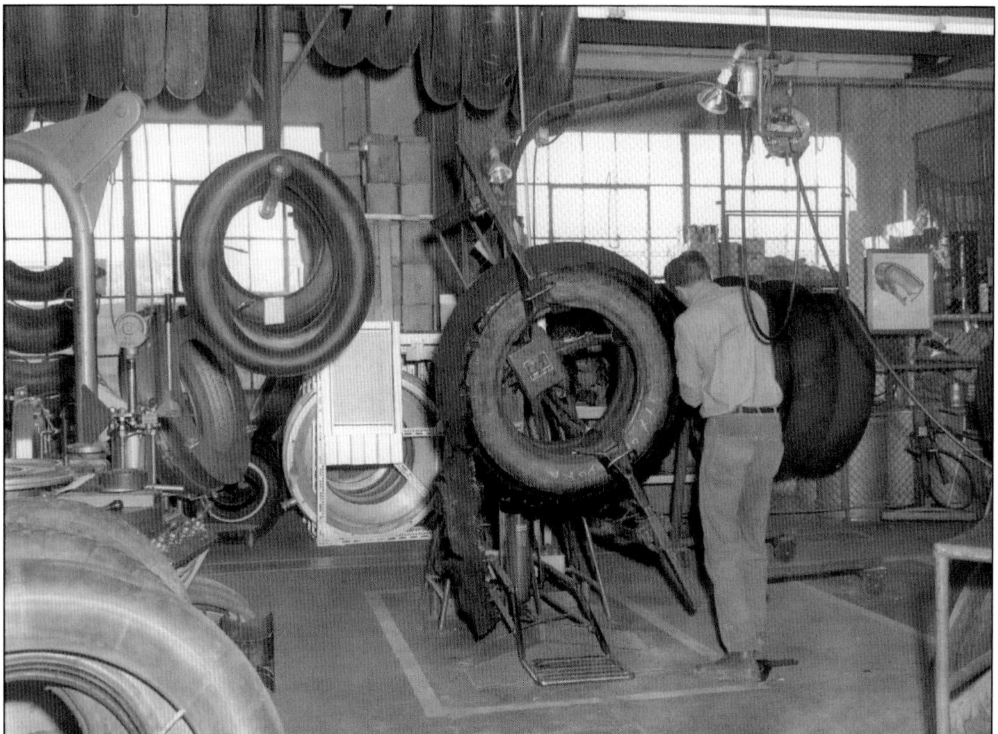

The tire recapping shop was operated by Prison Industries for many years. They recapped truck, school bus, and heavy equipment tires for schools and governmental agencies. The shop also conducted a vocational training class that included written material and a wider range of on-the-job experience than regular workers received. The shop was eventually closed.

The prison promoted many social and self-help groups, including Check Writers Anonymous, Jaycees, and Alcoholics Anonymous. At right, Iowa governor Herschel Loveless visits with an inmate at the 8th annual Alcoholics Anonymous banquet in 1958.

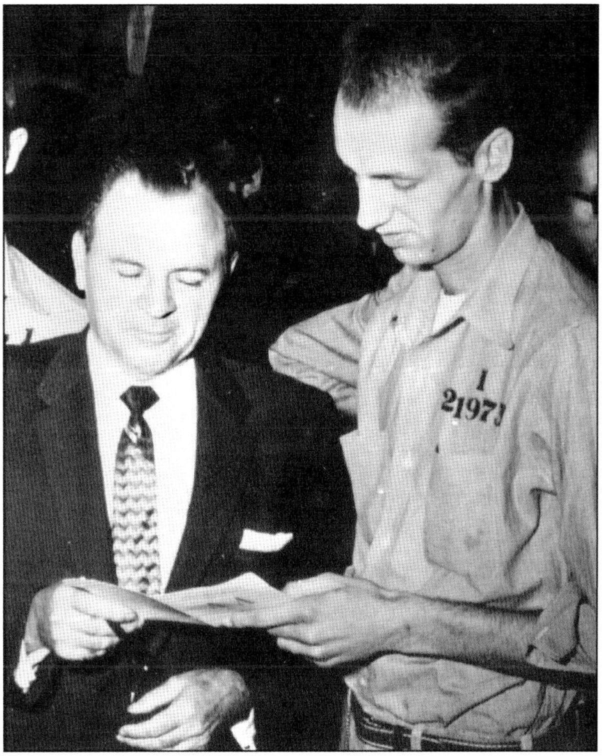

In the photograph below, Fr. Cyril Engler visits with a parishioner. The first treatment staff in most prisons were ministers or priests.

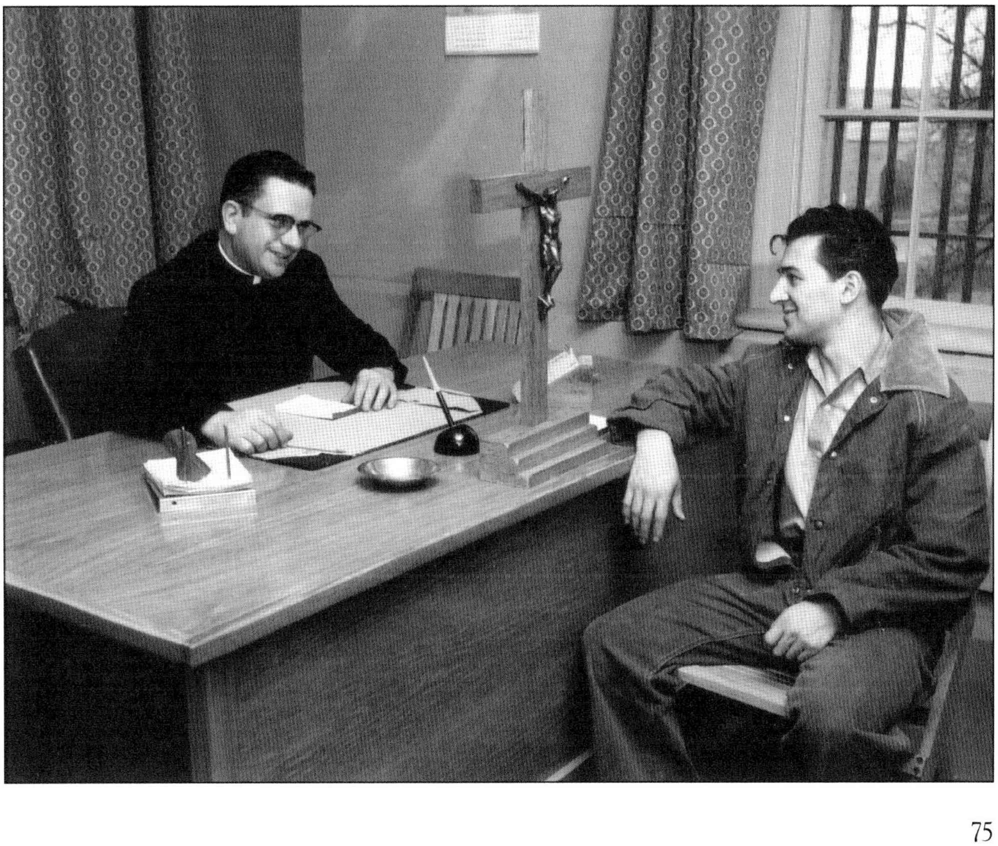

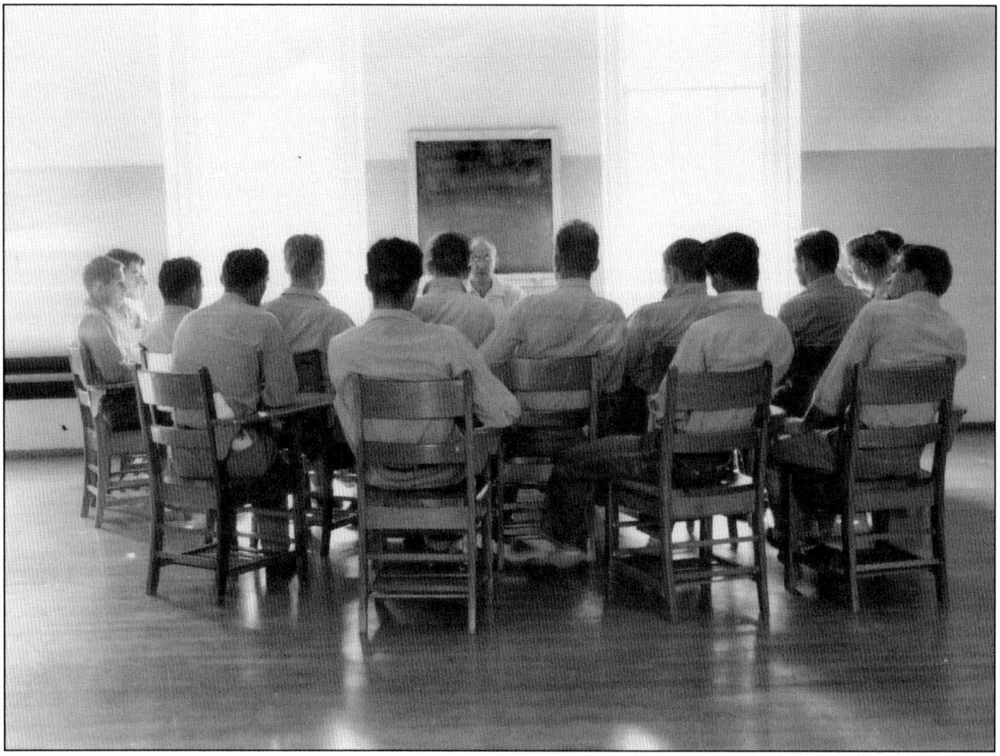

A classroom of inmates listens intently to their instructor.

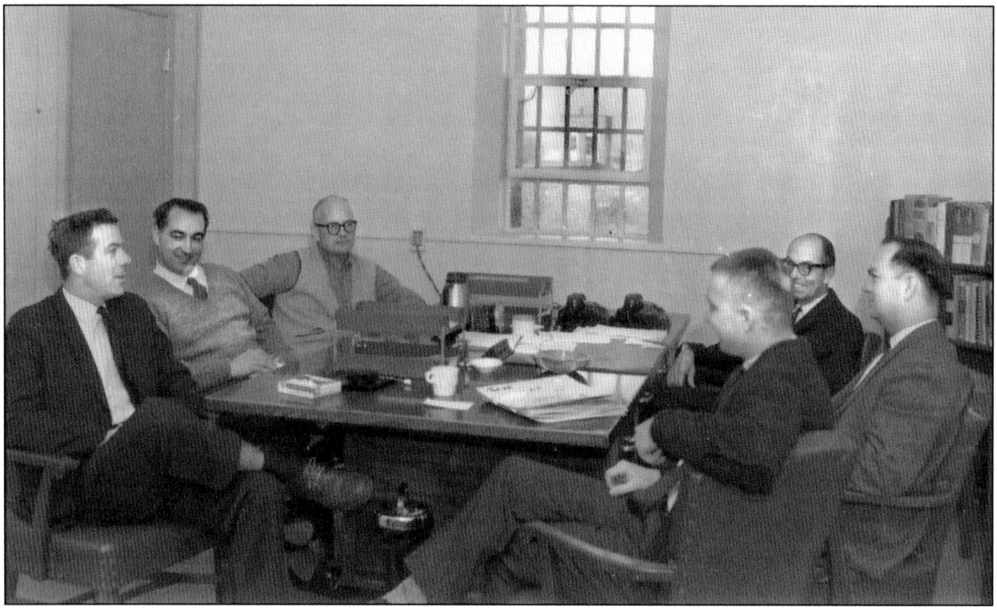

Staff meetings became more common as mental health treatment and counseling became part of the new psychiatric unit. This photograph was taken in the psychiatric unit of the prison hospital before the Iowa Security Medical Facility moved to their new unit at Oakdale.

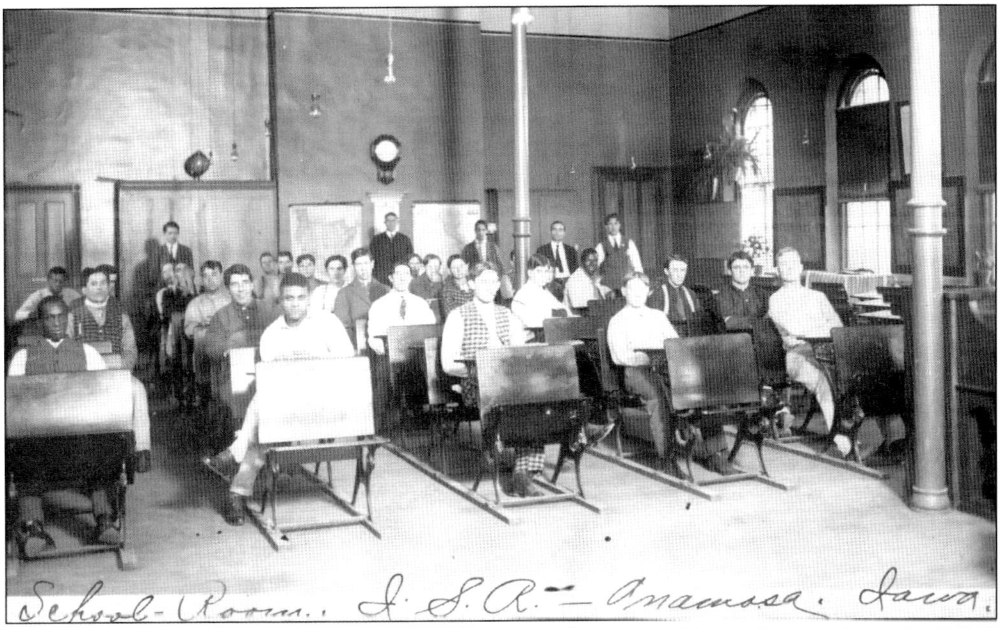

Located in the south wing of the center building, the schoolroom (shown here in the early 1900s) was later used as a recreation hall and now houses the dining hall's dishwashing area. A female instructor taught the female inmates and supervised the male inmates who taught the men.

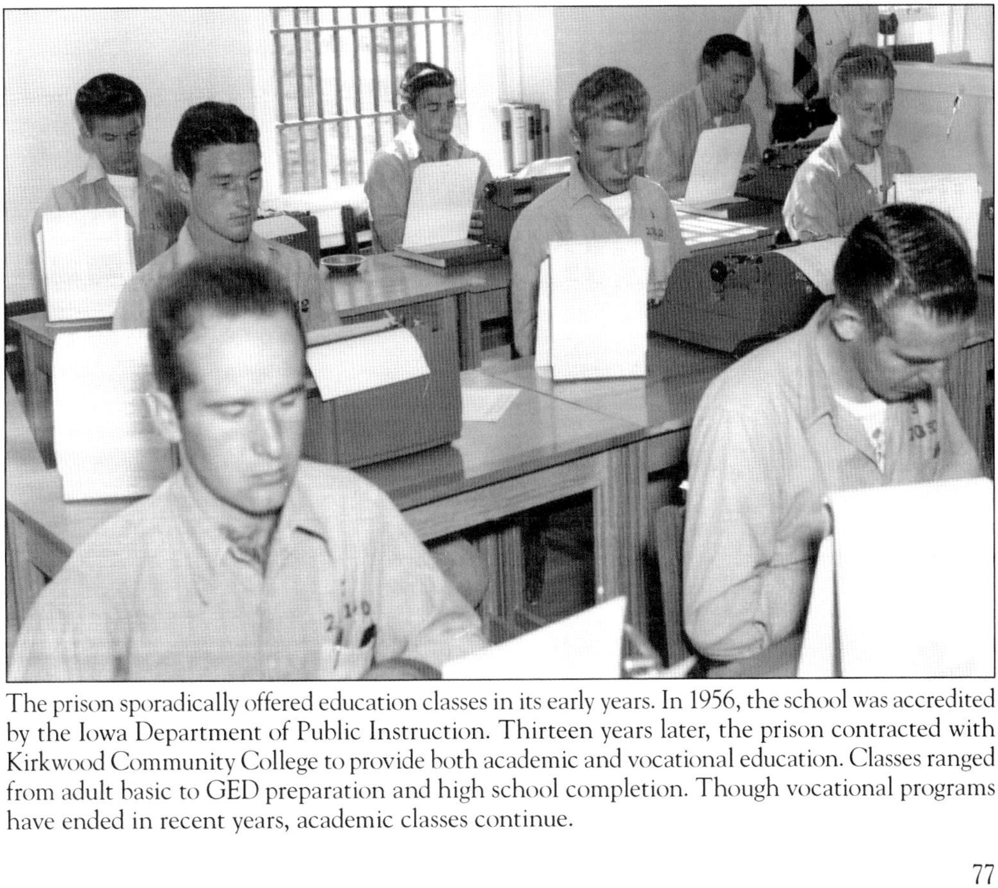

The prison sporadically offered education classes in its early years. In 1956, the school was accredited by the Iowa Department of Public Instruction. Thirteen years later, the prison contracted with Kirkwood Community College to provide both academic and vocational education. Classes ranged from adult basic to GED preparation and high school completion. Though vocational programs have ended in recent years, academic classes continue.

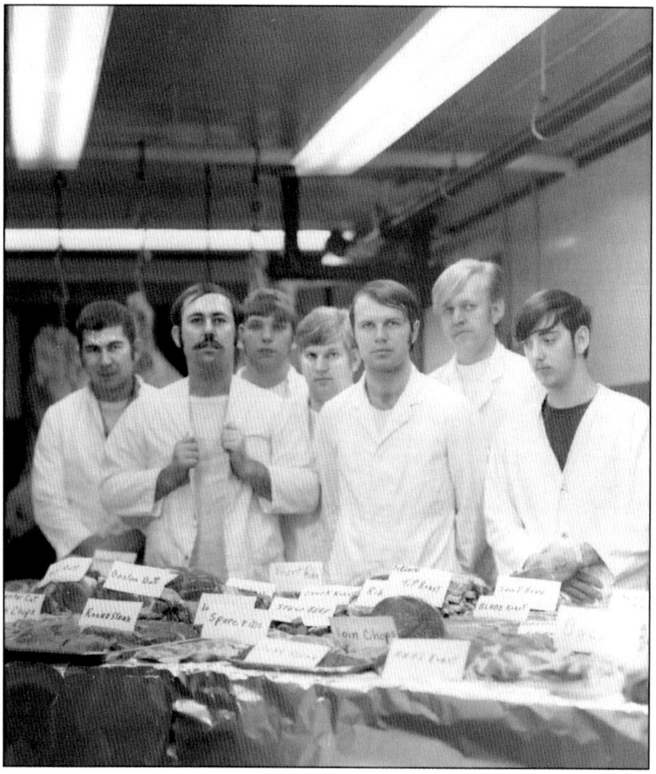

A vocational training program in meat cutting was started in the 1970s. This group of students illustrates the various cuts of meat they are learning about. The institution raised cattle and cut their own meat to be used in the prison kitchen until it became more economical to sell the beef and buy factory-cut boxed meat.

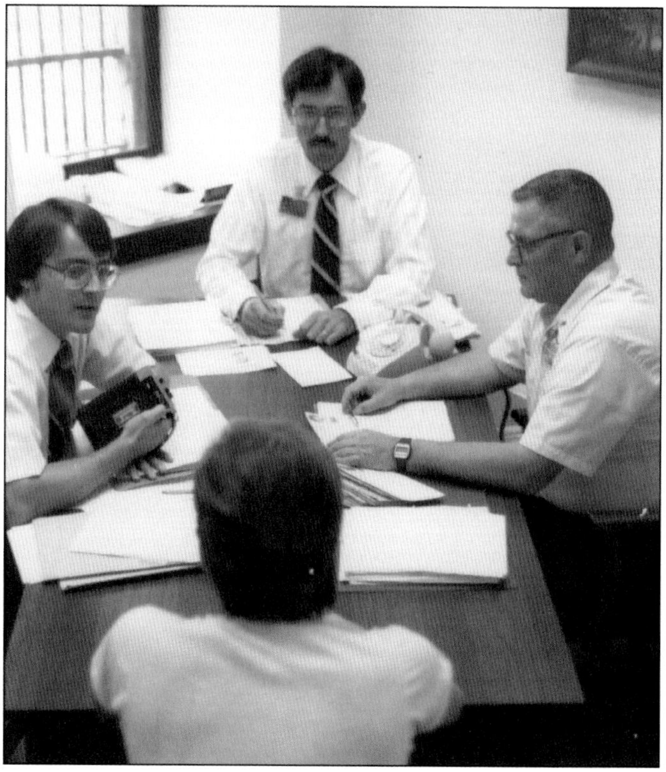

Clockwise from the left, counselor Steve Wendl, classification committee chairman Larry Brimeyer, and correctional officer Lloyd Peterson interview an inmate before making a recommendation.

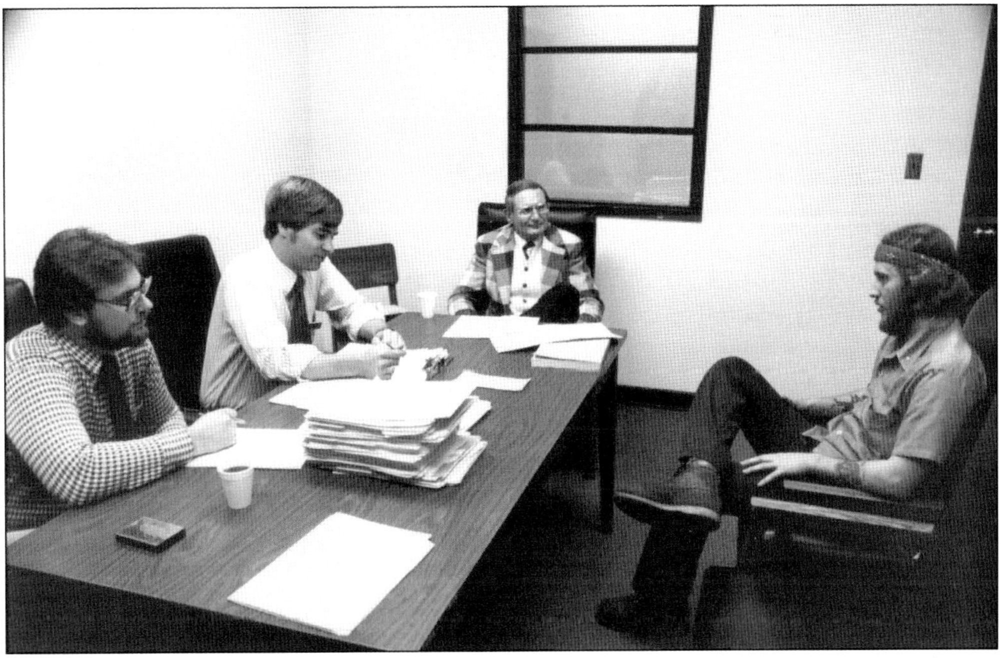

Psychologists Fred Pecharka (left) and Richard Snavely (center) review an inmate with psychiatric consultant Dr. Richard Lee.

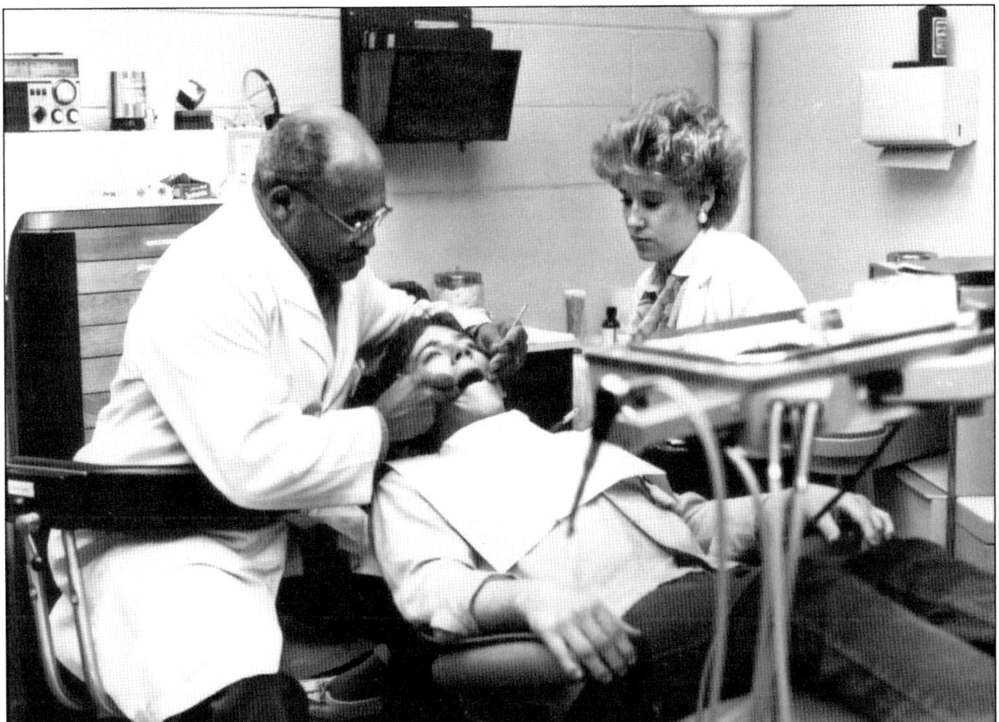

Dr. Russell Collins was the dentist at Anamosa from 1967 until his retirement in 1991. A graduate of Coe College, he completed flight training in the Tuskegee program just before the end of World War II. He later was a military pilot in the Korean Conflict before becoming a dentist.

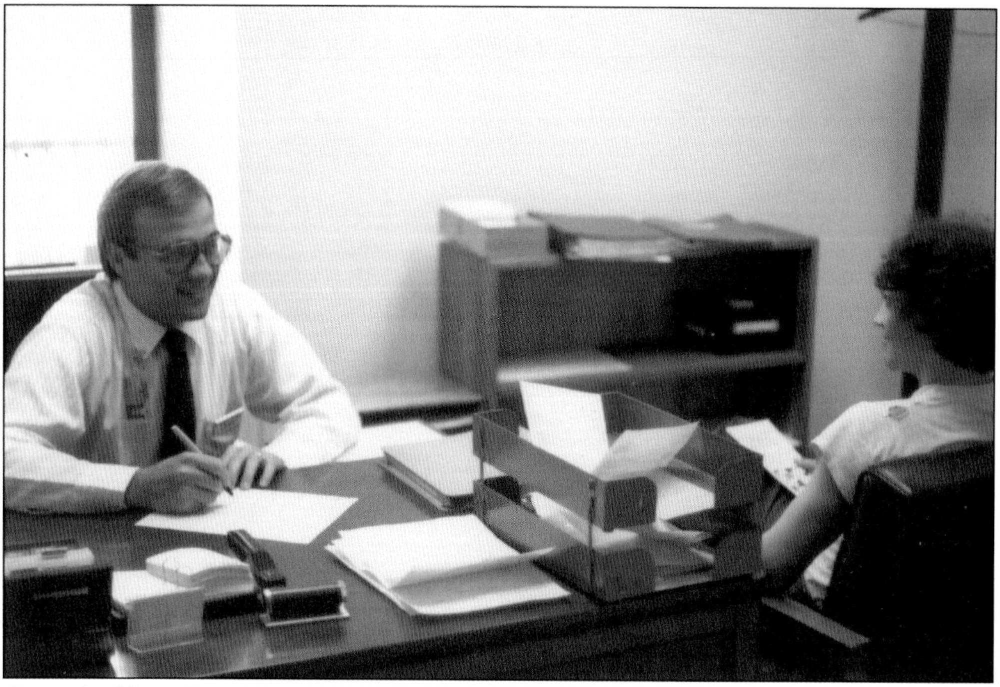

Counselor Harry Brown interviews an inmate. Raised on prison grounds since his father was a longtime supervisor, Brown is now the Associate Warden for Administration.

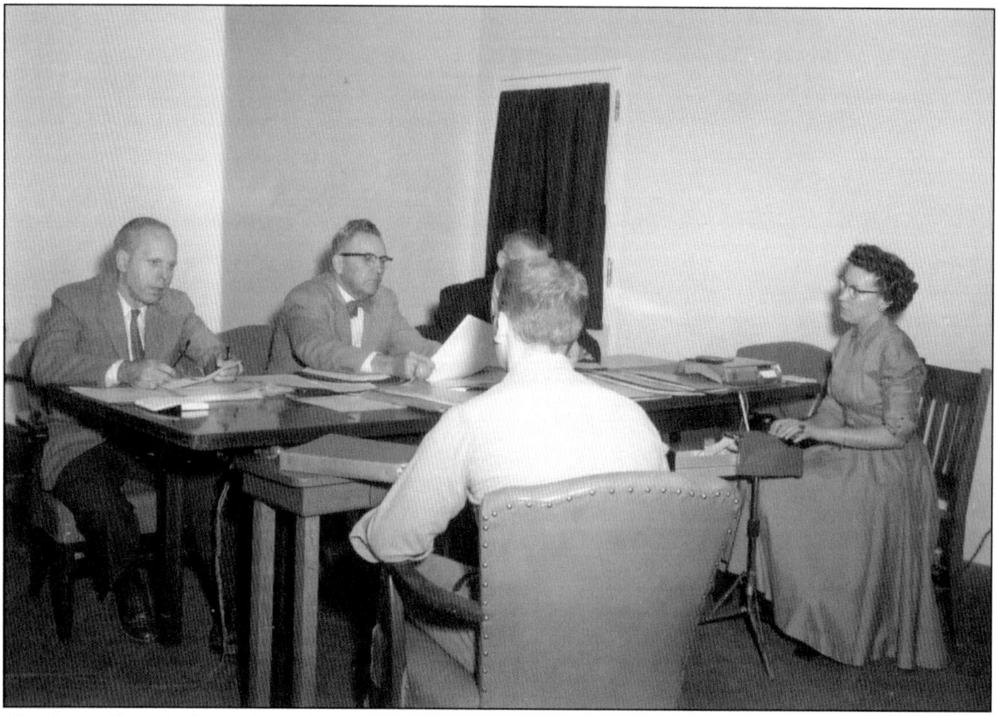

The Iowa Board of Parole is shown meeting at Anamosa in this 1960s photograph. The parole board now usually considers the offender after interviewing him over a two-way television network from their office in the State Capitol.

Seven

Day by Day

Hollywood would have difficulty making an exciting movie about the Anamosa Penitentiary. Daily life here consists primarily of routine. A prison, after all, is really a small city. Every community offers its citizens schools, religious facilities, athletic fields, hospitals, work opportunities, and a protected environment. A typical citizen develops a daily routine within this environment. Prisons and prisoners are no different. In fact, inmate slang for their cell is "house."

Since many prisoners led adrenaline-filled, drug-and-alcohol fueled lifestyles before prison, getting them into a more normal, sober, workaday existence is an important role for the prison. Contrary to popular opinion, most inmates are not locked in their cells all day long. At Anamosa, most inmates enjoy rather liberal yard privileges during daylight hours. When not otherwise assigned to work or treatment programs, inmates are free to mingle in the expansive prison yard or play sports. Many prefer the relative solitude of their cell, however, with television or a book to divert them. However, due to high prison populations over the last few decades, most inmates have at least one cellmate.

Prison life used to be quite austere—marching in lockstep and observing strict silence in the dining hall were part of daily life, and a price was to be paid for violating the rules. In Anamosa's early days, bread and water in isolation, or being handcuffed to the cell door for a period of time was used for control and punishment. An early method of encouraging compliance with prison rules remains effective even today—time off for good behavior. In addition, the inmate knows that violations of prison rules will be looked on unfavorably by the parole board.

Time has a different meaning here. Calendar pages hang in every cell. Days are counted down. The clock is watched. That's why they call it "doing time."

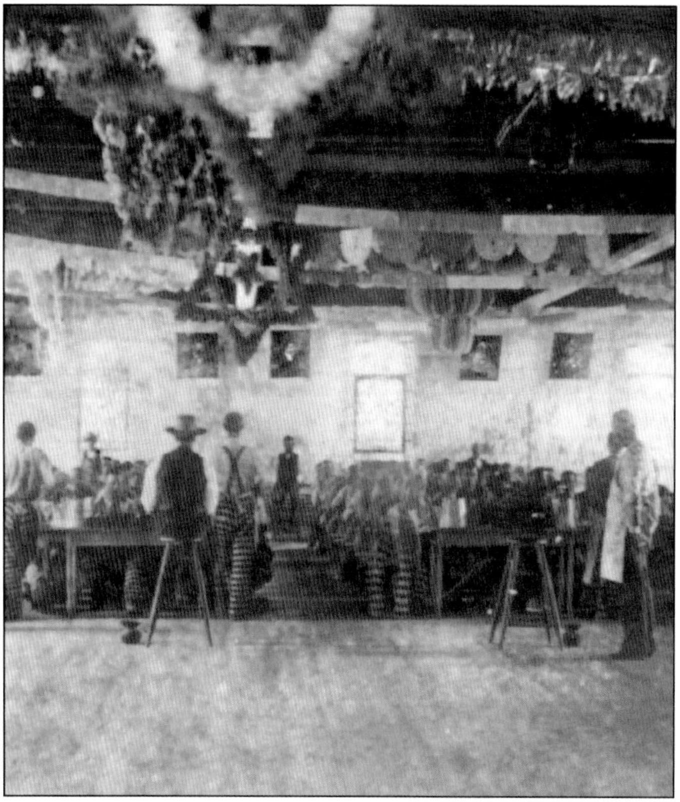

This image shows the old dining hall located in Shop No. 1. This was the first building constructed by the inmates, and it burned in 1896. Note the paintings hung on the bare stone wall in an apparent attempt to introduce some culture. What appear to be Christmas decorations hang from the ceiling. The guards are stationed around the room, sitting on tall stools next to strategically placed spittoons. (Courtesy Paul C. Juhl Collection ISHS.)

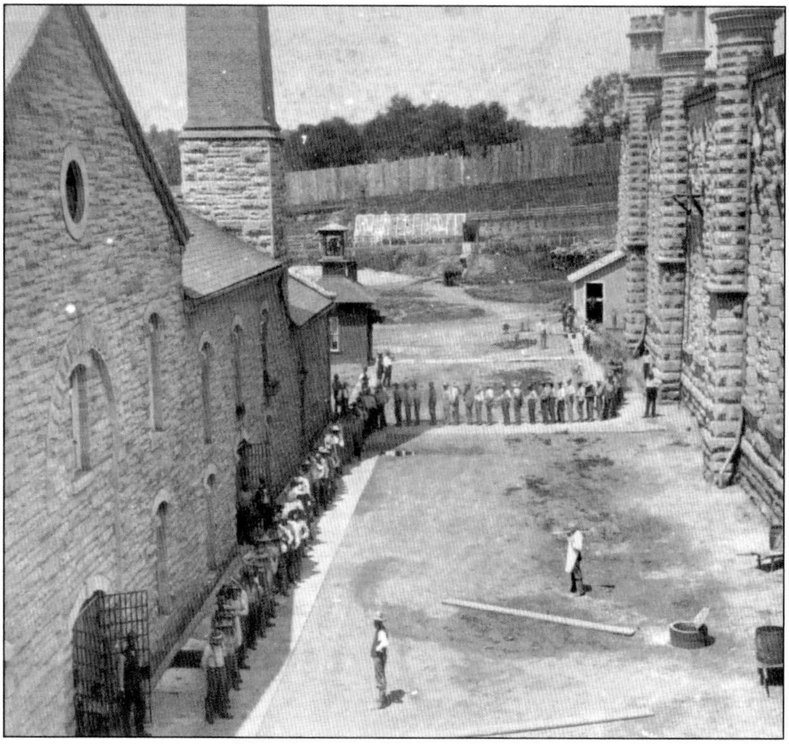

This early 1880s photograph shows inmates coming out of the cell house and apparently lined up to enter Shop No.1, perhaps for a meal. On the hill in the background is the wooden stockade that contained the prisoners until the stone wall was completed in 1885. Note the greenhouse just below the stockade. This view is looking north from Tower No. 2.

The northeast corner of the south cell house was used as the barbershop in the late 1800s. Note the officer holding a nightstick; they were still routinely carried until the 1960s.

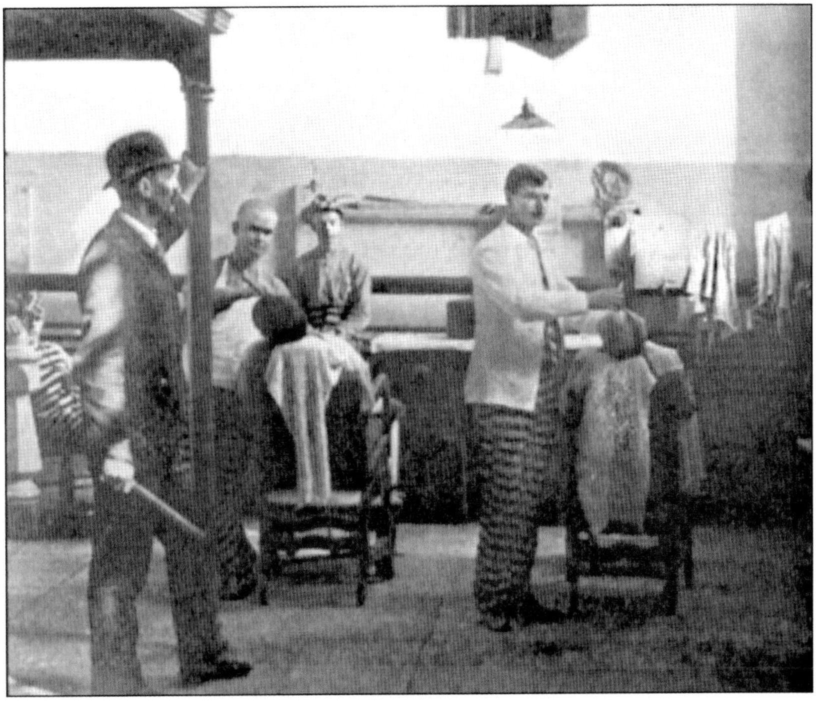

Below, inmates are pictured marching out of the south cell house.

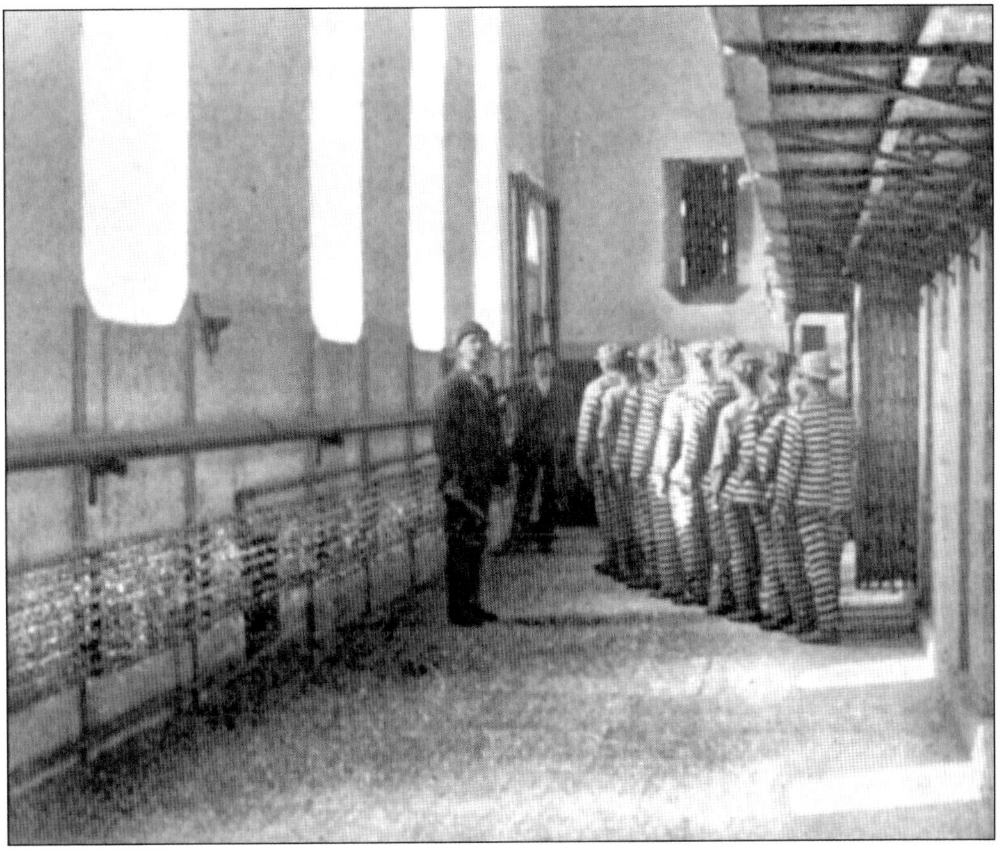

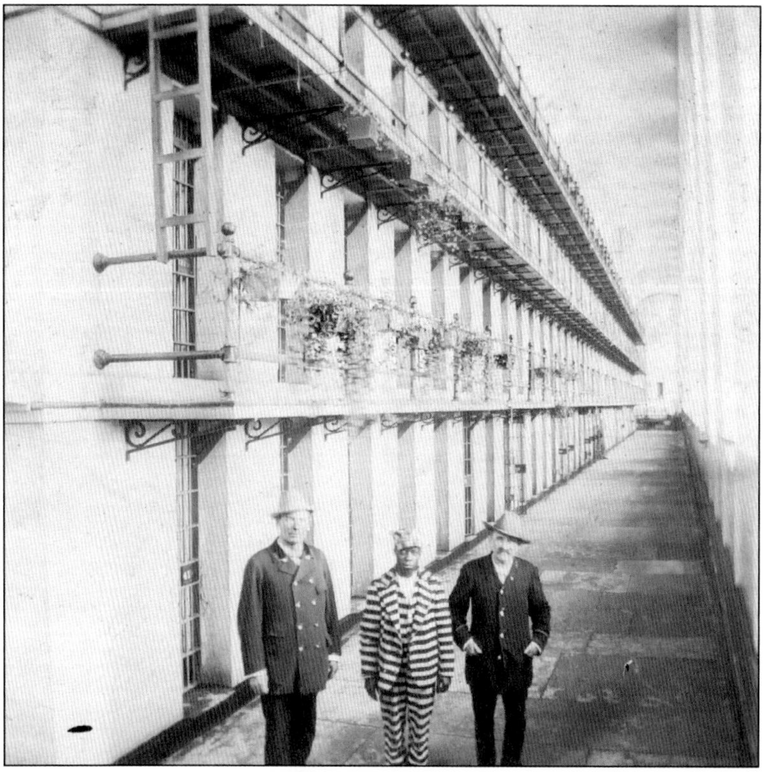

An inmate stands between two guards in the south cell house, probably about 1900. Note the planters along the railing, and the vines that do little to soften the harsh reality of the cellblock. This cell house remains in use today.

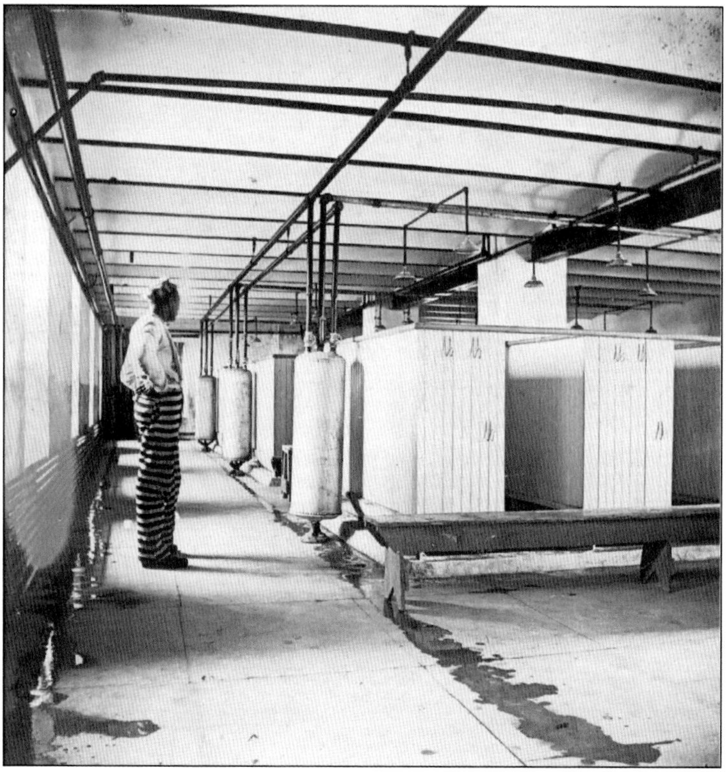

This shower room had hot and cold running water and was located in the lower level of the center building.

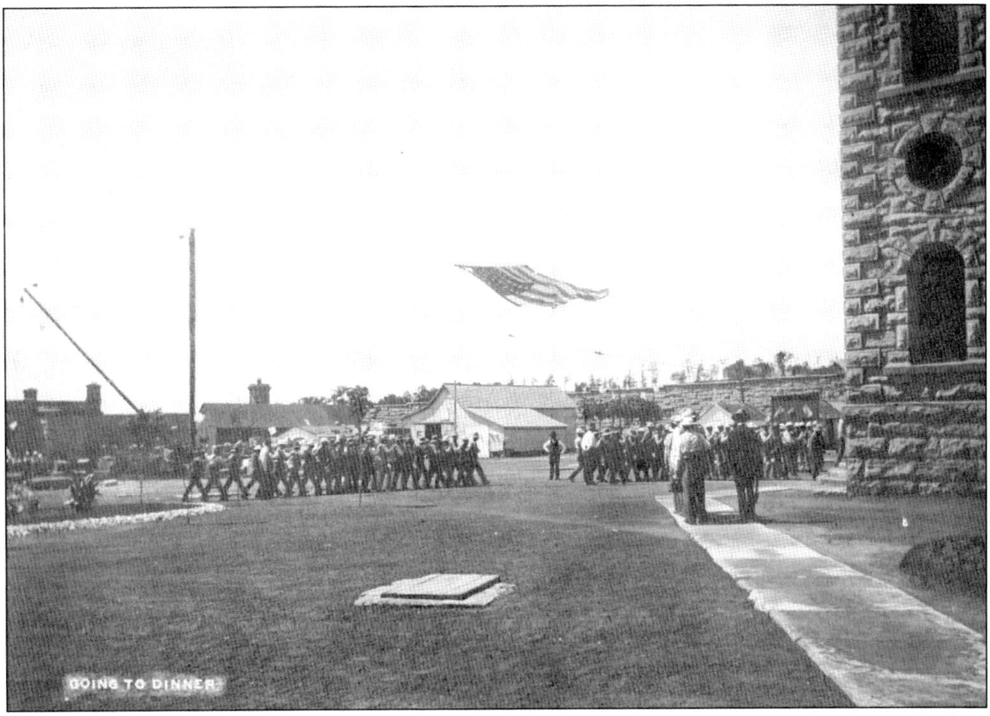

The image looks to the northwest and shows groups of inmates walking to the dining hall in lockstep. Each man had his right hand on the right shoulder of the man ahead of him, marching in unison. The cables in the photograph anchor the cranes used in the construction of the yet unfinished prison. The lockstep was abolished soon after this picture was taken about 1900.

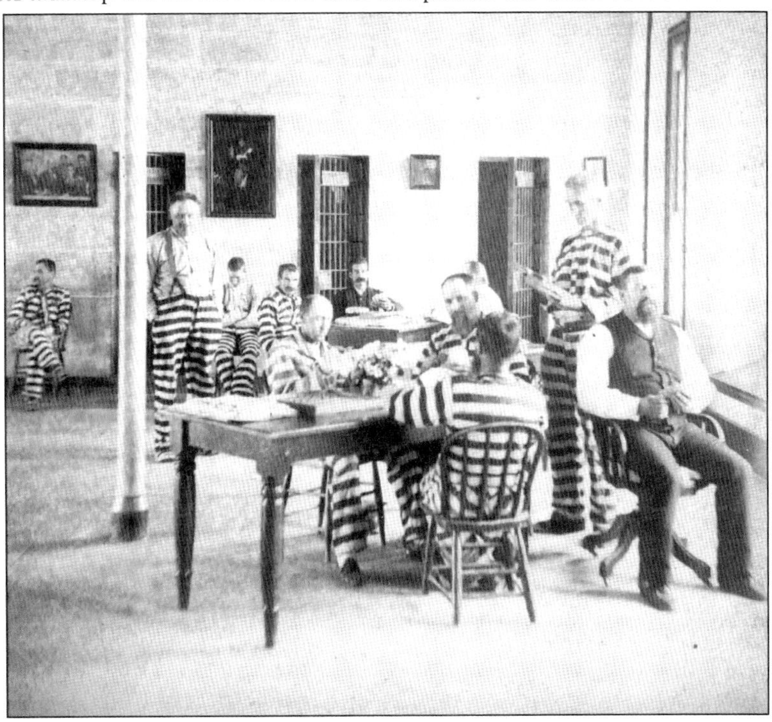

This view of the insane ward dates from the late 1800s. The patients appear to be playing a game of cards, while the staff member seems to be acting like he is not involved. The cards in his hands would suggest otherwise.

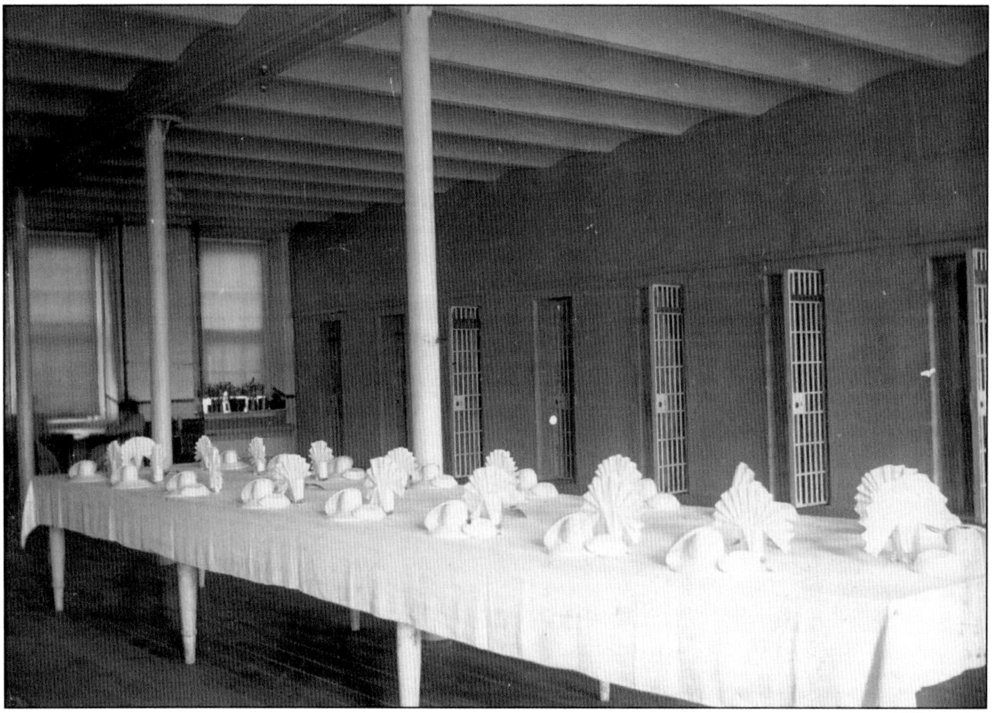

A fancy table setting has been prepared in the female ward of the hospital. The elegance of the table setting in front of the stark cell doors creates an interesting contrast.

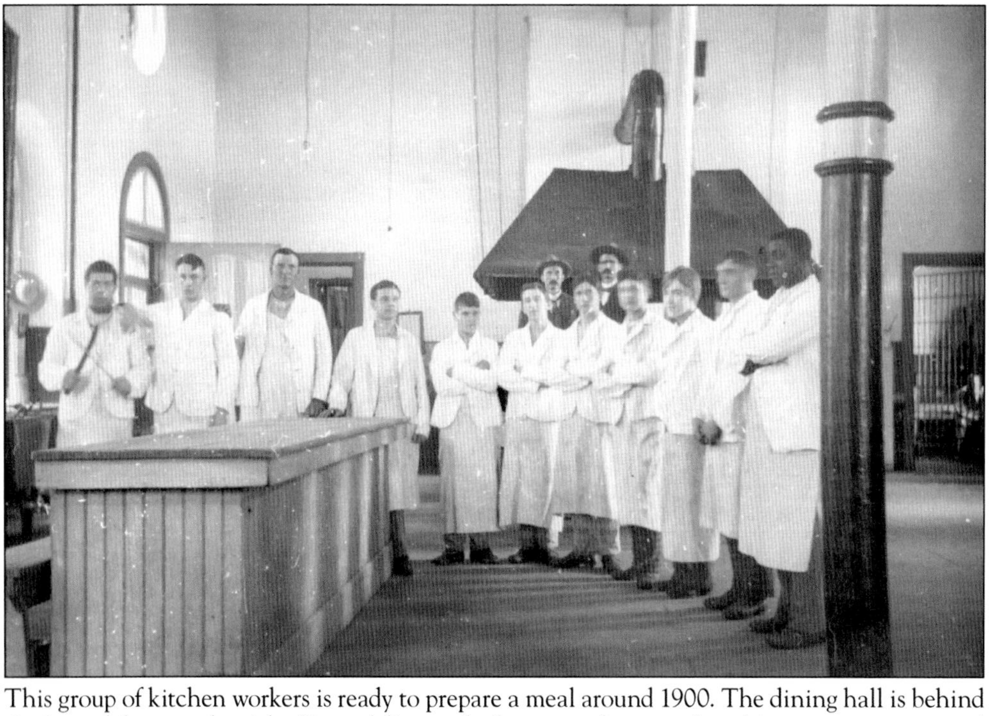

This group of kitchen workers is ready to prepare a meal around 1900. The dining hall is behind the barred door on the right. Remodeling took place over the years, but this same room was used to prepare meals until 2009.

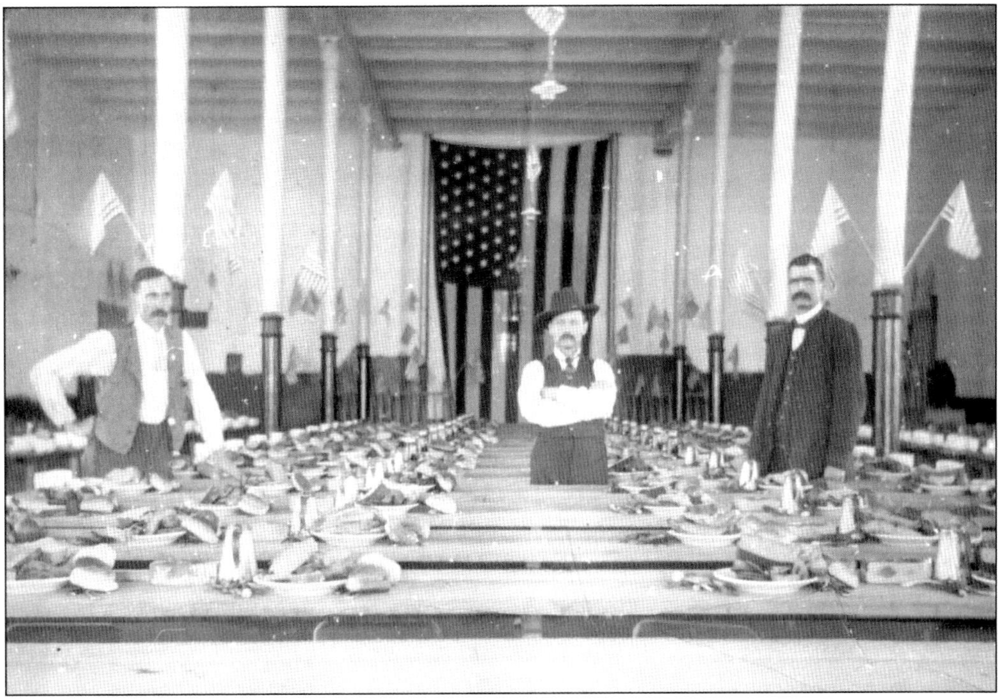

The penitentiary often celebrated holidays by decorations, special foods, athletic events, and allowing the inmates more hours out of their cells. This photograph appears to have been taken about 1900, and the many flags suggest a Fourth of July celebration. The slate tables in the dining hall are already set, complete with the meal.

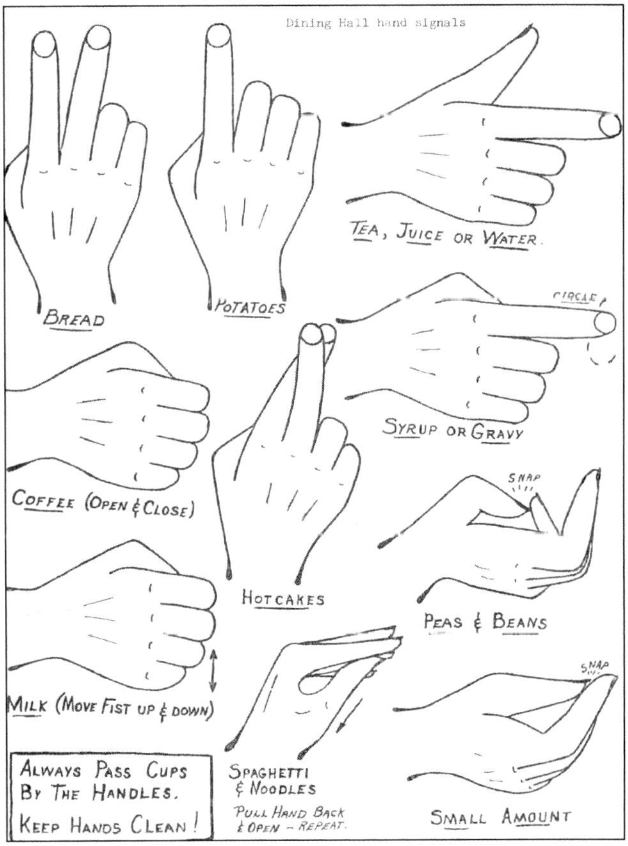

Prior to the mid-1960s, talking in the dining hall was forbidden. Inmates were usually escorted into the room by their work supervisor, who stood near his men. Food was served from large pots. These hand signals were used to request the food. When the work supervisor gave the order, his group left, either because they were finished or because they were getting too restless.

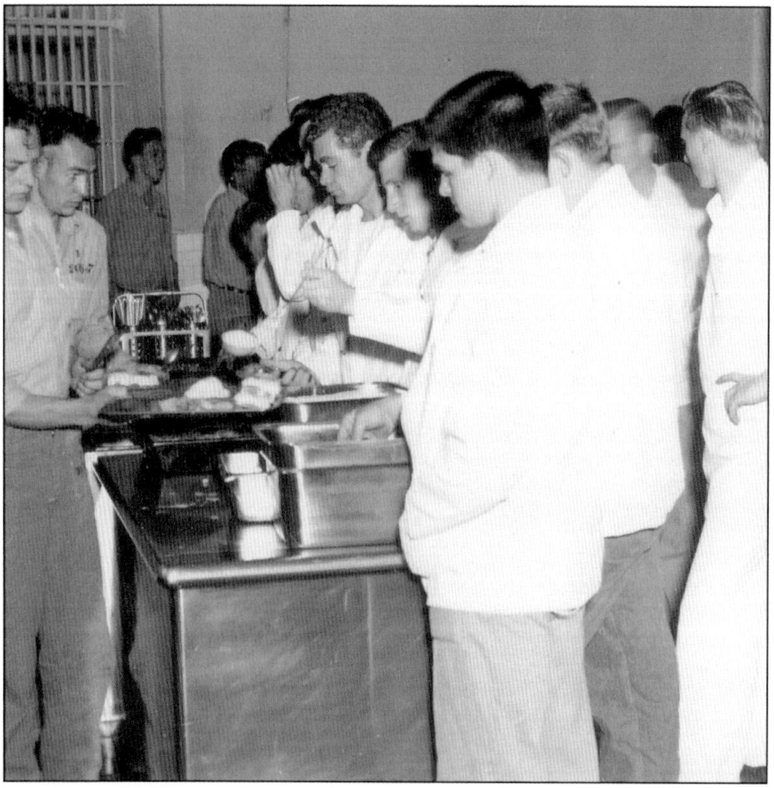

By the mid-1960s, the long slate tables were removed and the men could enter the dining hall on their own during scheduled meal times. The food was served on steel trays. Inmates could sit with whomever they chose, and talking was allowed. They were, however, expected to eat all the food they took.

Below, the dining hall is pictured about 1975.

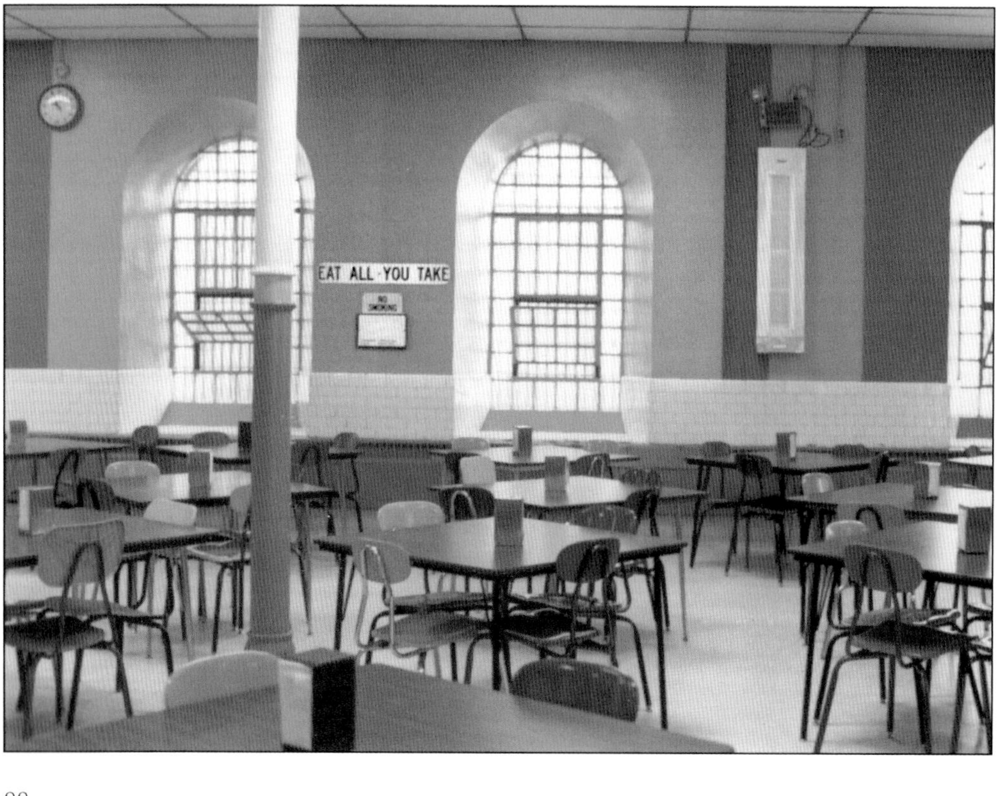

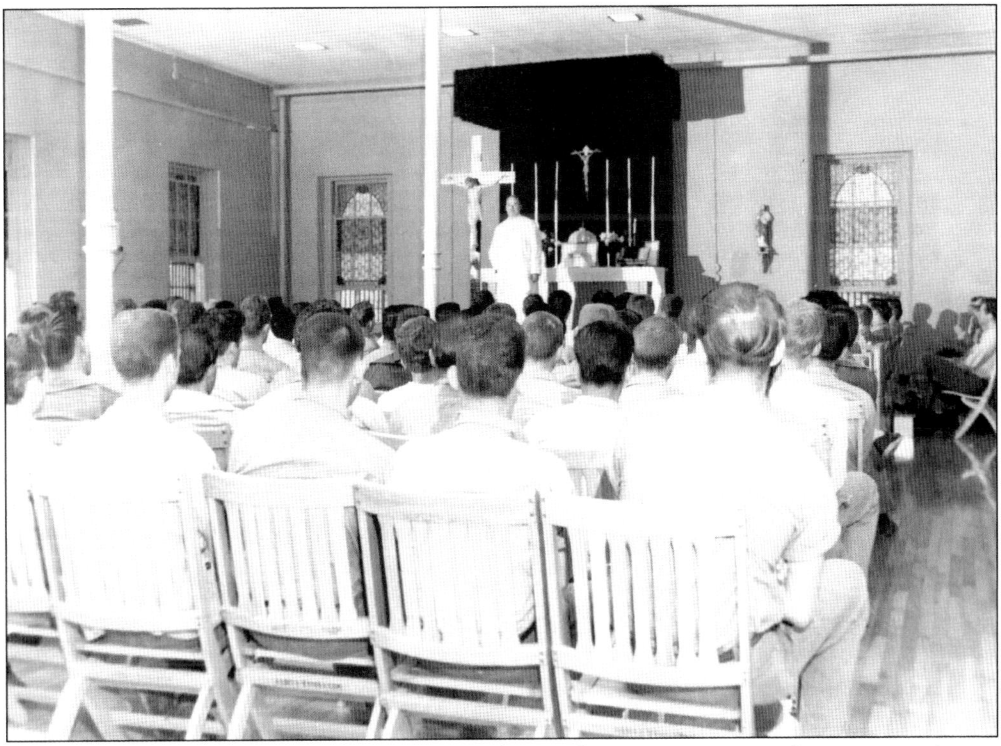

This photograph illustrates the interest in religion that many inmates demonstrate during their incarceration.

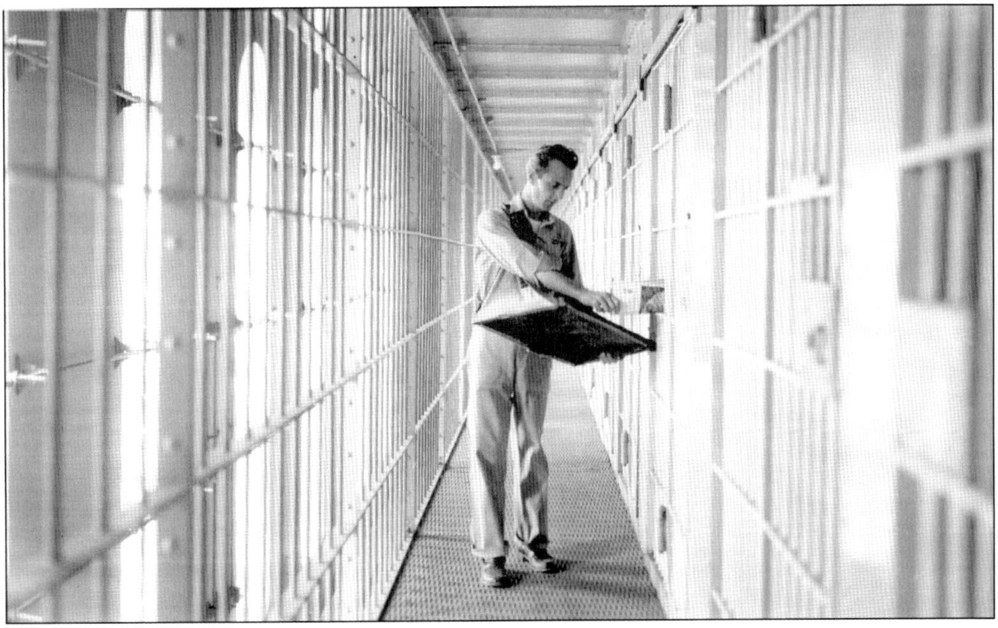

Here an orderly passes out mail in the north cell house. During the 1963 riot, inmates rocked back and forth in unison until the steel cell block swayed several feet at the top. It was later removed and the space remodeled to contain the visiting room, social services department, health services department, and a small housing unit.

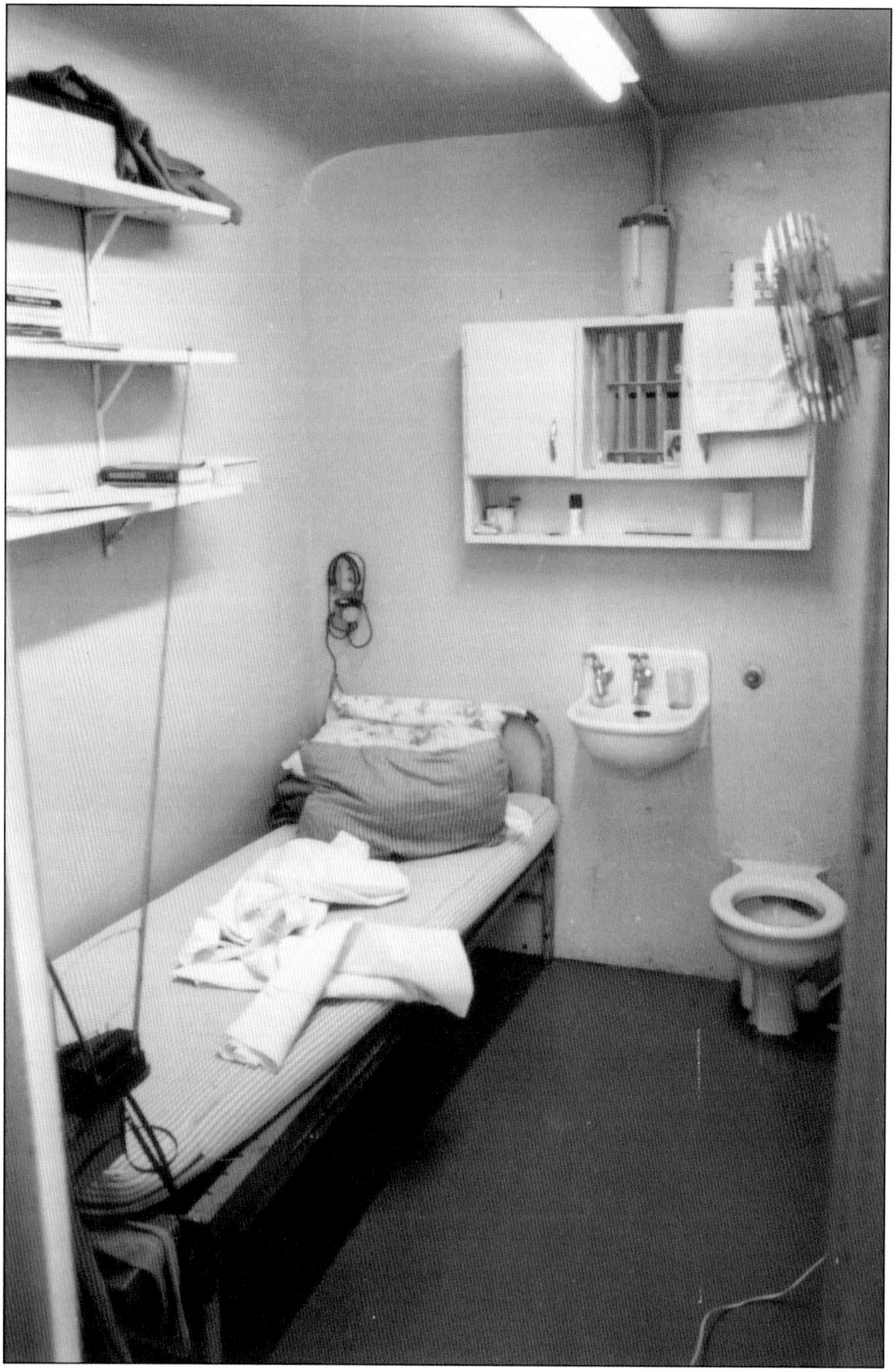

This is a cell in the south cell house that was opened in 1881. This unit is now a privileged area that men are eager to enter. The cell is small, but no cellmate is required for prisoners in this unit. The stone cellblock is also quieter than the newer steel block. Note the wires and headset hanging on the far wall, used to listen to the radio.

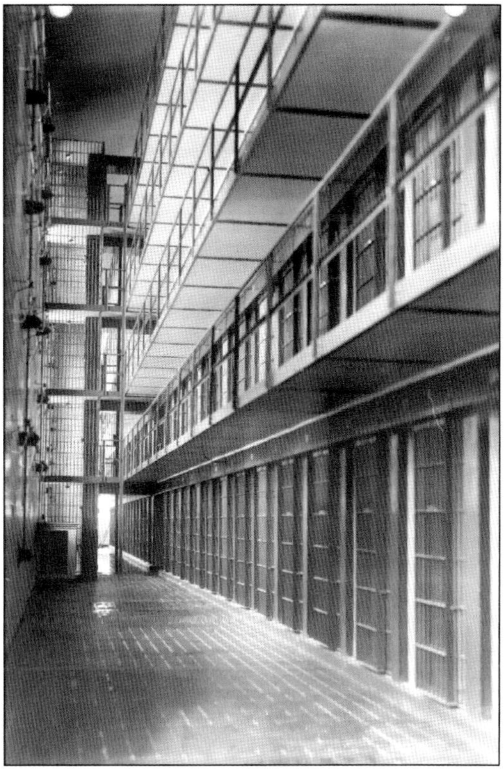

This is the interior of Living Unit B, the cell house built in the early 1930s to relieve the crowding that accompanied the Great Depression. The cells were bigger than the old south cell house, allowing the use of bunk beds to help deal with the growing population.

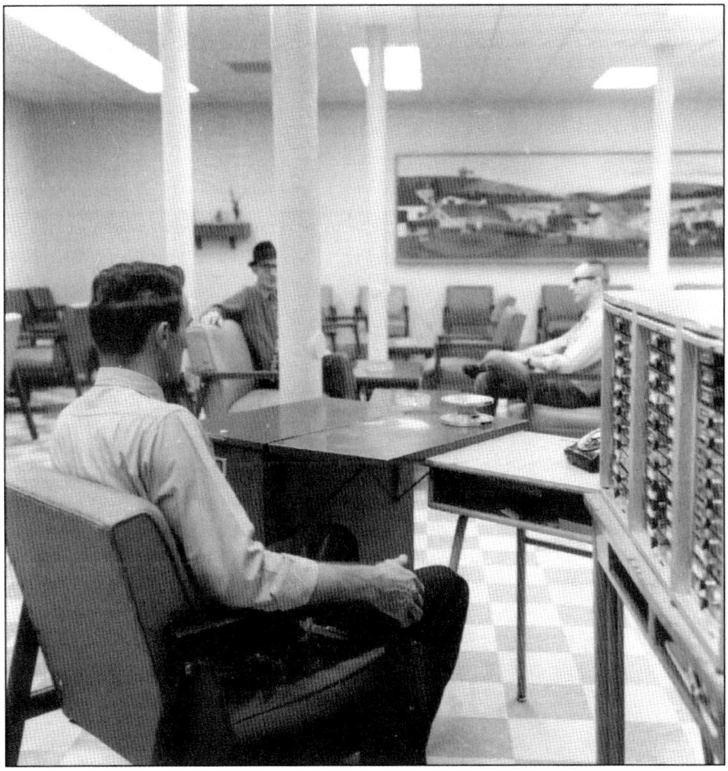

For many years, the visiting room was located above the control center, where the library used to be. Note the pillars forming a circle where the old rotunda was located. This area now houses the records office.

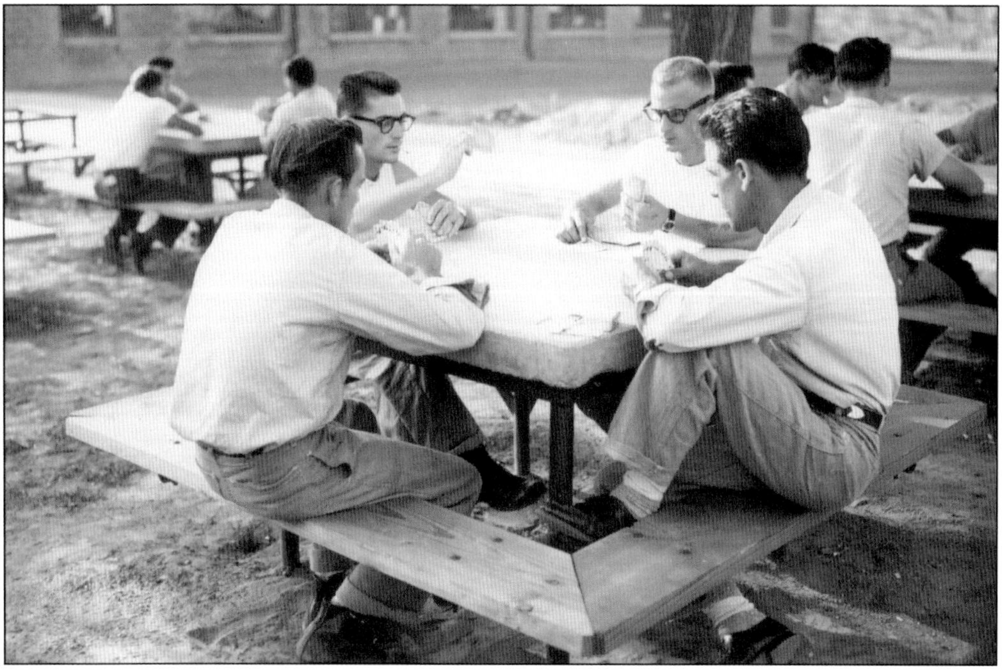

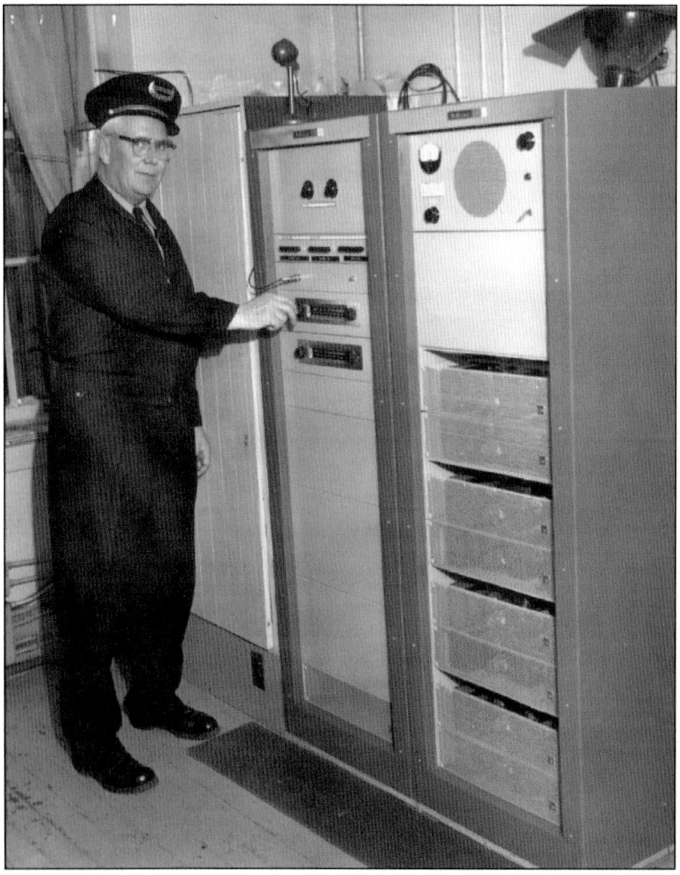

The 1960s image above shows the yard tables used for table games. Construction includes frames of steel pipe sunk into cement, seats of thick lumber, and table tops of four-inch cement. However, durability is not the only reason for the design—in case of disturbances, including fights that might break out over a "friendly" game of cards, the material in the tables would be difficult to use for a weapon.

Cells are wired to receive a choice of radio stations in order to satisfy different musical tastes. Headphones plug into a switch box in each cell and allow for late night listening without disturbing others. This unit controls the radio system.

At the right, an inmate makes his way down the long narrow walkway in the south cell house.

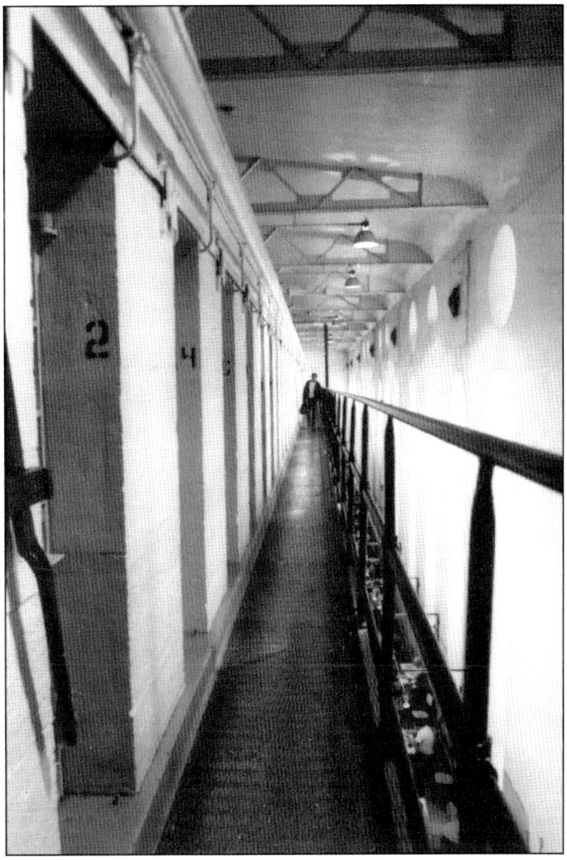

Below, a laundry worker loads a washing machine in the prison laundry.

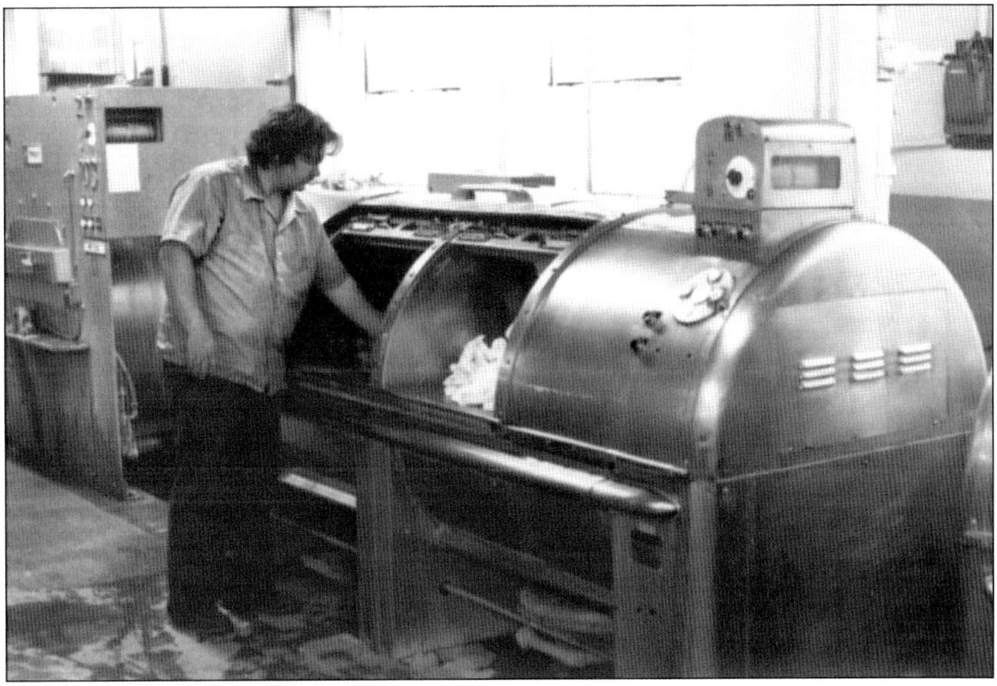

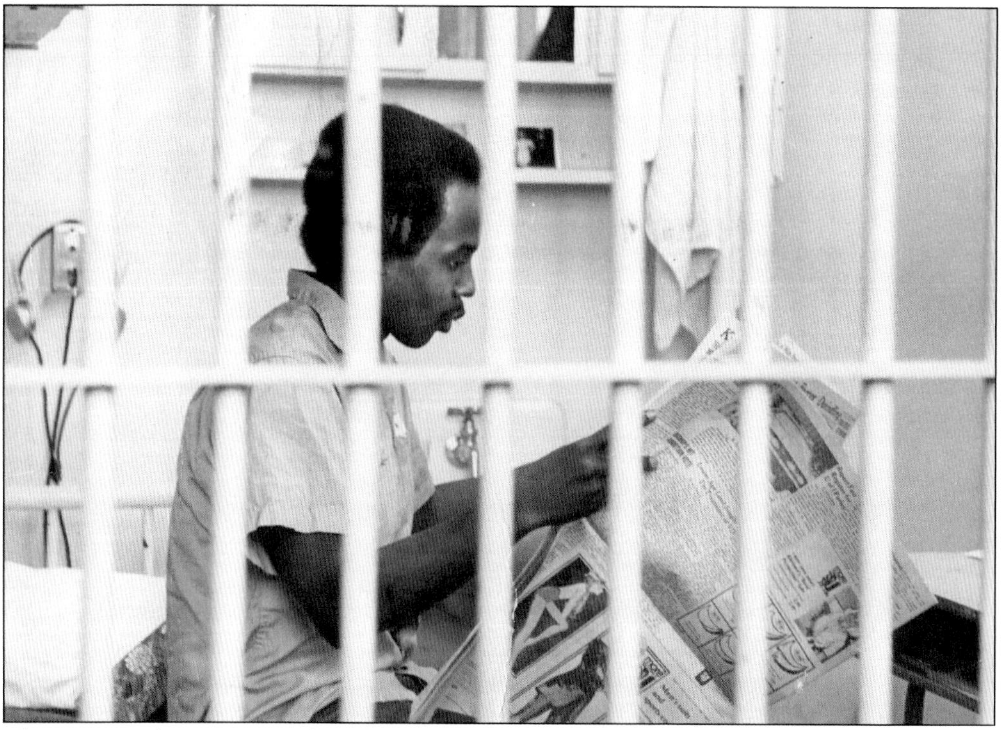

This inmate is keeping in touch with news from home. Due to security reasons, friends and family are not allowed to send newspapers, but subscriptions from the publishers are allowed.

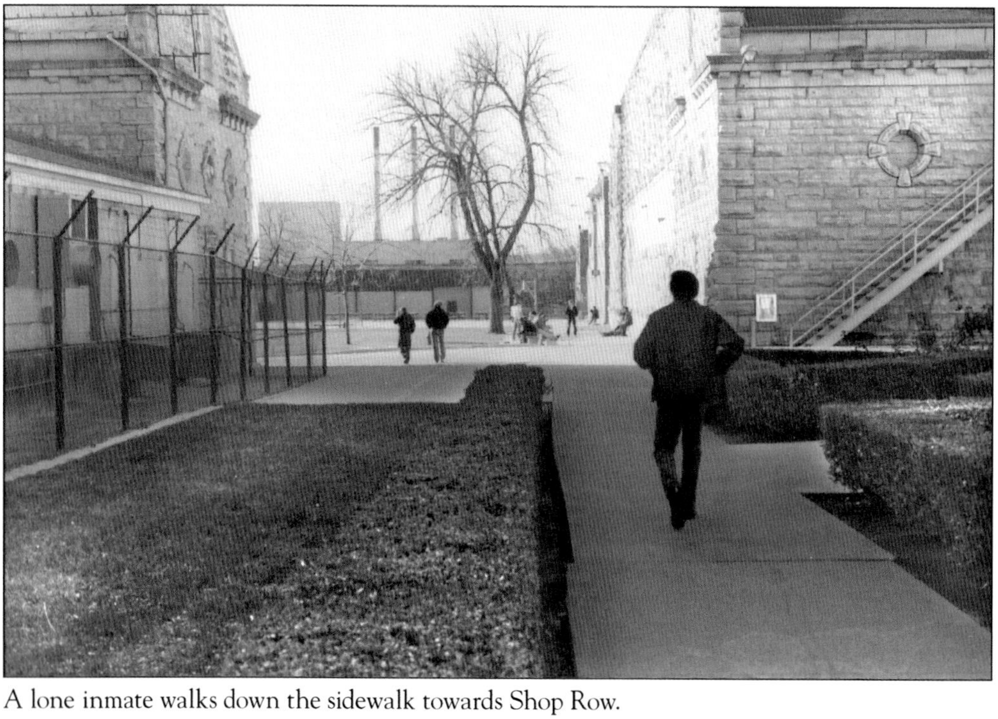

A lone inmate walks down the sidewalk towards Shop Row.

Eight

Escapes

Few prison events capture the imagination of the public like riots and escapes. They are standard fodder for movies, television dramas, and print media. Fortunately, Anamosa has had very few riots during its history. Escapes, however, are another matter. Inmates have proven endlessly creative in devising ways to, in prison parlance, take a "cornfield parole." Escapes were common before the massive stone wall was completed. A wooden stockade fence preceded the wall, and its construction was apparently an inexact science—at first, the boards were nailed from the outside, thus allowing escaping inmates the luxury of simply kicking away a plank to make their escape.

Sharp shooting tower officers were prized in those early days, and most inmates were reluctant to test their aim. Those who did usually regretted it. In 1886, an escape attempt by four inmates drew rifle fire from all parts of the wall, killing two. On another occasion, a guard's bullets failed to stop an escaping inmate who was hotfooting it down the railroad tracks that led away from the prison. Thinking he was overshooting, the guard lowered his aim, felling the man. Later it was discovered that his original aim had been true, but the escapee had taken the precaution of padding his upper body and legs with magazines to absorb the bullets. His heels, however, were not so protected and proved to be his downfall.

Most escapes were not as dramatic. Walkaways from the prison quarry were fairly commonplace. In fact, Anamosa's first quarry escape occurred only two weeks after the first inmates arrived. Three inmates were involved. One of them, Andrew Costa, was apprehended a year later in Missouri, when he had the incredibly bad luck of shopping at a meat market owned by a former guard, who recognized him and aided in his capture.

In modern times, escapes are, fortunately, very rare. However, this was not always the case. Here are a few stories from those earlier days when prison security and inmate ingenuity often went head-to-head.

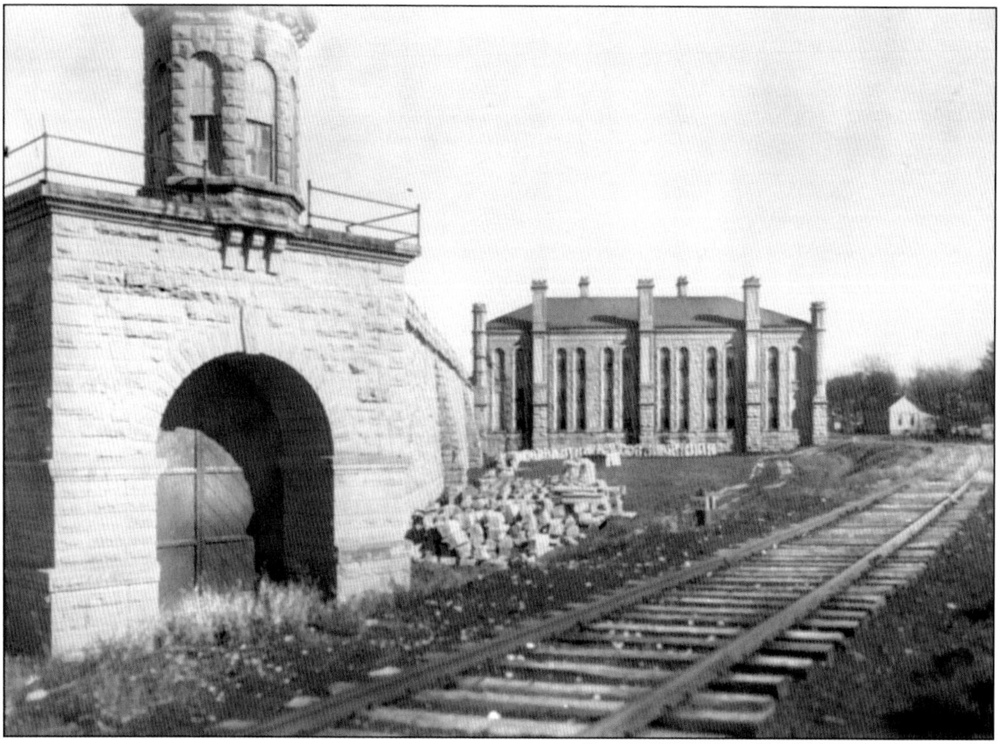

Before the massive iron gate was installed, a wooden version was a tempting escape target. In 1886, two inmates were shot dead by gun guards as they tried to chop through the door with an axe.

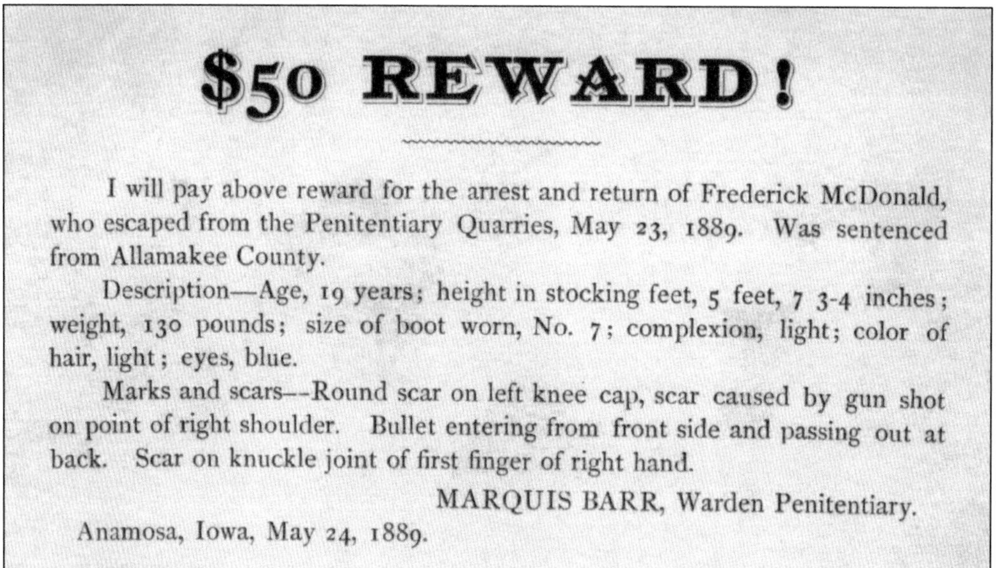

$50 REWARD!

I will pay above reward for the arrest and return of Frederick McDonald, who escaped from the Penitentiary Quarries, May 23, 1889. Was sentenced from Allamakee County.

Description—Age, 19 years; height in stocking feet, 5 feet, 7 3-4 inches; weight, 130 pounds; size of boot worn, No. 7; complexion, light; color of hair, light; eyes, blue.

Marks and scars--Round scar on left knee cap, scar caused by gun shot on point of right shoulder. Bullet entering from front side and passing out at back. Scar on knuckle joint of first finger of right hand.

MARQUIS BARR, Warden Penitentiary.

Anamosa, Iowa, May 24, 1889.

This postcard was sent to Iowa law enforcement officers in 1889 to announce the search for an Anamosa inmate who escaped from the quarry. The reward of $50 would be equal to a month's pay for a penitentiary guard at that time. The inmate was serving a 30-month sentence for burglary and had entered the prison only a few months before his escape. Based on his marks and scars, he may have lived an eventful life.

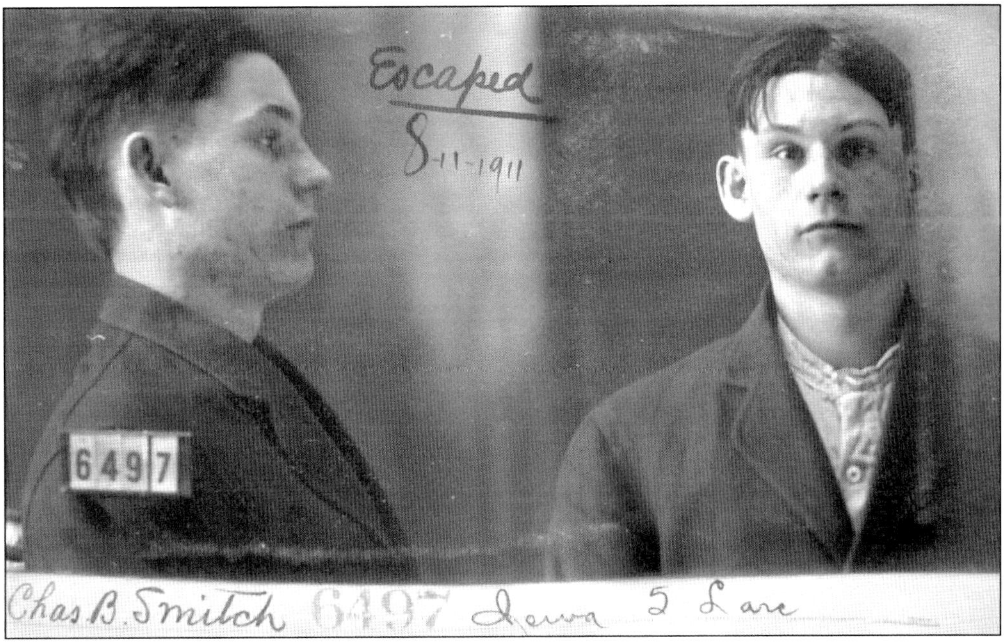

On August 11, 1911, Charles Smitch (above) was being escorted back to the prison by guard Alan Hamaker to visit his attorney. The attorney was actually Smitch's brother, Bert Mecum (below), who set up the ruse to free his brother. Hamaker was shot but survived. The brothers fled to Canada and were a two-man crime wave in Winnipeg (later resulting in the decision to arm the local police). After escaping yet again, they were given stiff prison terms before being returned to Iowa to face the music for their 1911 escapade.

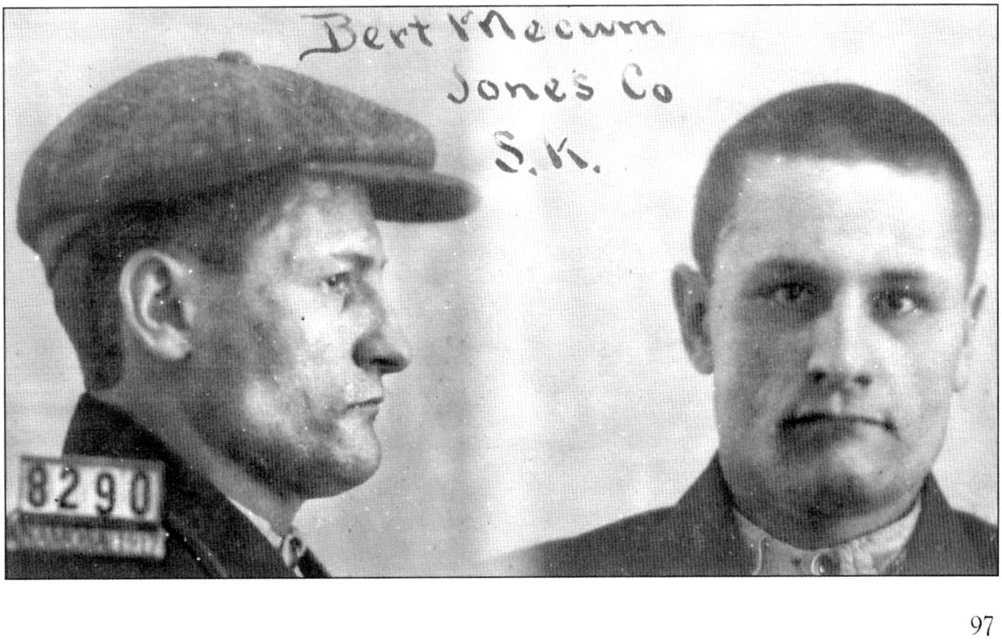

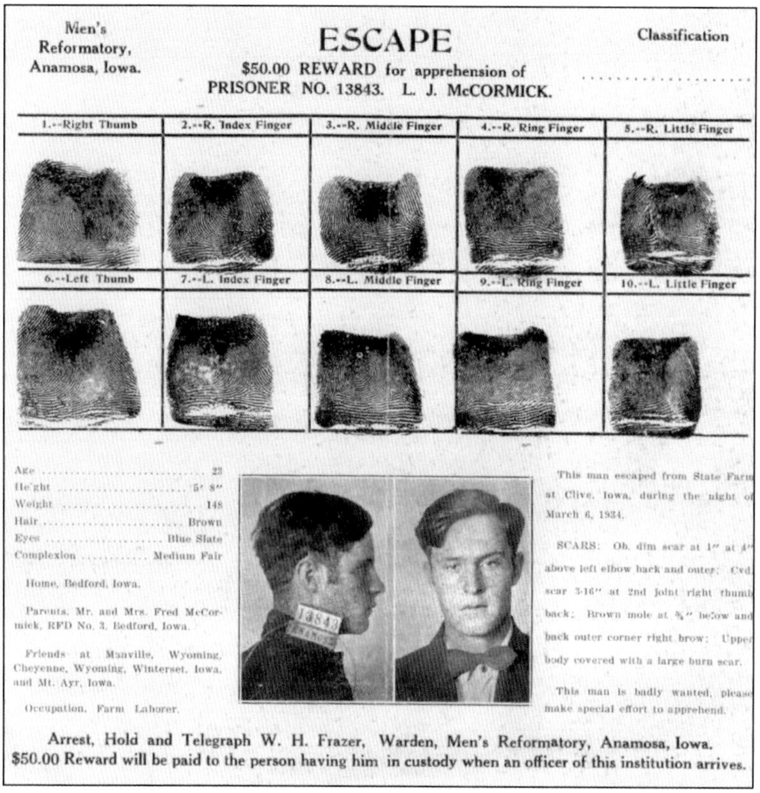

Men's Reformatory, Anamosa, Iowa.

ESCAPE

Classification ....

$50.00 REWARD for apprehension of PRISONER NO. 13843. L. J. McCORMICK.

1.--Right Thumb	2.--R. Index Finger	3.--R. Middle Finger	4.--R. Ring Finger	5.--R. Little Finger
6.--Left Thumb	7.--L. Index Finger	8.--L. Middle Finger	9.--L. Ring Finger	10.--L. Little Finger

Age 23
Height .... 5' 8"
Weight 148
Hair .... Brown
Eyes .... Blue Slate
Complexion .... Medium Fair

Home, Bedford, Iowa.

Parents, Mr. and Mrs. Fred McCormick, RFD No. 3, Bedford, Iowa.

Friends at Manville, Wyoming, Cheyenne, Wyoming, Winterset, Iowa, and Mt. Ayr, Iowa.

Occupation, Farm Laborer.

13843

This man escaped from State Farm at Clive, Iowa, during the night of March 6, 1934.

SCARS: Ob. dim scar at 1" at 4" above left elbow back and outer; Cvd. scar 3-16" at 2nd joint right thumb back; Brown mole at ⅜" below and back outer corner right brow; Upper body covered with a large burn scar.

This man is badly wanted, please make special effort to apprehend.

Arrest, Hold and Telegraph W. H. Frazer, Warden, Men's Reformatory, Anamosa, Iowa.
$50.00 Reward will be paid to the person having him in custody when an officer of this institution arrives.

A wanted poster from 1934 announces the escape of Anamosa inmate L. J. McCormick from the Clive Honor Farm near Des Moines. The escapee was at large for over six years, being returned to Anamosa in 1940.

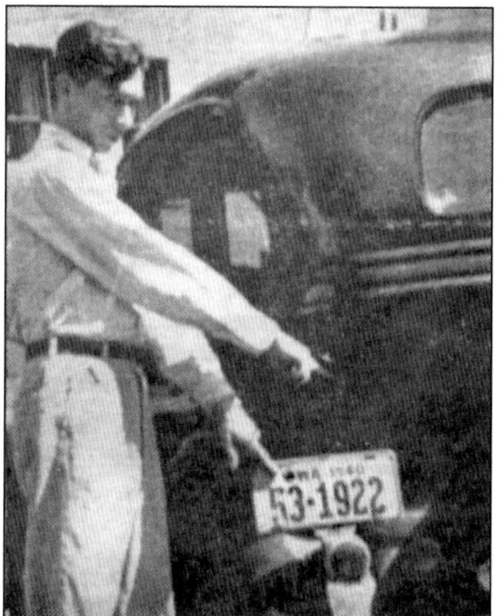

Bob Lohr points to bullet holes placed in his car by pursuers who caught the two convicts who stole Lohr's car. A slug from a .32 hit the pavement, glanced up and punctured the left front tire.

A wild car chase resulted from this 1940 escape. During their recapture, the beating that the two inmates publicly received from prison staff resulted in an investigation.

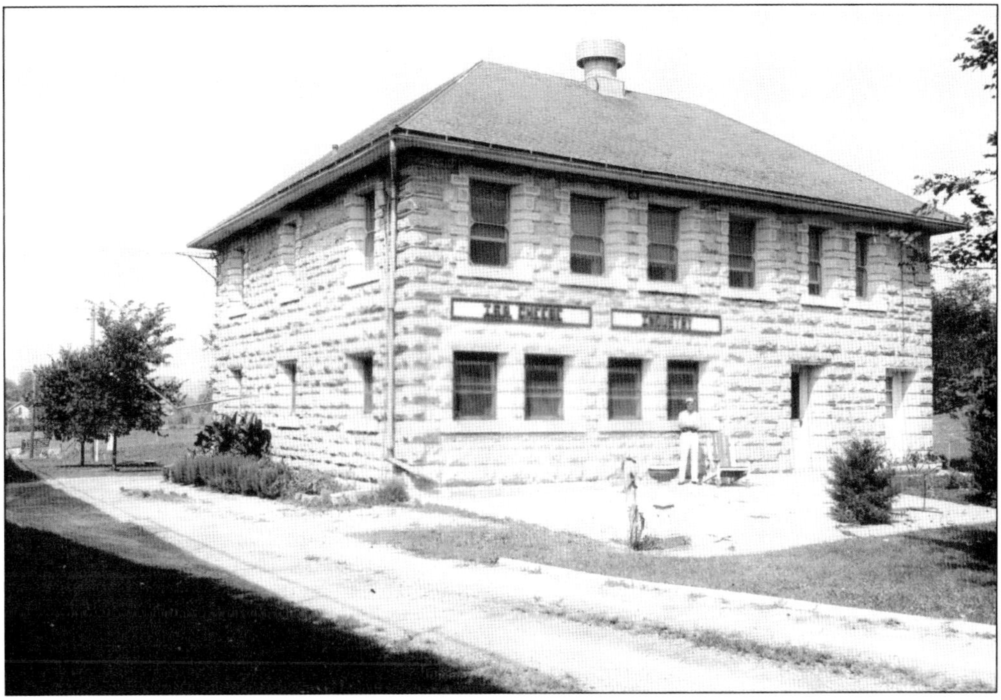

John H. Hinz is pictured in front of the reformatory cheese factory, adjacent to the prison. In June 1946, he was attacked and severely beaten by two inmates who stole his car and escaped. He died two days later. Quickly apprehended, one escapee was sentenced to hang and the other was given 104 years. Despite this, both were released within 21 years after commutations and paroles. The Anamosa Penitentiary Museum is now located in this building.

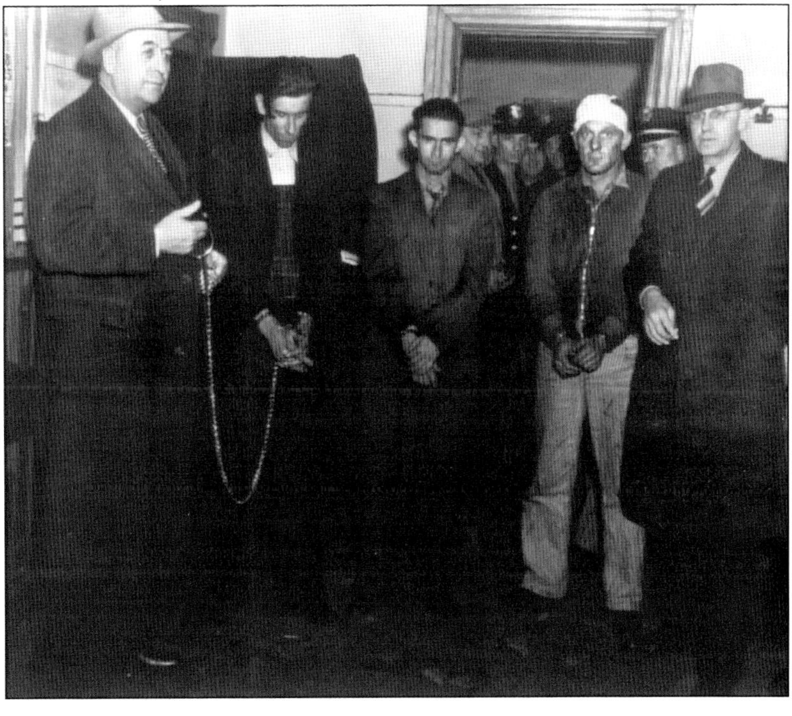

On New Year's Day, 1944, four inmates overpowered a deputy warden and guard and drove their hostages through the main gate. After terrorizing a family in a nearby town, all four were captured in Davenport, Iowa, the next day. Warden Foss Davis (far right) poses with the dejected convicts.

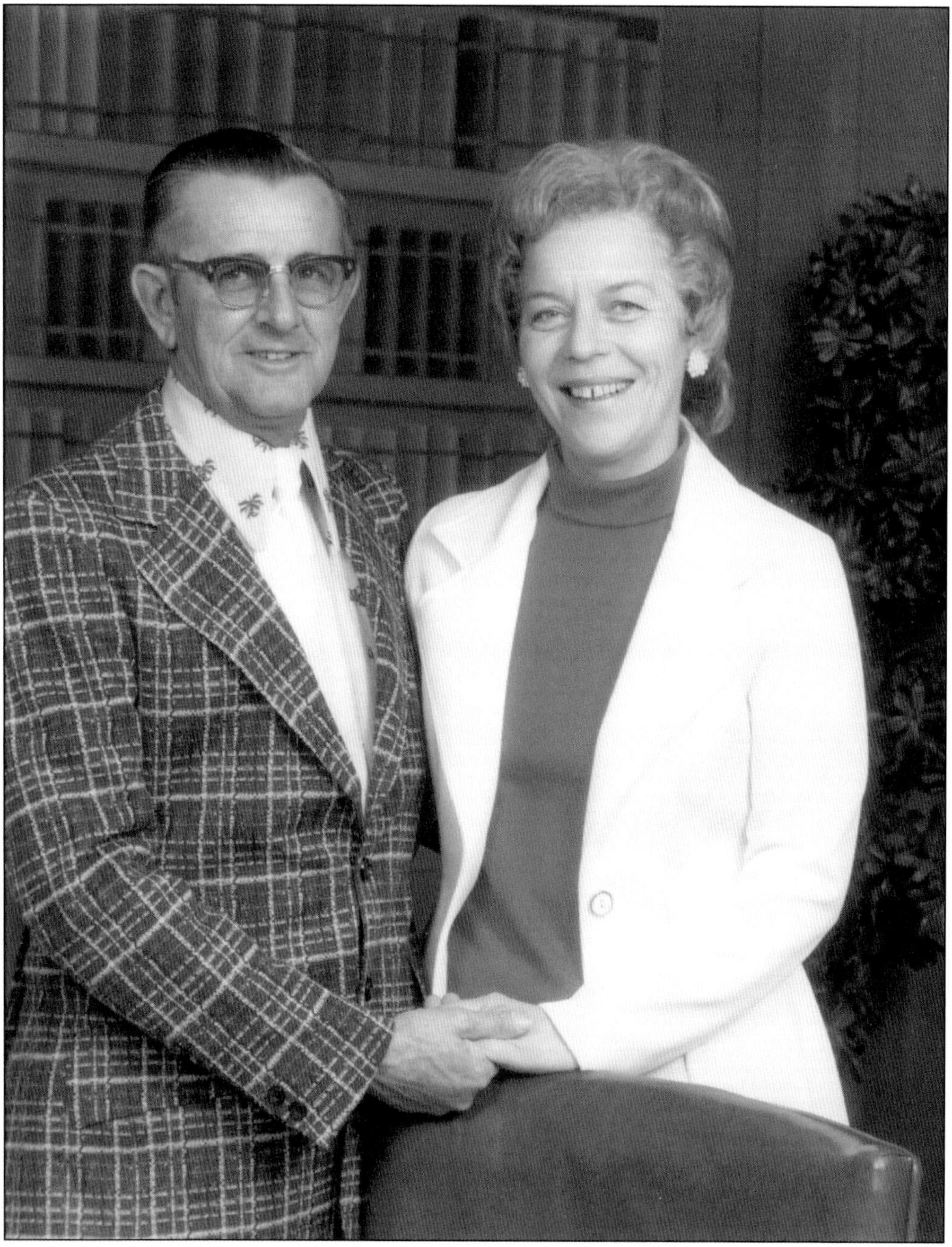

In January 1975, lifer Ron Brewer was being escorted from the prison to provide first aid training to a local group when he escaped and killed Clarence and Patricia Edwards in their Anamosa home. Patricia Edwards worked at the institution as an employee of Kirkwood Community College. This shocking event changed policies regarding prisoner management almost overnight. Many of the liberal policies from the 1960s regarding inmate trips were quickly tightened. The escorting officer was later determined to have aided in the escape, and he was subsequently convicted and served a prison sentence. (Courtesy Edwards family.)

Nine

Views

The penitentiary, by virtue of its attention-grabbing architecture and location among the gently rolling Eastern Iowa hills, make it an often-photographed place. The administration building is arguably the most striking feature, with its soaring height and wide, open porticos. From the air, one quickly gets perspective of the prison's location at the very edge of Anamosa's city limits. On the east, literally across the street, are private homes. On the west, just beyond the wall, the farm fields begin, some of them state-owned, some private. It is a pastoral, peaceful scene, a sharp contrast with what one expects to see around a maximum-security state prison.

The views inside the walls changed dramatically during the main construction years. Even the very shape of the institution was fluid. In fact, the completed look of the modern-day penitentiary was not achieved until the 1940s. Early views of the prison's interior are rather uninspiring. In fact, the place was a real mess for a while. Piles of stone and other building materials were everywhere. As quickly as practical, however, prison administrators endeavored to create a neat and attractive prison yard, with flowers, grass, and trees. In fact, flowers and flowerbeds have always been an important part of the prison, both inside and out, perhaps because the color and beauty of the flowers helps temper the harshness of the stone. Enjoy this collection of very different views of the Anamosa Penitentiary.

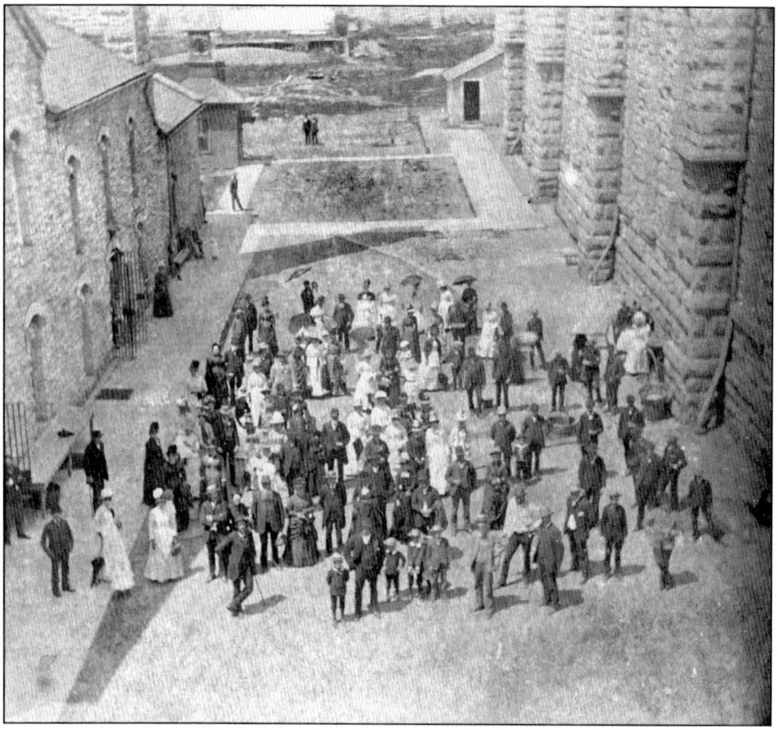

A group of local citizens appears to be visiting the Additional Penitentiary in this 1880s view. The prisoners are probably all locked safely in their cells, as they often were then unless working, eating, or attending chapel. (Courtesy Paul C. Juhl Collection, ISHS.)

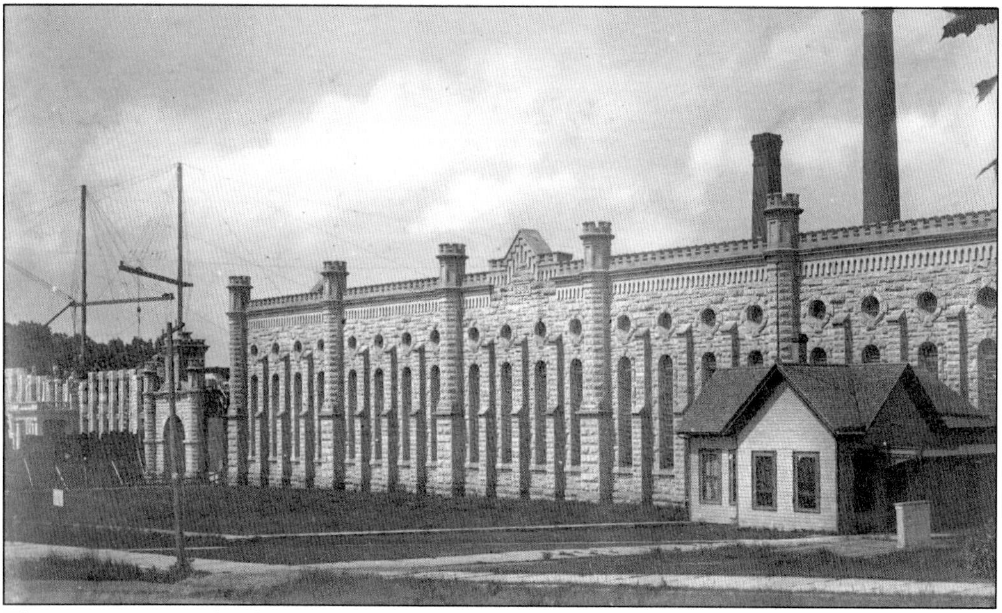

The temporary wooden-frame warden's office was later replaced by the administration building. Note that construction on the female department building was underway at the far left in this late 1880s image.

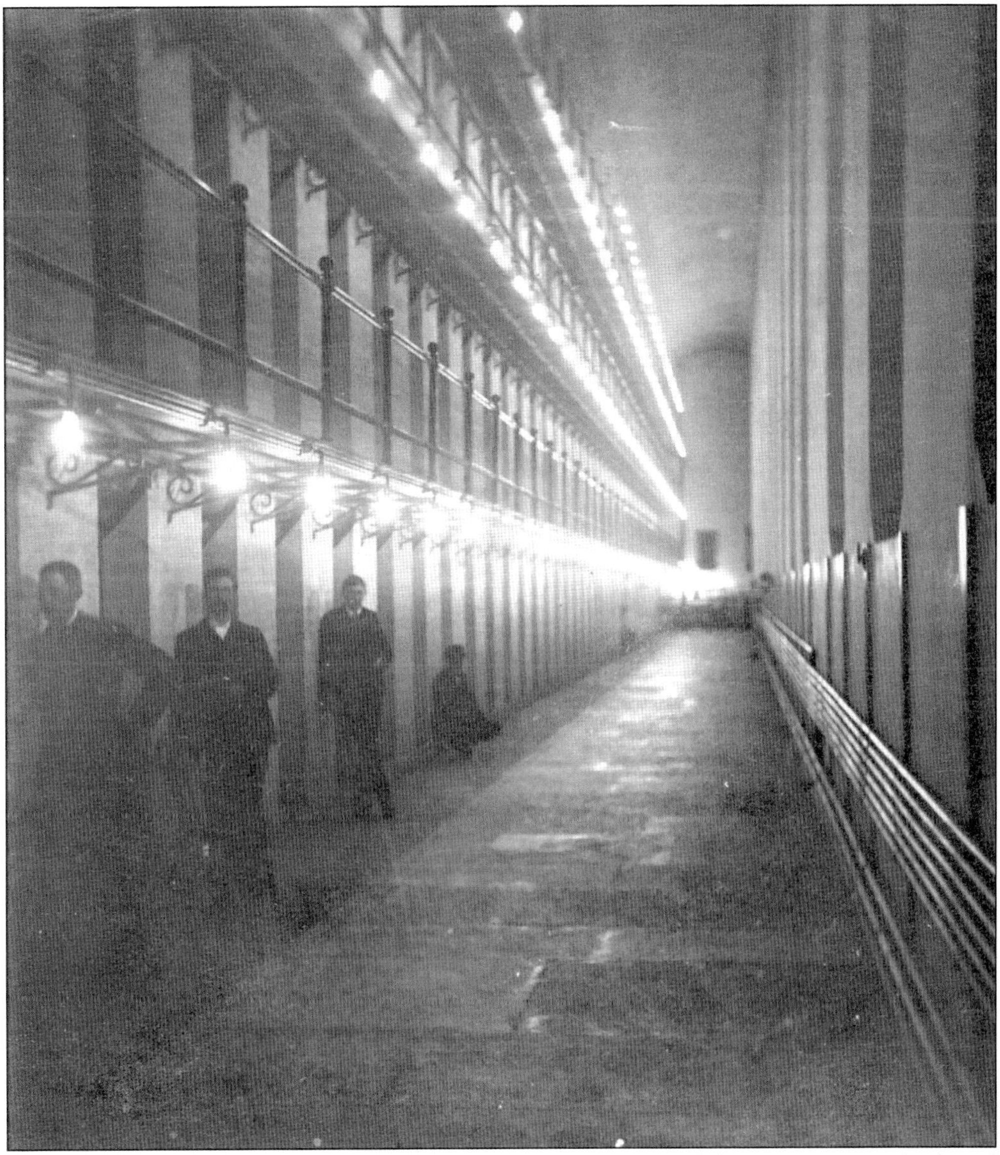

Opened in 1881, the south cell house was the first permanent cell house. Four tiers high and 241 feet long, the stone cell block held 320 cells. With steam heat, a ventilation system, and an electric light bulb outside of every cell, it was one of the most modern cell houses in the country. Pictured here as a new building, it continues to be used today. (Courtesy Ernie Rairdin.)

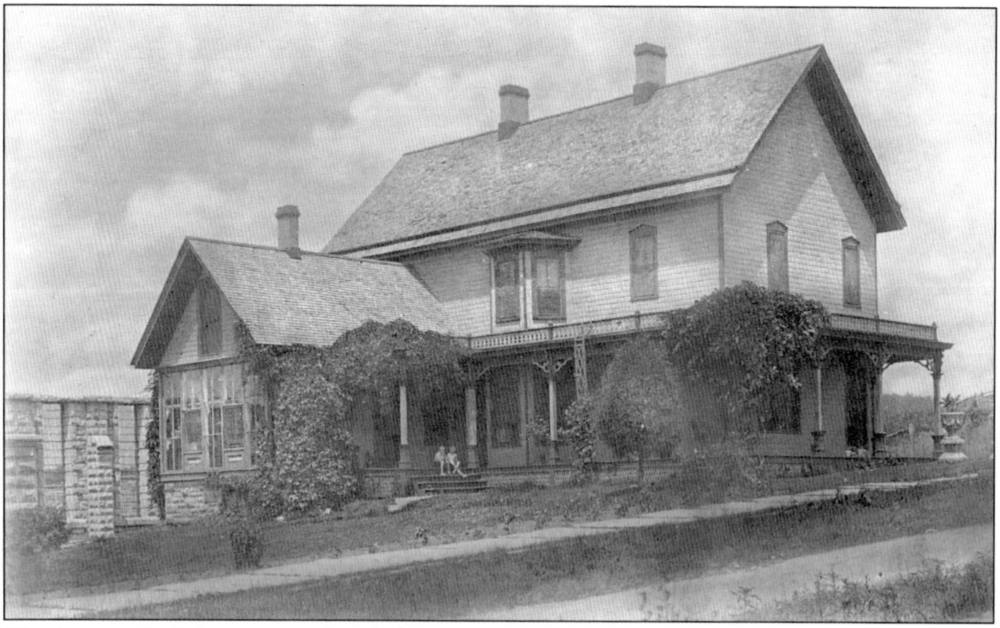

The first warden's house, completed about 1880, was said to have been finished with trim and wall hangings in the latest style obtained from Chicago and New York City. On the left is the east wall of the prison where the window openings covered with iron bars would eventually be windows for the north cell house.

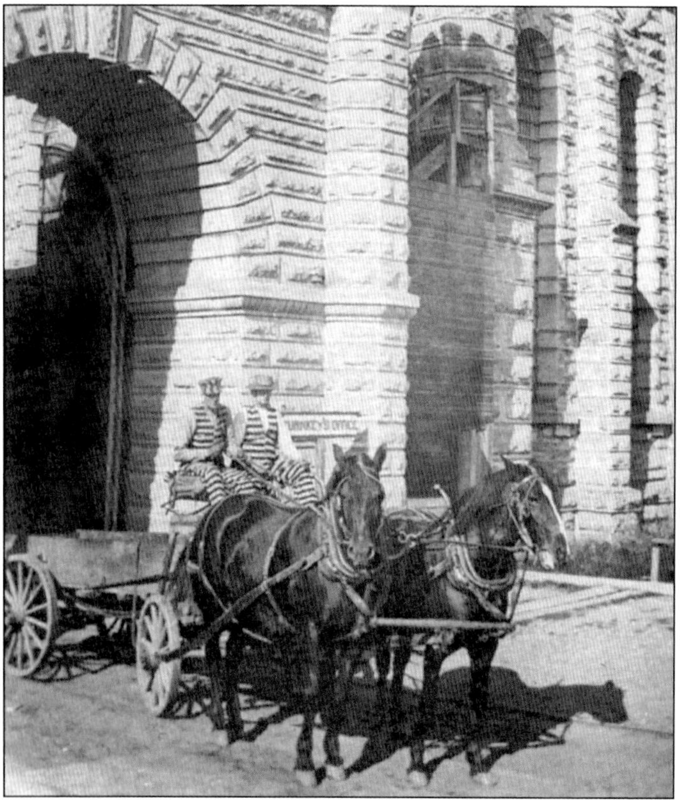

The train gate was often also referred to as the wagon gate for obvious reasons. As late as the 1970s, supervisors were reminding staff to call it the vehicle entrance, evidence that both time and traditions pass slowly in prison.

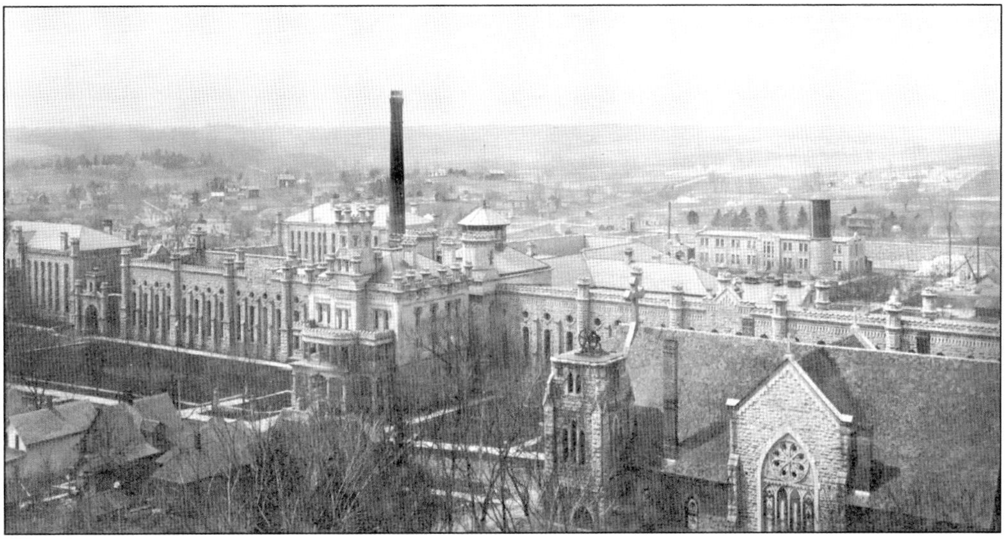

The sanitarium in Anamosa overlooked the prison, and the vantage point provided a rare peek into the prison yard. This photograph was taken around 1920.

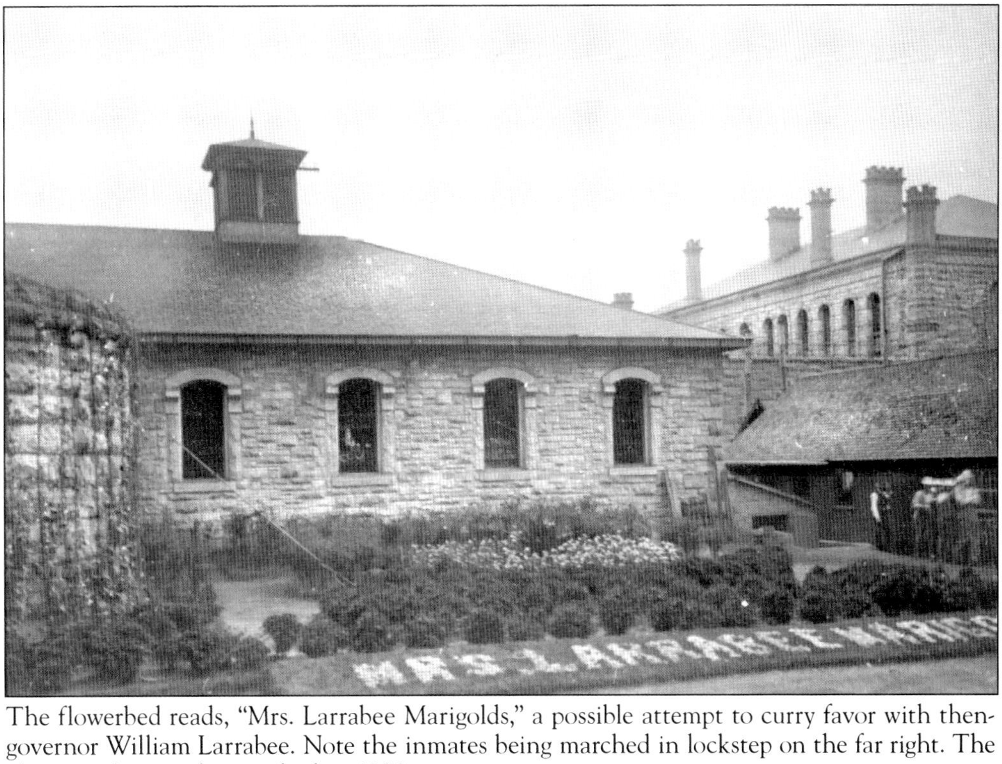

The flowerbed reads, "Mrs. Larrabee Marigolds," a possible attempt to curry favor with then-governor William Larrabee. Note the inmates being marched in lockstep on the far right. The photograph was taken in the late 1880s.

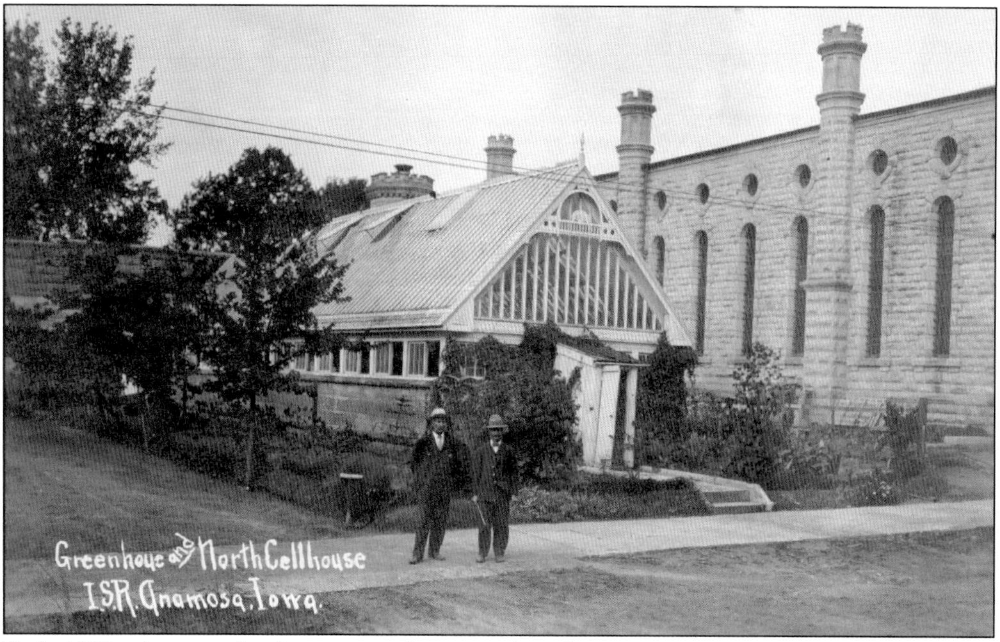

Early 1880s photographs show a greenhouse within the prison. There appear to have been at least four different greenhouses over the years, all in about the same area of the institution. They were used to start plants for the vegetable gardens that supplied food for the prisoners and to start flowers for the elaborate flowerbeds for which the prison has become known.

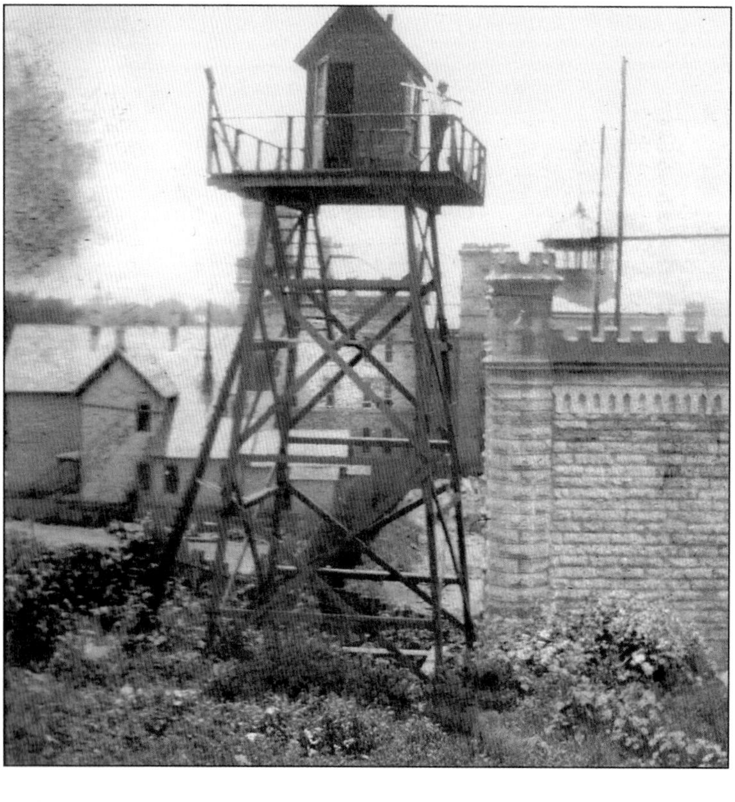

A temporary tower overlooks the northeast corner of the prison in this early 1900s photograph. The guard holds a gun on his shoulder, while a rocket leans on the railing behind him to warn others in case of an escape. Cranes from the construction of the north cell house can be seen. The new warden's residence/administration building rises behind and above the original warden's house.

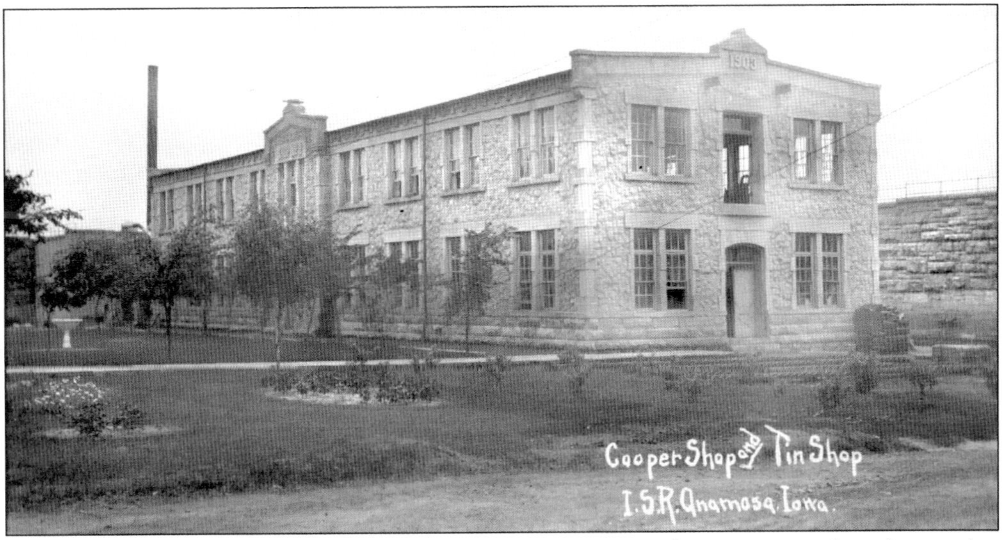

Shop No. 2 was completed in 1903 for the American Cooperage Company to replace the wooden structure that burned in 1902. After the cooperage business ended, the building housed the tin shop, the apron factory, and during the 1930s, the stone cutting shop. After several years of being used for storage, it housed the Ford School, and then the metal furniture shop. In 1989, the building was razed.

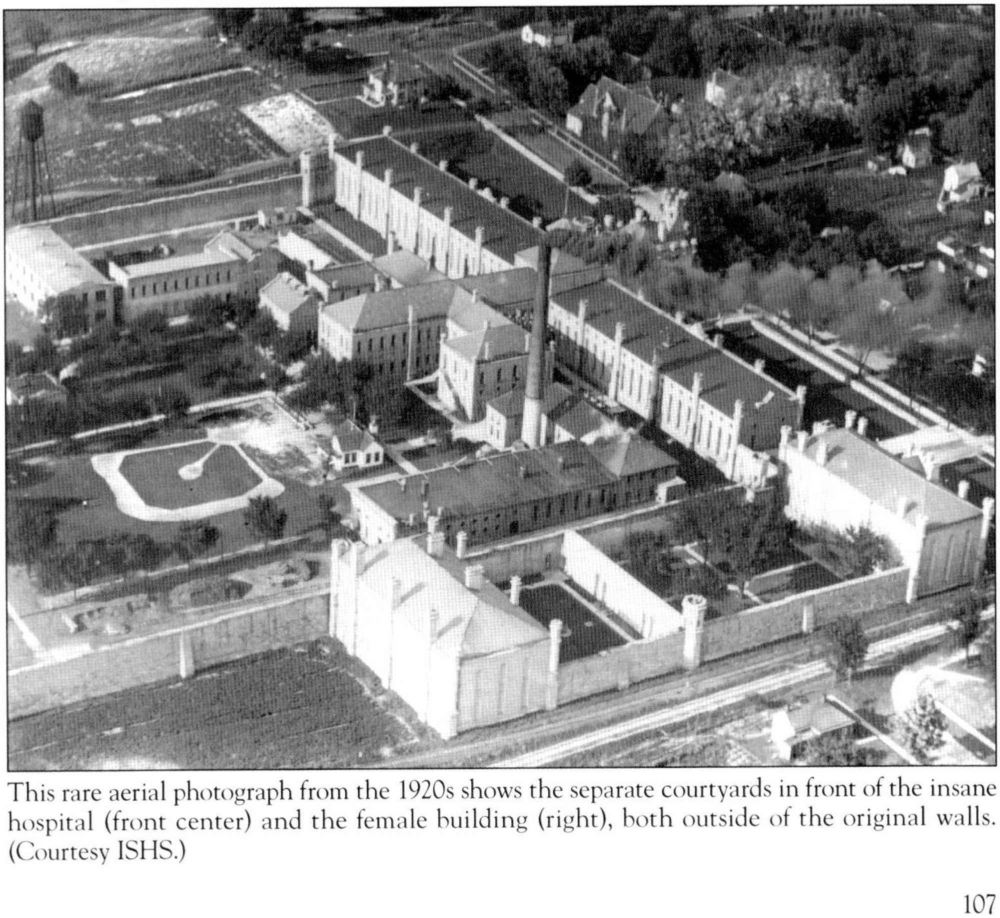

This rare aerial photograph from the 1920s shows the separate courtyards in front of the insane hospital (front center) and the female building (right), both outside of the original walls. (Courtesy ISHS.)

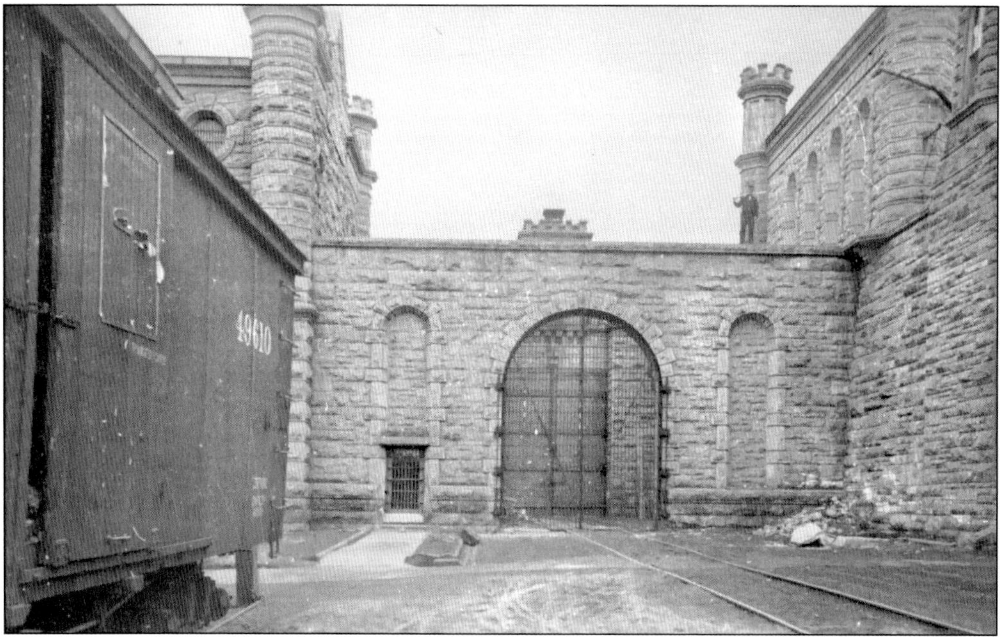

This was the train gate as viewed from the inside in about 1930. The iron outside gate, and the second barred gate, allowed train cars and wagons to be brought into the prison yard without opening both gates at the same time. This discouraged impulsive escape attempts, as did the armed gun guards on the wall in the two towers overlooking the gate.

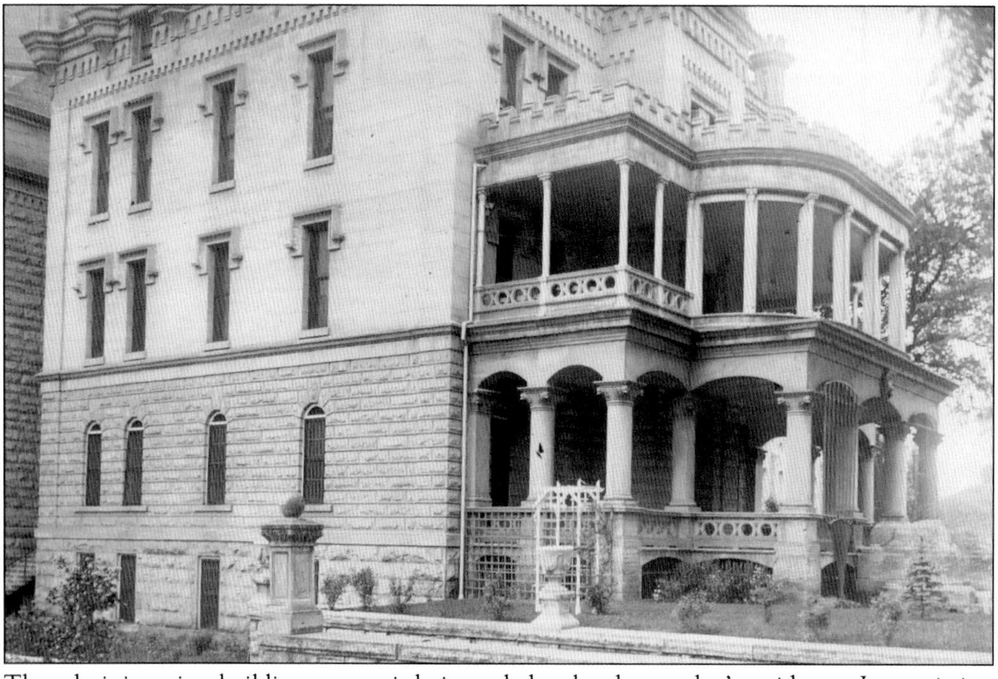

The administration building was mainly intended to be the warden's residence. Large sitting rooms, bedrooms, a dining room, and a ballroom on the top three floors made it the finest home in town. Four large offices comprised the main floor. Built by inmate labor for a cost of $10,500, officials estimated that if contractors had been hired, the cost would have been $130,629.

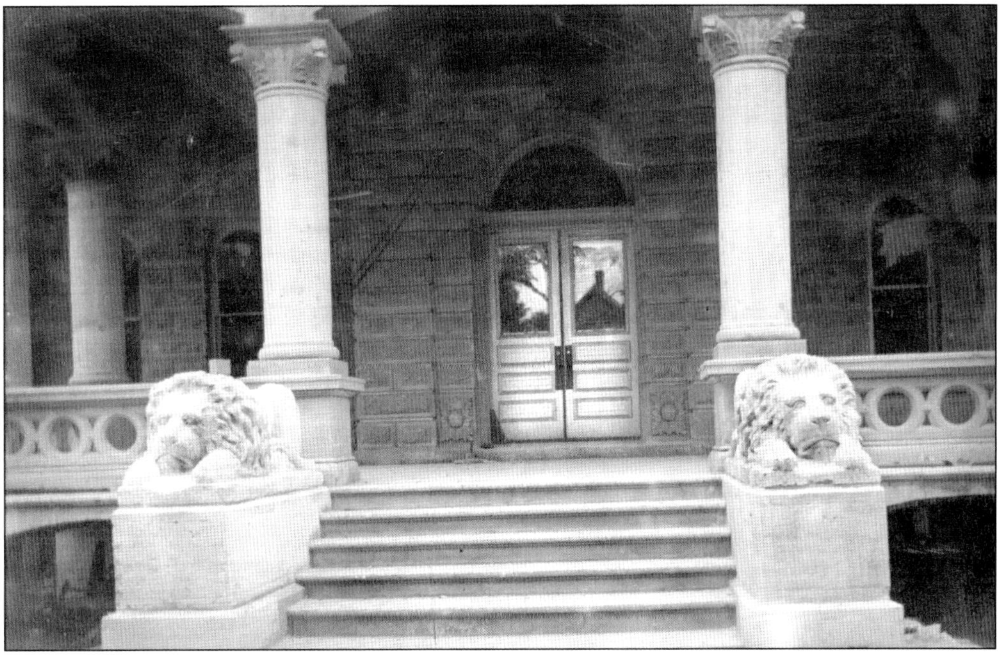

The entrance to the administration building is guarded by two stone lions carved by inmate Ed Munford. The lions were said to weigh five tons each. Munford had to hurry his work, as his release was fast approaching. One of these lions was nicknamed "Sappho" by the inmates.

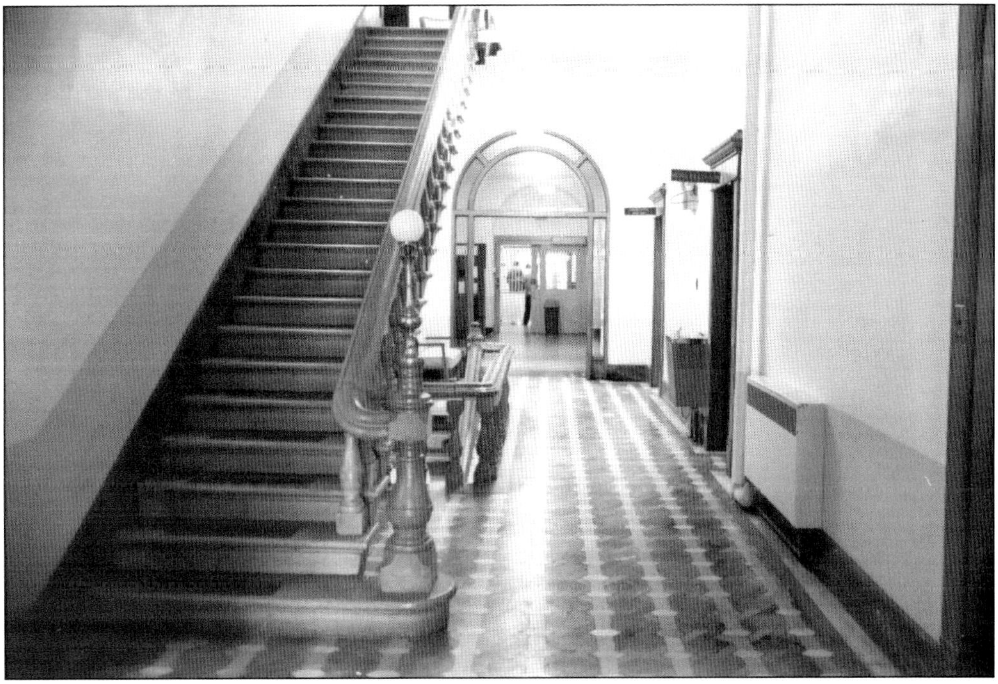

Upon entering the front door of the administration building, one is quickly impressed with the craftsmanship of the late 1890s inmate workers. When bids for the marble floor went beyond the architect's projected budget, scrap marble was located at a significant savings. The workers cut and shaped the stones into a beautiful floor that continues to shine after 110 years.

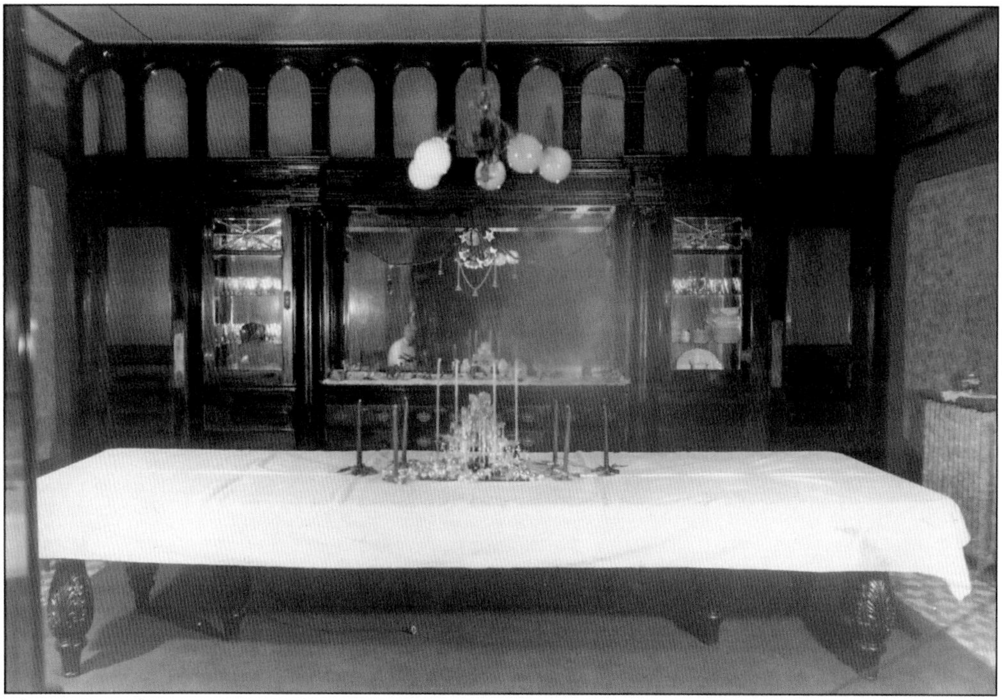

This ornate dining room in the warden's residence on the second floor featured inmate servants and had meals (made in the basement kitchen) brought up by a dumbwaiter and served by inmates. As late as the early 1960s, the noon meal was presided over by the warden's wife, who would be joined by those with business to conduct at the institution. It was said that sheriffs would time their delivery of prisoners in order to enjoy the noon meal. (Courtesy Jones County Historical Society.)

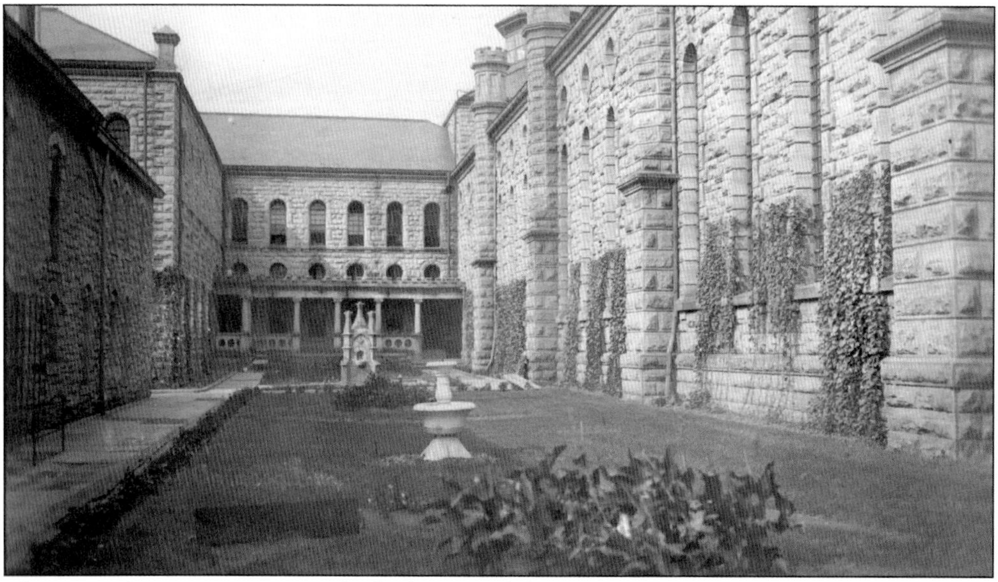

This view of an interior courtyard is looking north from under Tower No. 2. The south cell house is on the right and the center building is in the background. It looks much the same today, except the two buildings on the left have been reconstructed over the years.

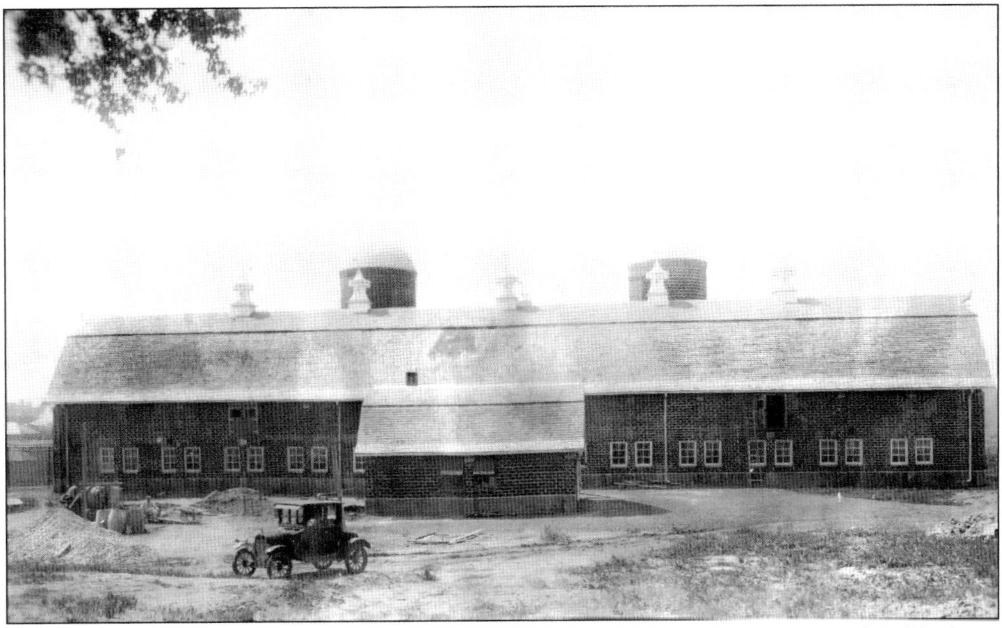

At its 1929 completion, the new dairy barn was said to be the largest barn in Iowa. A public barn dance celebrated the occasion, with music provided by the 12-piece prison band. Attendance at the event suffered, however, when a rainstorm turned the barn road into a quagmire.

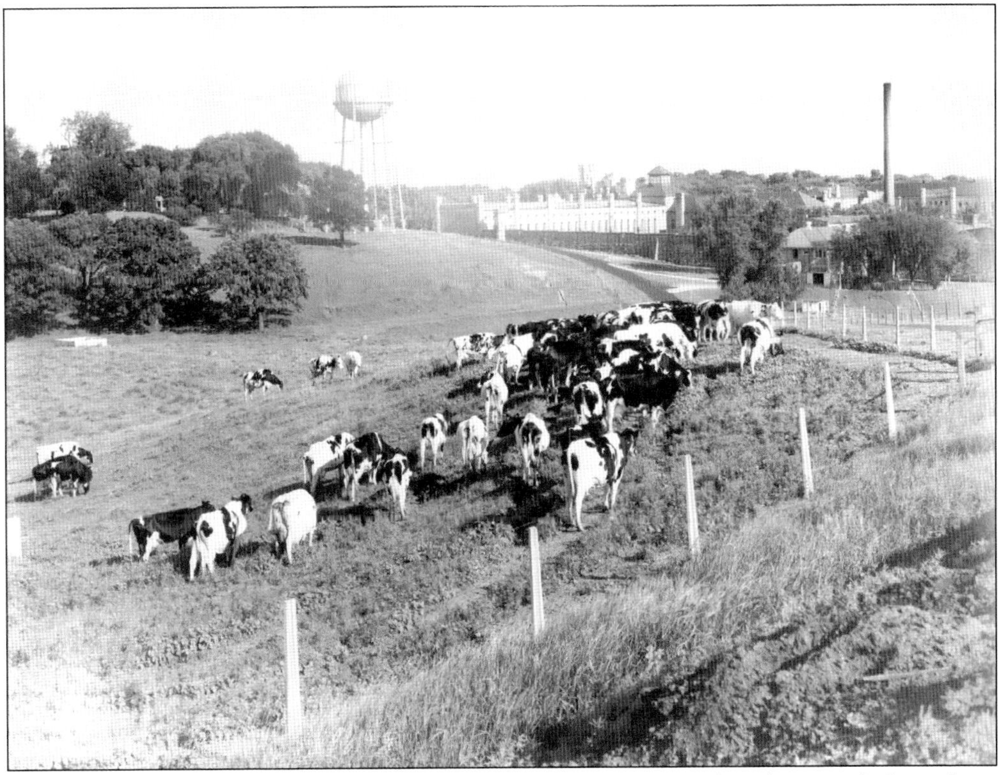

Part of the prison's extensive dairy herd grazes near the prison in this photograph from about 1960. The herd had a national reputation for its milk production before being sold in 1970.

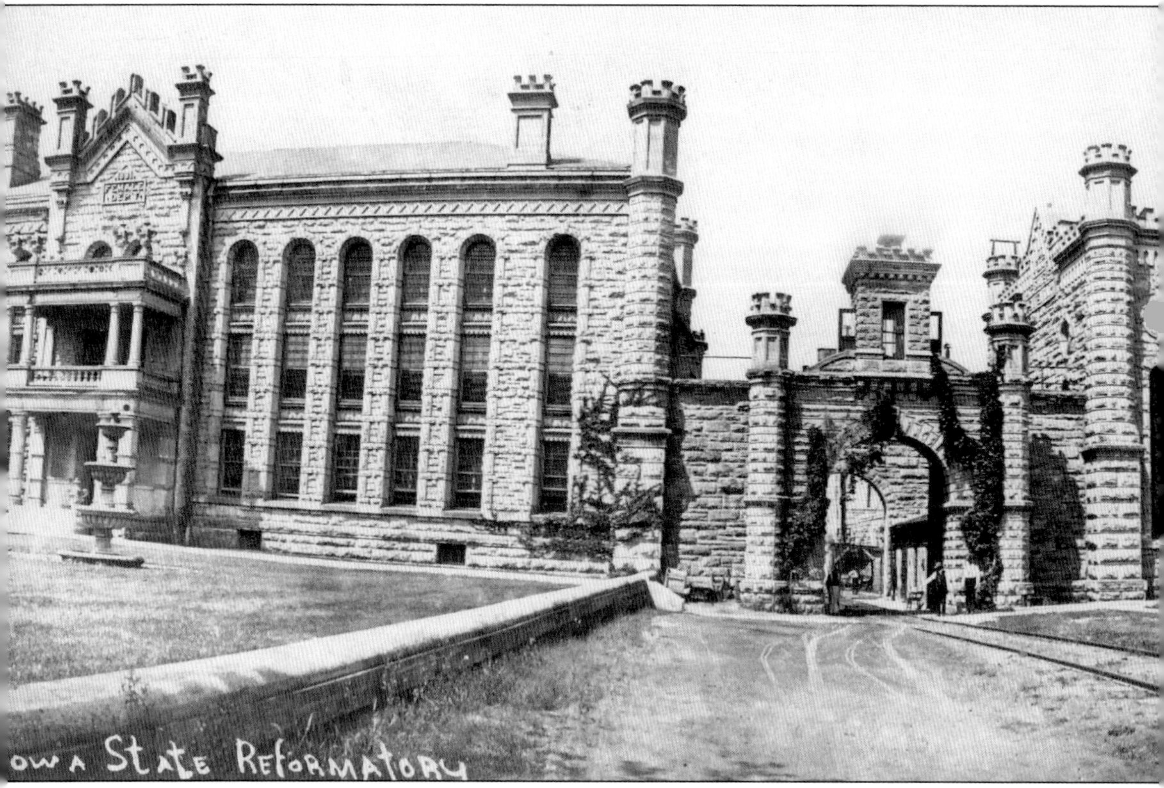

A wide-angle view of the southeast front of the institution is pictured here. The female department and the train gate are on the left, with the south cell house and the warden's residence/administration

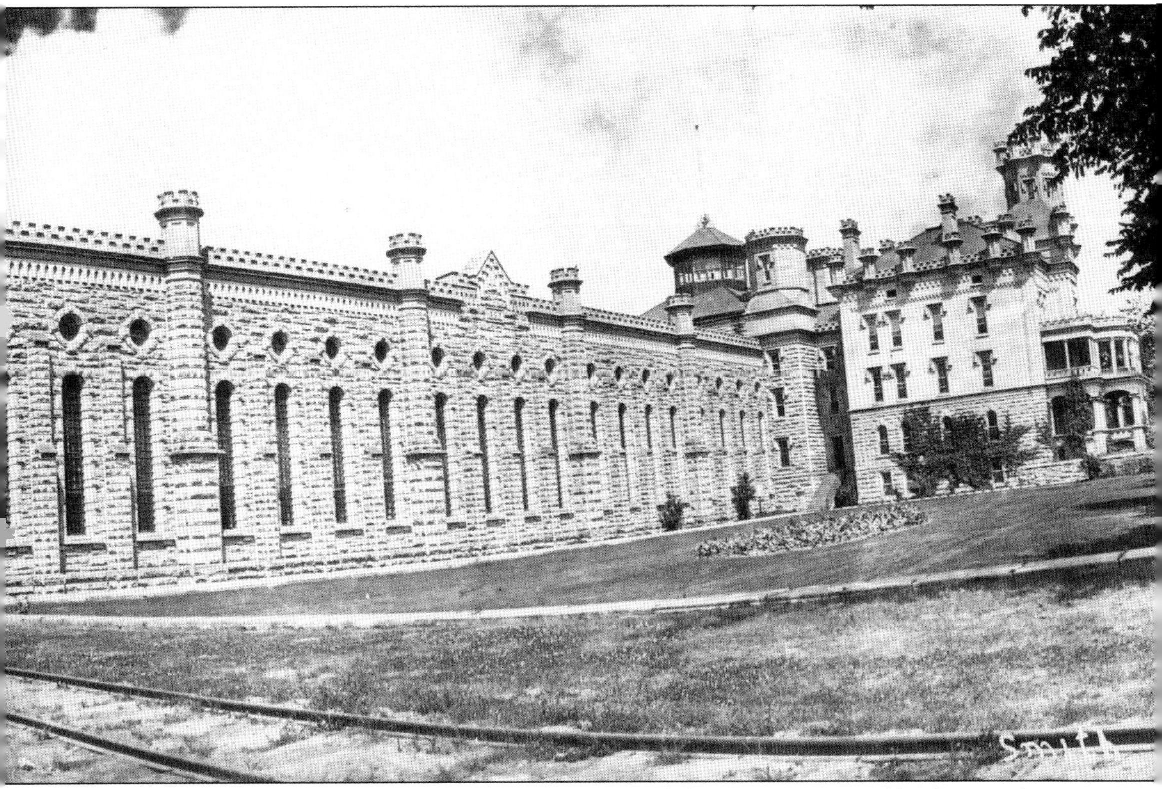

building on the right. Note the black smudge at the top of the open gate caused by the soot from the many steam trains that hauled coal to the power plant. (Courtesy Cecilia Hatcher.)

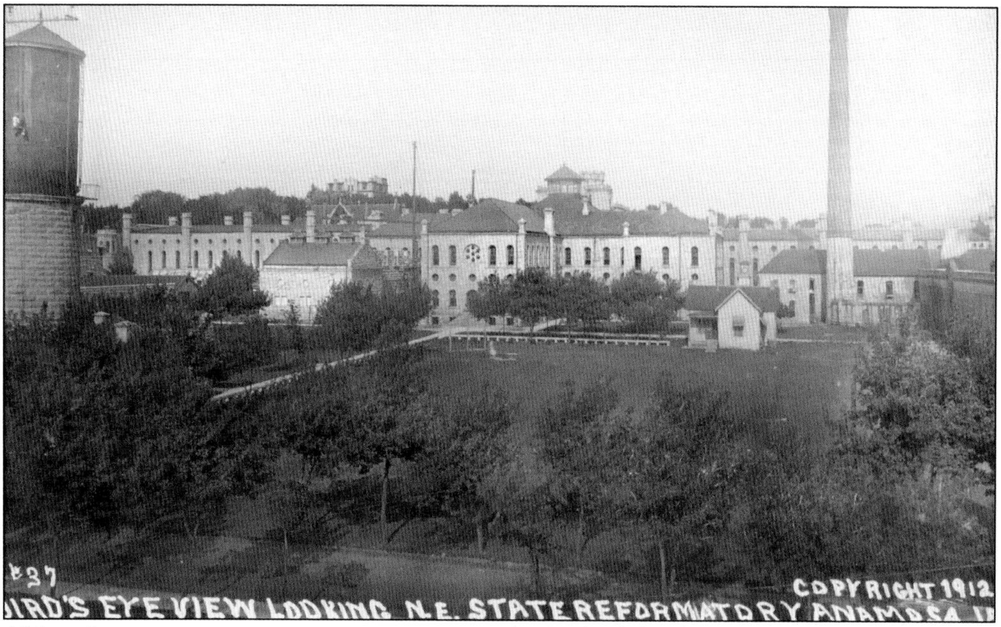

Although one construction crane remains near the back of the chapel, much of the prison was complete in this 1912 photograph. Trees and grass have replaced dirt and gravel, as landscaping is now an obvious priority. The frame house that served outside the walls as the warden's office is now inside, being used as the yard captain's office.

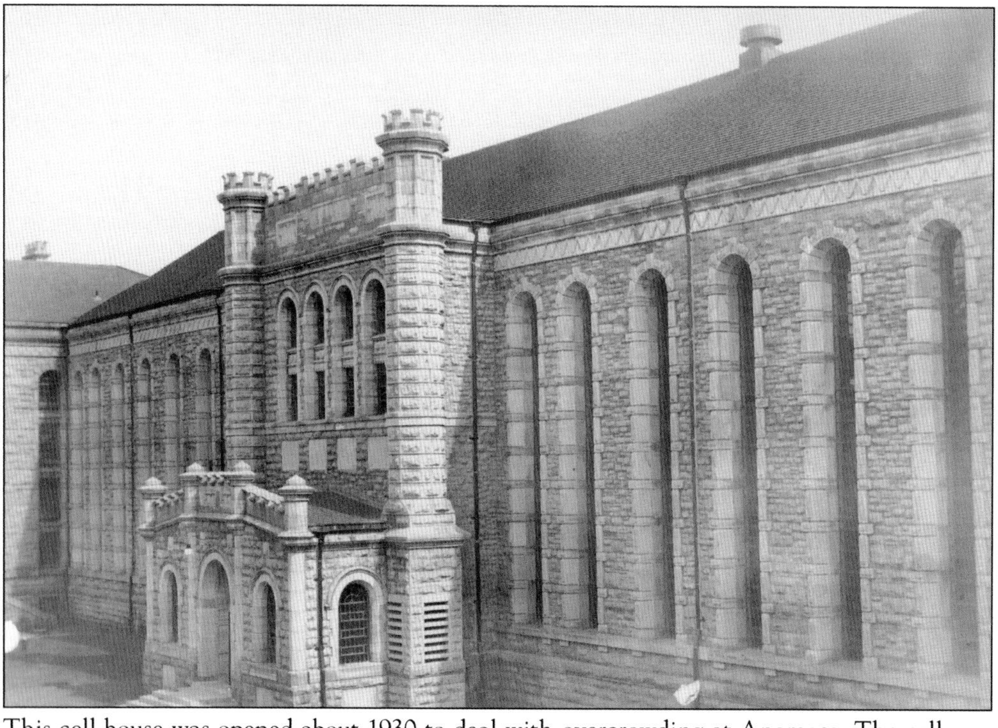

This cell house was opened about 1930 to deal with overcrowding at Anamosa. The cells are larger than those in the 1881 cell house, and today most hold two inmates by using bunk beds. For 30 years after it was built, it was still often referred to as the new house.

Ten

TAILINGS

Those connected to the penitentiary for any length of time have a whole album of images burned into their memory. Life seems more intense inside the walls, and the memories formed are long-lasting. Some images are whimsical, others piercing. Some are quite funny, others painful. Life happens here. So does death. This chapter presents a few of those images.

In its formative years, the penitentiary was a very popular tourist attraction, and the signature image of the administration building found its way onto spoons, cups, plates, and postcards. The public could not seem to get enough. Tours were so frequent that a staff member, usually an aging prison veteran, was assigned to guide the tours. The price of admission was 25¢, which was used to buy books for the inmate library.

The first inmate death occurred only six months after the first inmates arrived. When an inmate died, and the family could not or would not claim the body, the responsibility for burial fell to the state. The first "Boot Hill" was located a short distance from the west wall, on an elevation facing the rising sun at the prison farm. In 1914, when the land was needed for farm expansion, the cemetery's 35 occupants were moved to its current location, a quarter-mile uphill in a serene, picturesque spot. Cows graze in a field nearby, and the prison complex broods massively and silently in the valley below. It is another image for the album.

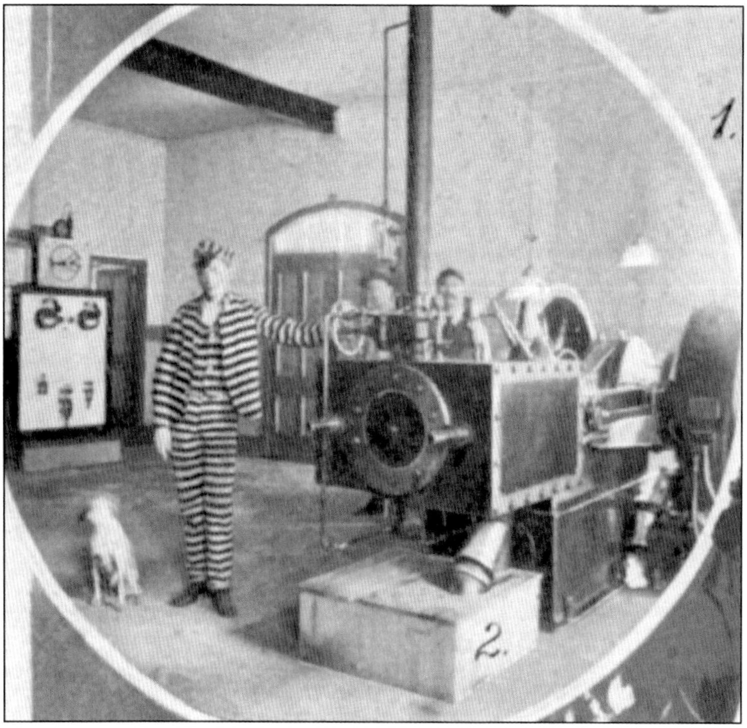

What is thought to be the institution's first steam-driven electric generator is pictured at left. The prison had electric light bulbs by 1882 and was the first state institution in Iowa to be electrified. (Courtesy Cecilia Hatcher.)

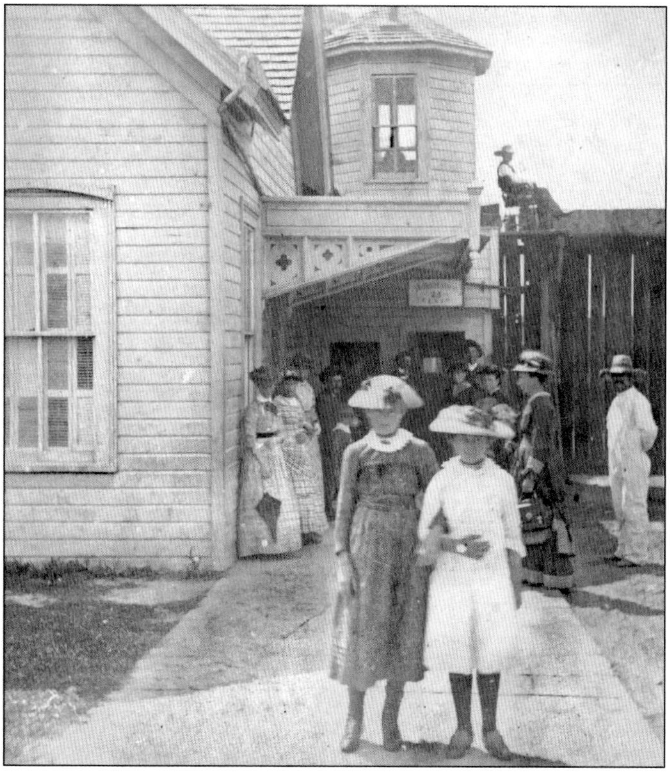

Ladies and gentlemen line up outside the prison, waiting for the tour to begin. The sign above the doorway reads "Admittance 25 cents." Proceeds were used to support the inmate library fund. Note the gun guard sitting on top of the stockade fence, keeping an eye on the proceedings. This photograph is from the 1880s and was taken on the site where the future administration building would be built.

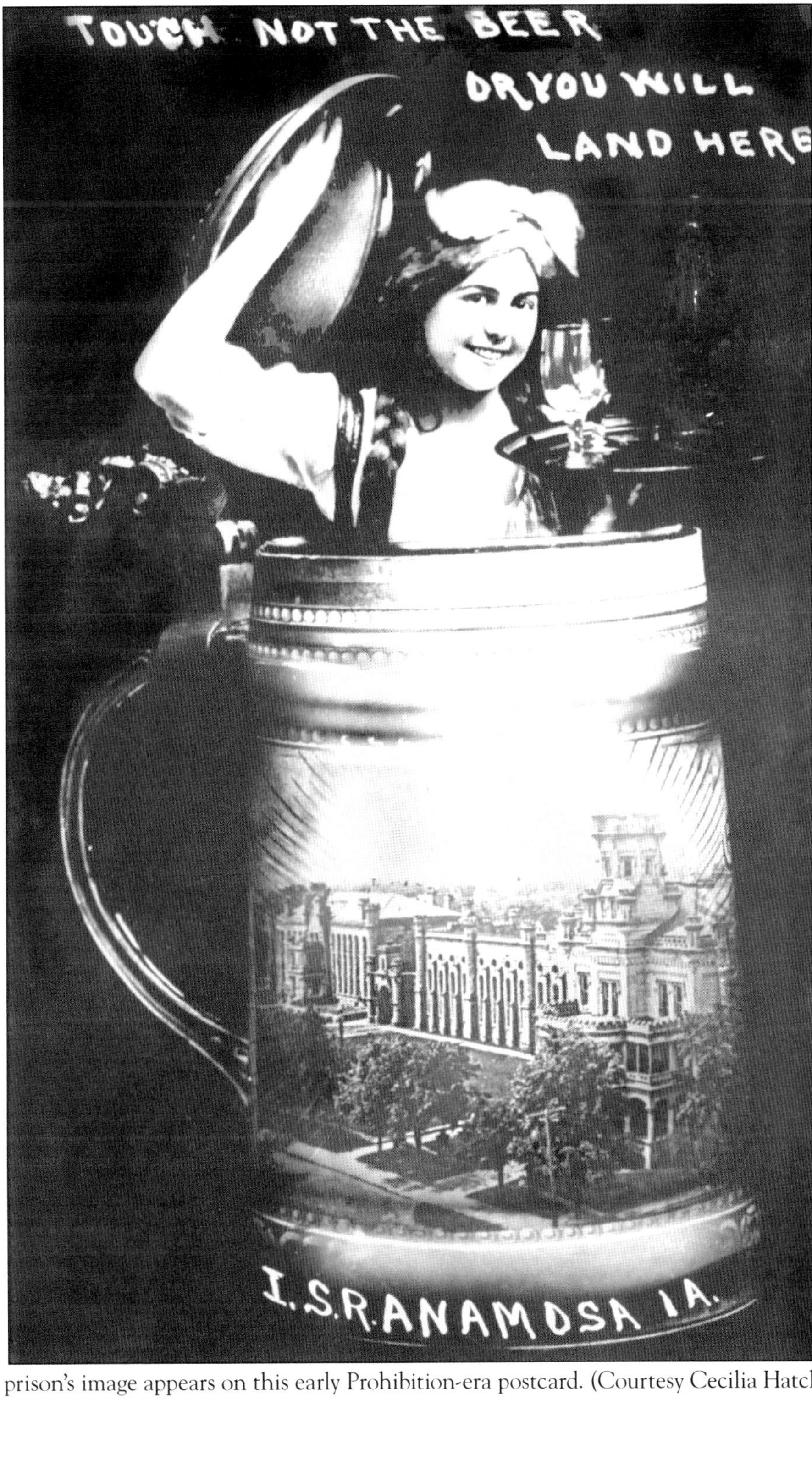

The prison's image appears on this early Prohibition-era postcard. (Courtesy Cecilia Hatcher.)

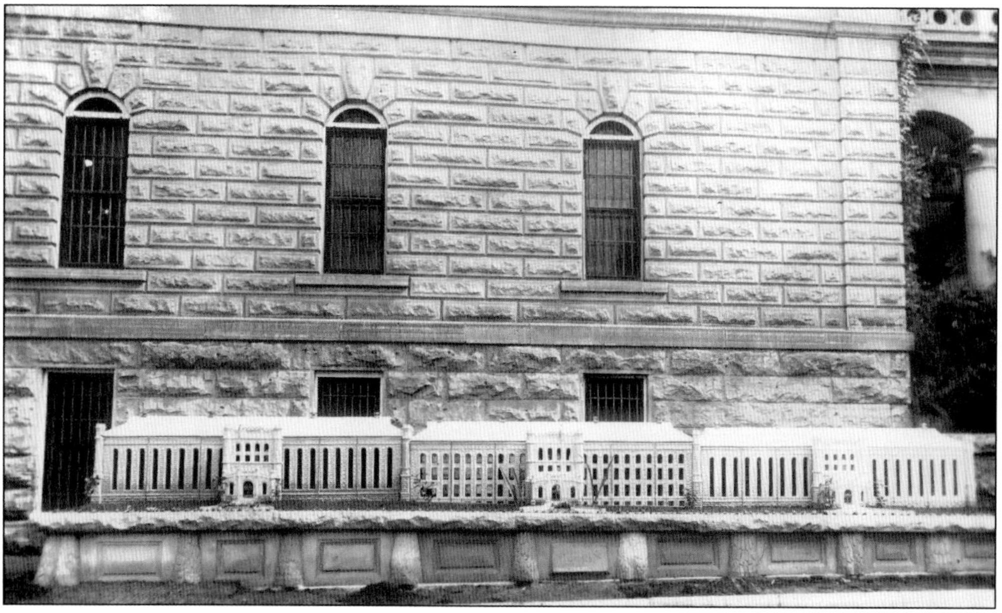

This carved stone model of the planned 1930s construction was displayed at the base of the administration building for over 25 years. The building at the far right was never constructed, and only a few small pieces of the model remain.

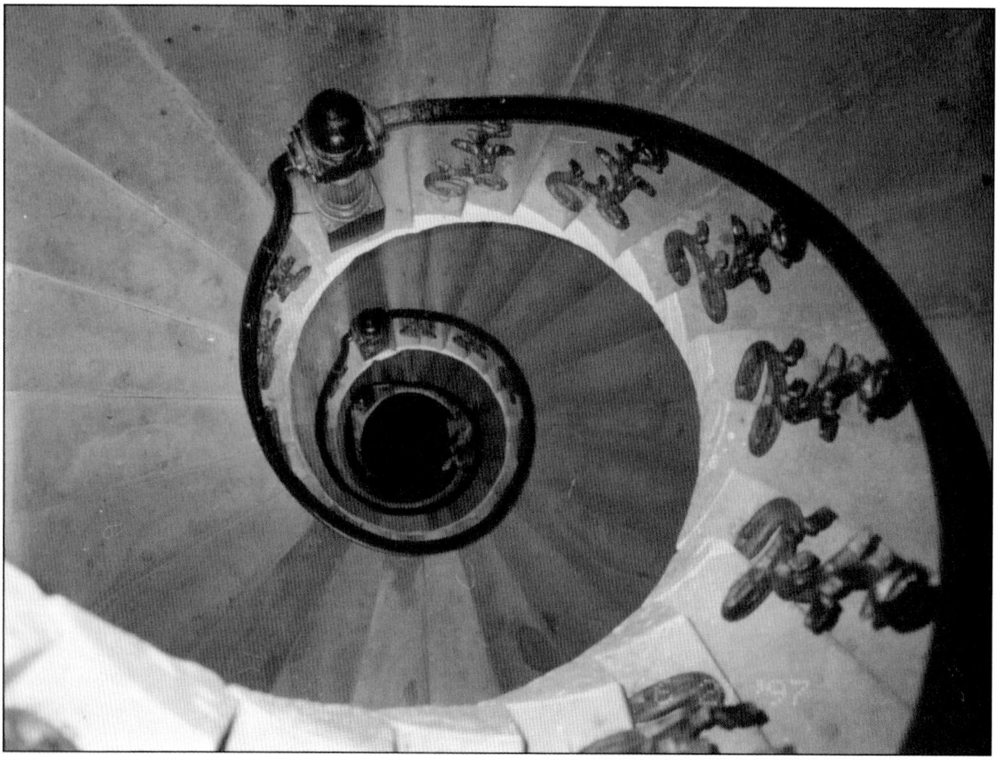

All old institutions have interesting features the public never sees. This staircase extends from the basement of the administration building to the fourth floor and provides access for tower officers. The banisters were cast in the prison foundry.

When the prison cemetery was moved to its current location in 1914, groups of remains were buried together under a common stone. The names marked "unknown" indicate that prison officials had difficulty identifying some of the remains.

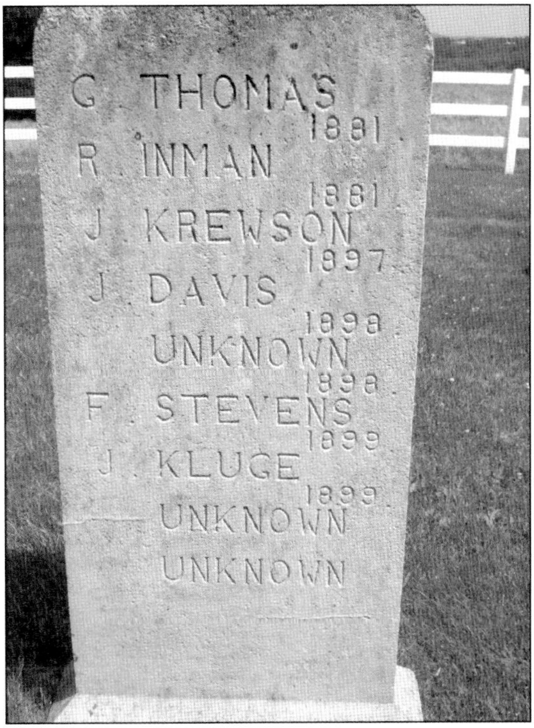

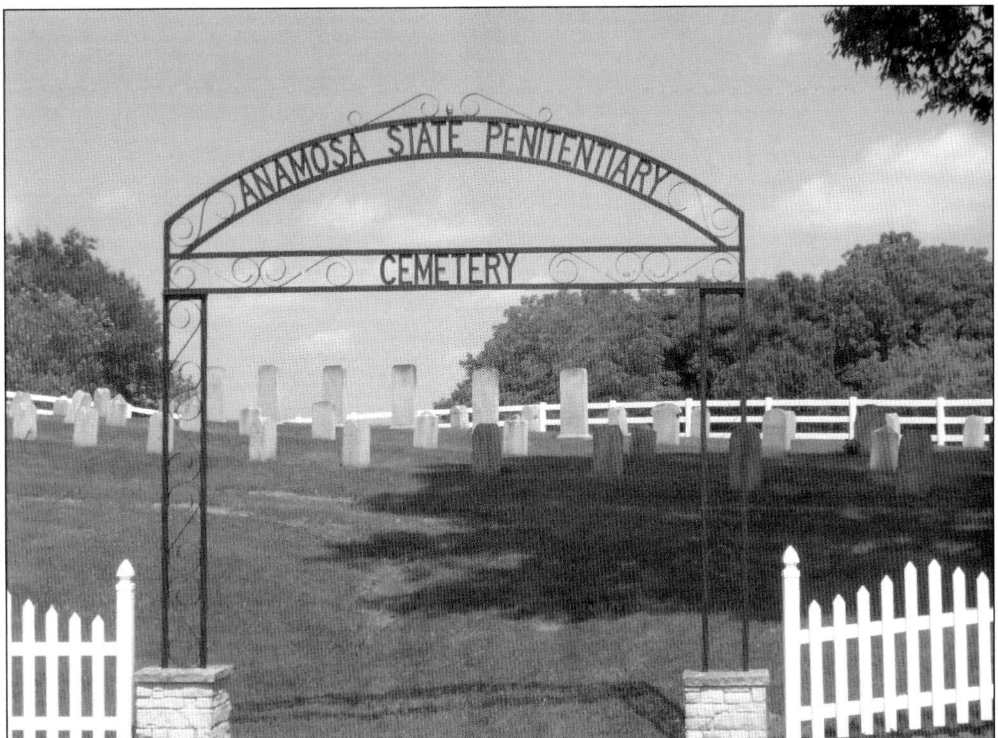

Approximately 150 inmates are buried in the prison cemetery, which is located high on a ridge overlooking the city of Anamosa and the prison, about a mile outside of town.

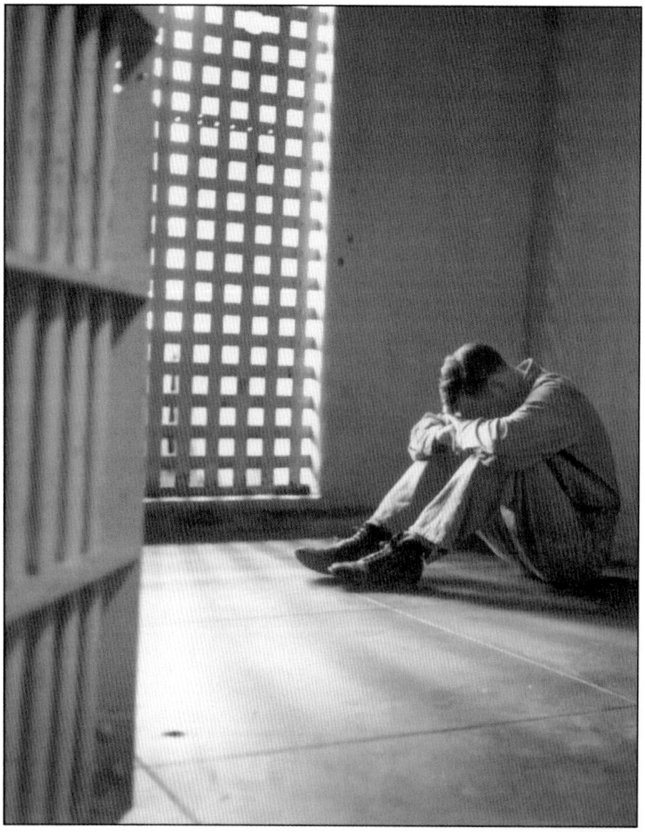

An inmate ponders his predicament.

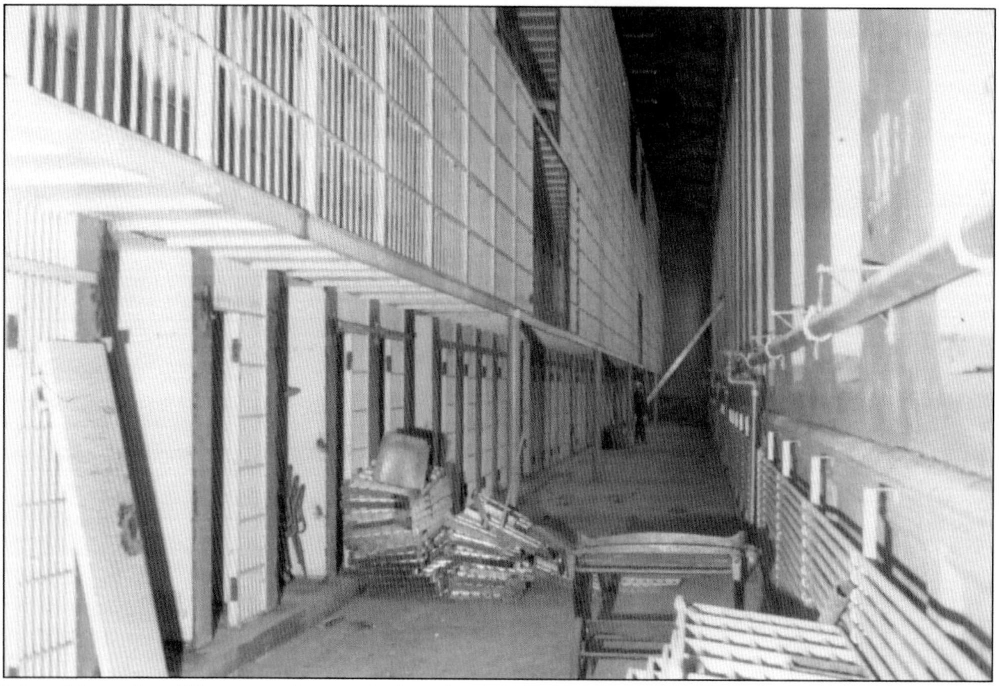

The old north cell house is dismantled in the 1970s.

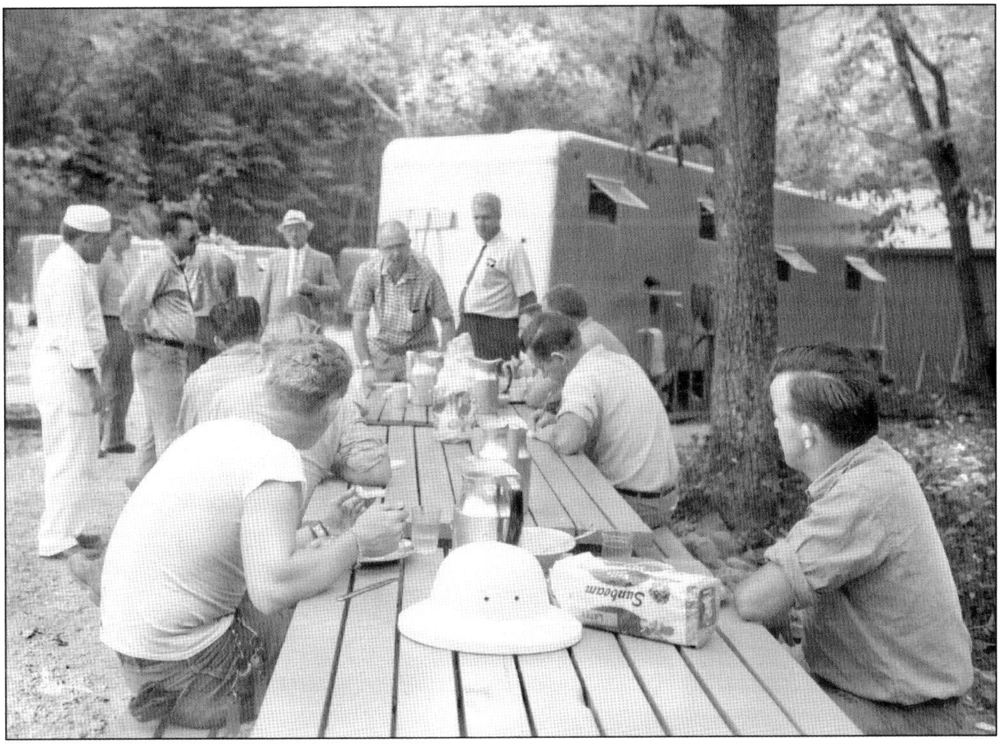

In July 1963, the Luster Heights camp was opened at the Yellow River State Park near Harpers Ferry, about two hours north of Anamosa. The 40-bed unit was operated in cooperation with the State Conservation Commission to utilize prison labor to develop the park. Initially the inmates were housed in trailers until the permanent buildings were constructed. The camp is still operated by the penitentiary as a satellite unit for minimum-security inmates. The picture below shows the facility in the present day.

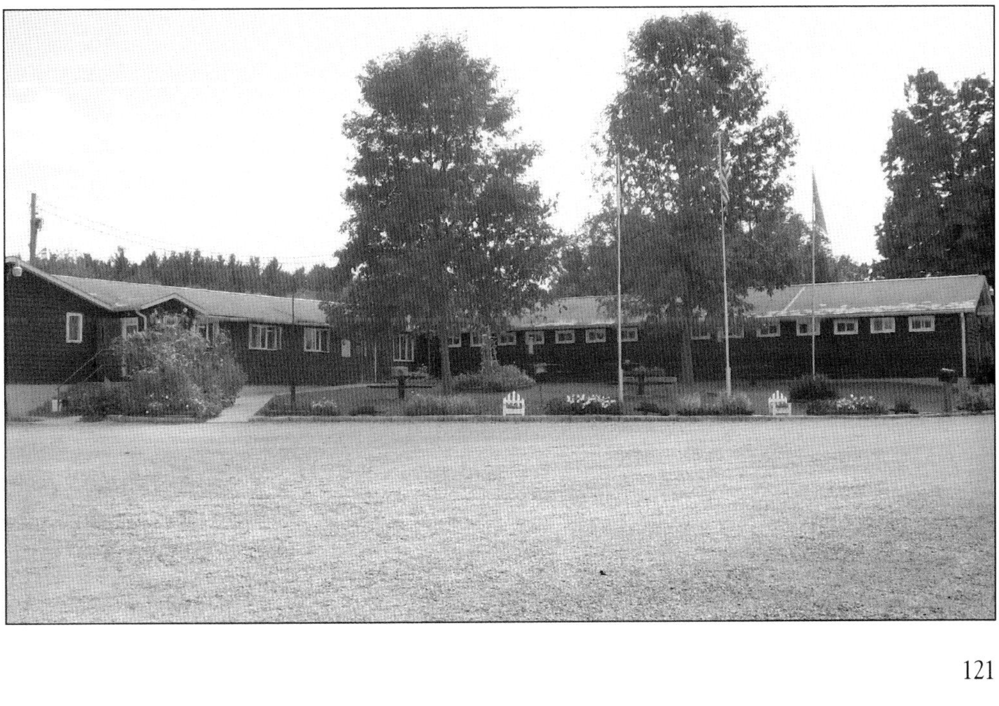

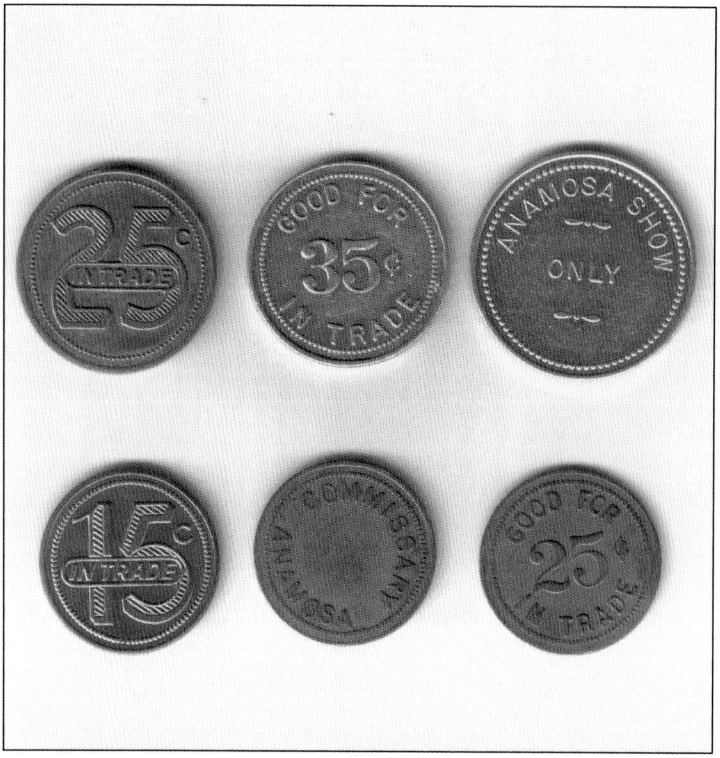

Inmates can purchase tokens from their commissary account, as cash is not allowed. Pop tokens, also known as commissary tokens, will purchase soft drinks from vending machines. The denomination changed as the price of soda increased. Movie tokens were used as admission to the movies before they were ended several years ago.

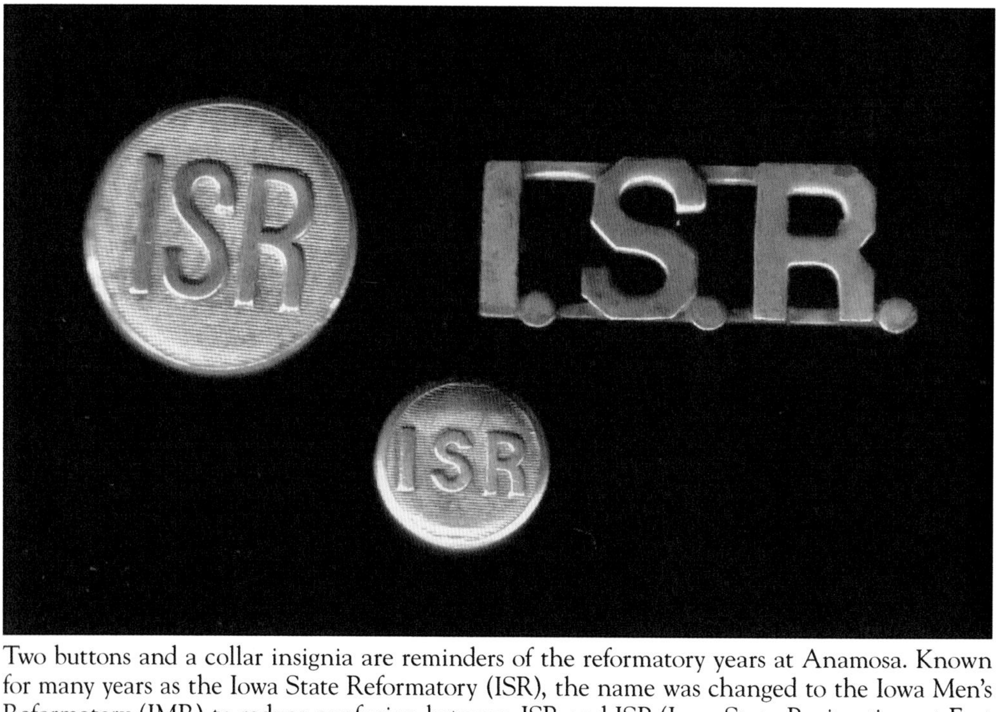

Two buttons and a collar insignia are reminders of the reformatory years at Anamosa. Known for many years as the Iowa State Reformatory (ISR), the name was changed to the Iowa Men's Reformatory (IMR) to reduce confusion between ISR and ISP (Iowa State Penitentiary at Fort Madison). The real confusion was probably between 1884 and 1907, when both Anamosa and Fort Madison were called Iowa State Penitentiary.

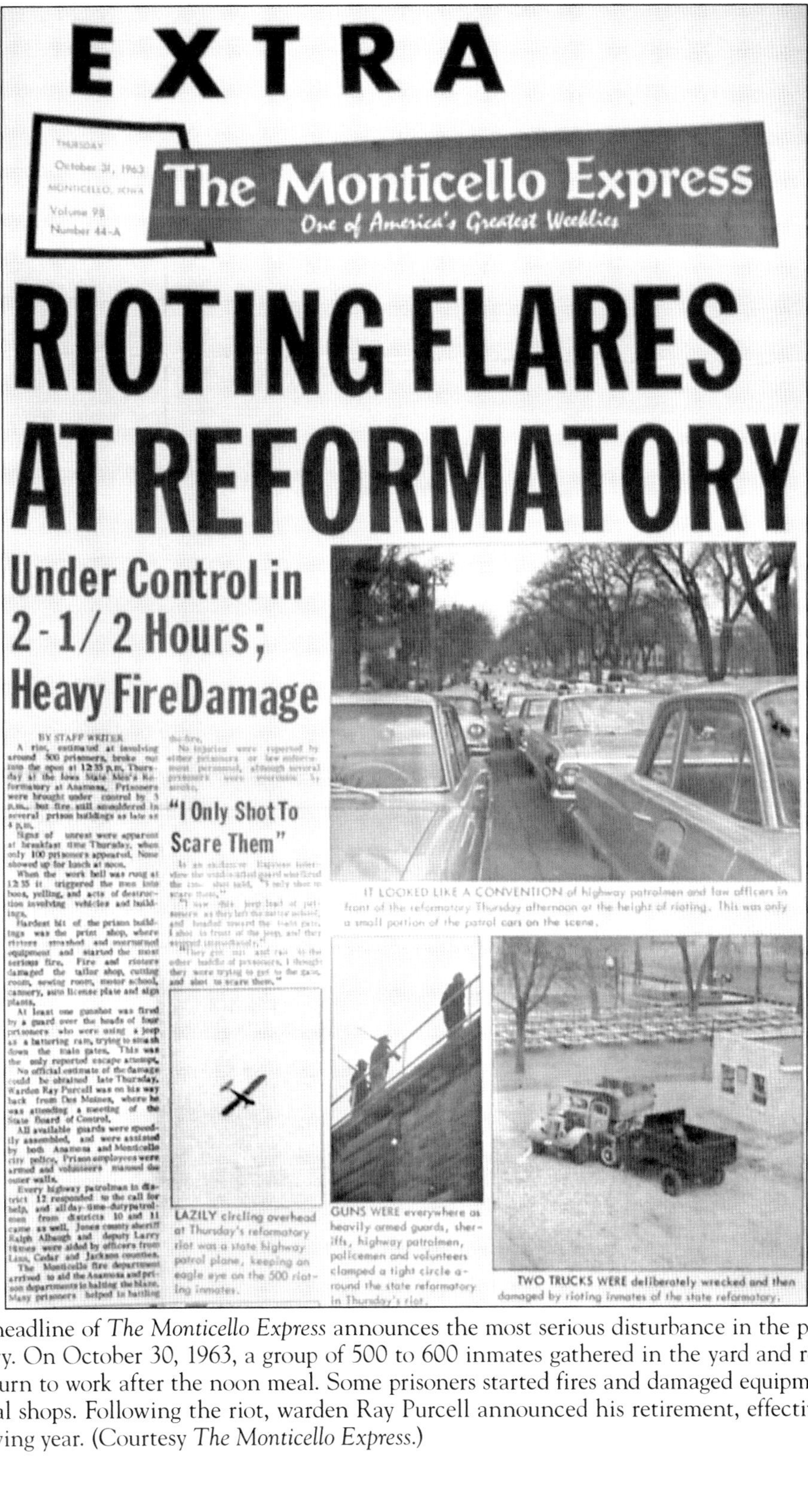

EXTRA

THURSDAY
October 31, 1963
MONTICELLO, IOWA
Volume 98
Number 44-A

The Monticello Express

One of America's Greatest Weeklies

RIOTING FLARES AT REFORMATORY

Under Control in 2-1/2 Hours; Heavy Fire Damage

BY STAFF WRITER

A riot, estimated at involving around 500 prisoners, broke out into the open at 12:35 p.m. Thursday at the Iowa State Men's Reformatory at Anamosa. Prisoners were brought under control by 3 p.m., but fire still smouldered in several prison buildings as late as 4 p.m.

Signs of unrest were apparent at breakfast time Thursday, when only 100 prisoners appeared. None showed up for lunch at noon.

When the work bell was rung at 12:35 it triggered the men into boos, yelling, and acts of destruction involving vehicles and buildings.

Hardest hit of the prison buildings was the print shop, where rioters smashed and overturned equipment and started the most serious fire. Fire and rioters damaged the tailor shop, cutting room, sewing room, motor school, cannery, auto license plate and sign plants.

At least one gunshot was fired by a guard over the heads of four prisoners who were using a jeep as a battering ram, trying to smash down the main gates. This was the only reported escape attempt.

No official estimate of the damage could be obtained late Thursday. Warden Ray Purcell was on his way back from Des Moines, where he was attending a meeting of the State Board of Control.

All available guards were speedily assembled, and were assisted by both Anamosa and Monticello city police. Prison employees were armed and volunteers manned the outer walls.

Every highway patrolman in district 12 responded to the call for help, and all day-time-duty patrolmen from districts 10 and 11 came as well. Jones county sheriff Ralph Albaugh and deputy Larry [illegible] were aided by officers from Linn, Cedar and Jackson counties.

The Monticello fire department arrived to aid the Anamosa and prison departments in halting the blaze. Many prisoners helped in battling the fire.

No injuries were reported by either prisoners or law enforcement personnel, although several prisoners were overcome by smoke.

"I Only Shot To Scare Them"

In an exclusive Express interview the unidentified guard who fired the [illegible] shot said, "I only shot to scare them."

"I saw this jeep load of prisoners as they left the [illegible] school, and headed toward the [illegible] gate. I shot in front of the jeep, and they stopped immediately."

"They got out and ran to the other bundle of prisoners. I thought they were trying to get to the gate, and shot to scare them."

IT LOOKED LIKE A CONVENTION of highway patrolmen and law officers in front of the reformatory Thursday afternoon at the height of rioting. This was only a small portion of the patrol cars on the scene.

LAZILY circling overhead at Thursday's reformatory riot was a state highway patrol plane, keeping an eagle eye on the 500 rioting inmates.

GUNS WERE everywhere as heavily armed guards, sheriffs, highway patrolmen, policemen and volunteers clamped a tight circle around the state reformatory in Thursday's riot.

TWO TRUCKS WERE deliberately wrecked and then damaged by rioting inmates of the state reformatory.

The headline of *The Monticello Express* announces the most serious disturbance in the prison's history. On October 30, 1963, a group of 500 to 600 inmates gathered in the yard and refused to return to work after the noon meal. Some prisoners started fires and damaged equipment in several shops. Following the riot, warden Ray Purcell announced his retirement, effective the following year. (Courtesy *The Monticello Express*.)

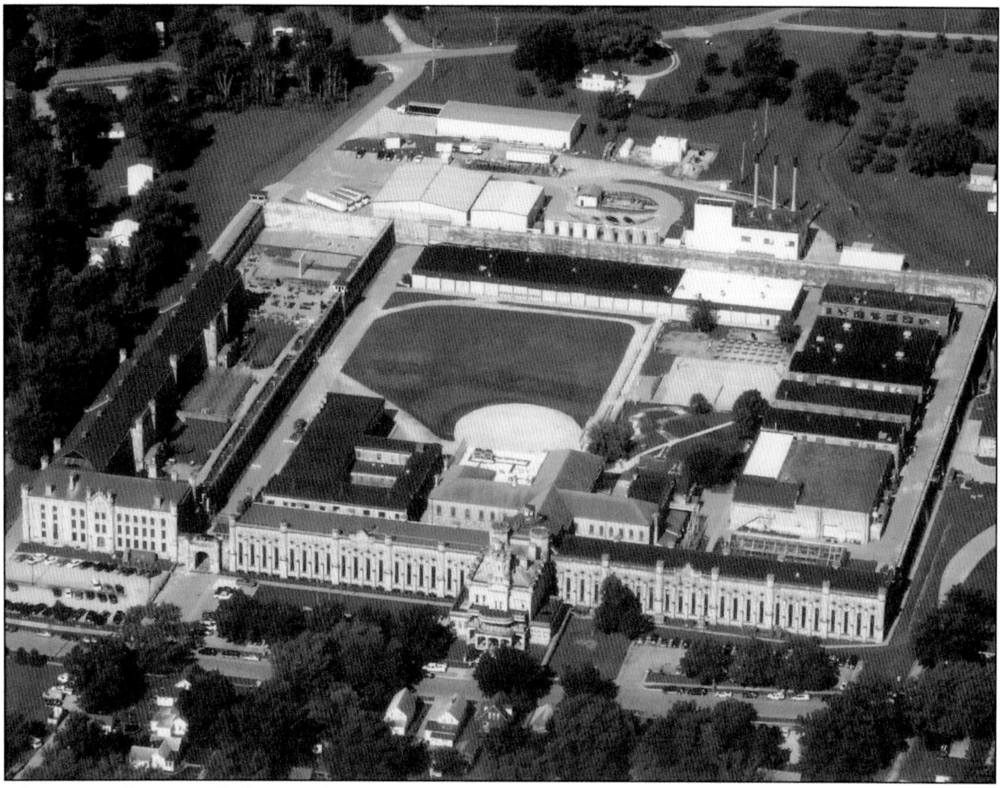

This 2009 photograph depicts the Anamosa State Penitentiary as it looks today. The large square portion is the original 11 acres contained by the wooden stockade and later by the stone wall. The rectangular portion to the left was enclosed during the 1930s when the count escalated during the Depression. (Courtesy the authors.)

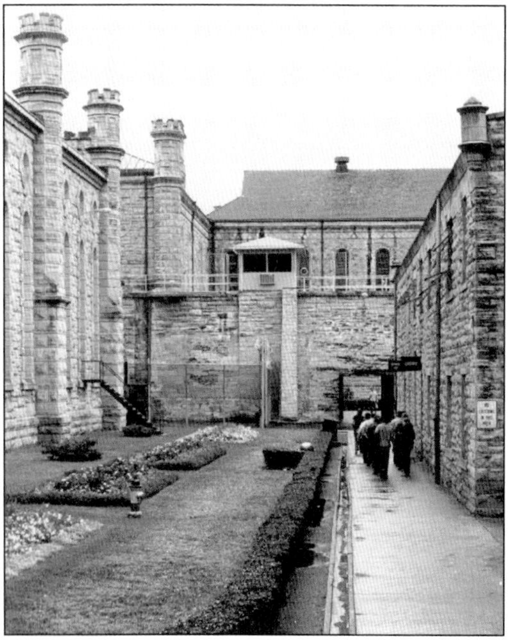

Several inmates walk down the sidewalk toward Tower No. 2. The opening in the original south wall provides passage to the cell house and hospital that were added during the 1930s construction. This photograph was taken after the new-style towers were introduced in the 1970s.

This is an early photograph of Tower No. 2 taken from the south. The end of the south cell house can be seen to the right. The tower would eventually be surrounded by the prison but stands above the original south wall in the photograph.

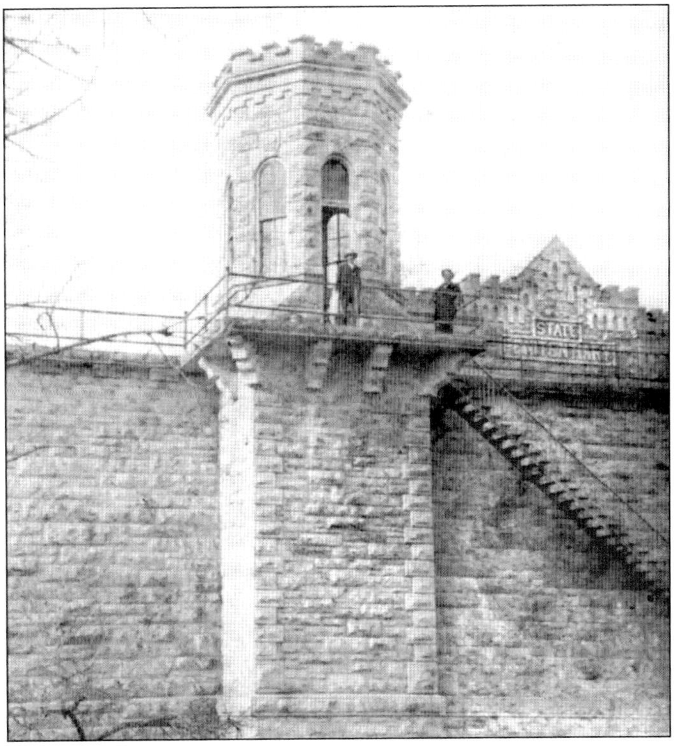

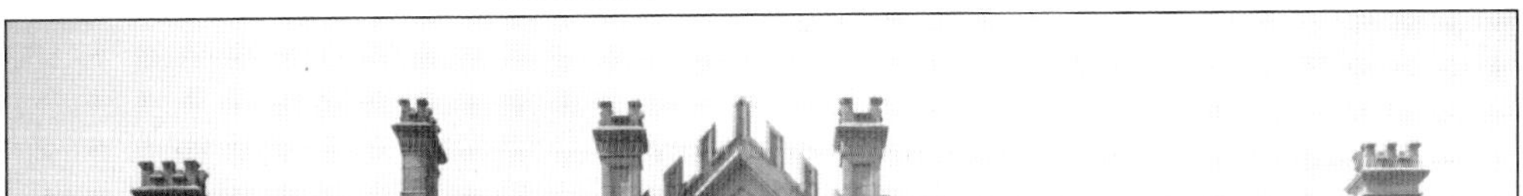

An early view of the female department building shows the entrance that led to the warden's office in the late 1890s. After the administration/warden's residence was completed, the female prisoners were moved here from the hospital. Little-used for years after the female prisoners left in 1918, it now houses the academic school, a storeroom, and a small living unit for minimum-security inmates.

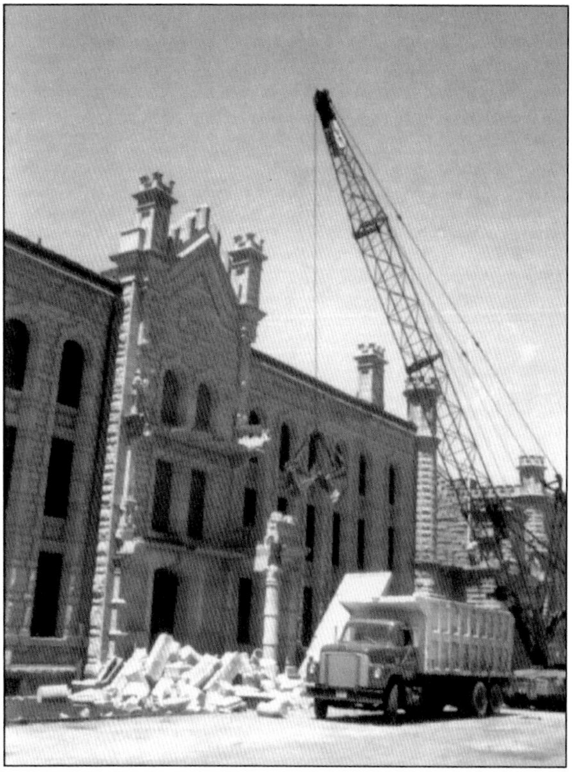

By the 1970s, the two-level porch on the female department building had became unstable and needed repair. Funds were not available, so the porch was removed. The building continues to be used for a storeroom, the academic school, and a small housing unit in the old female cell block.

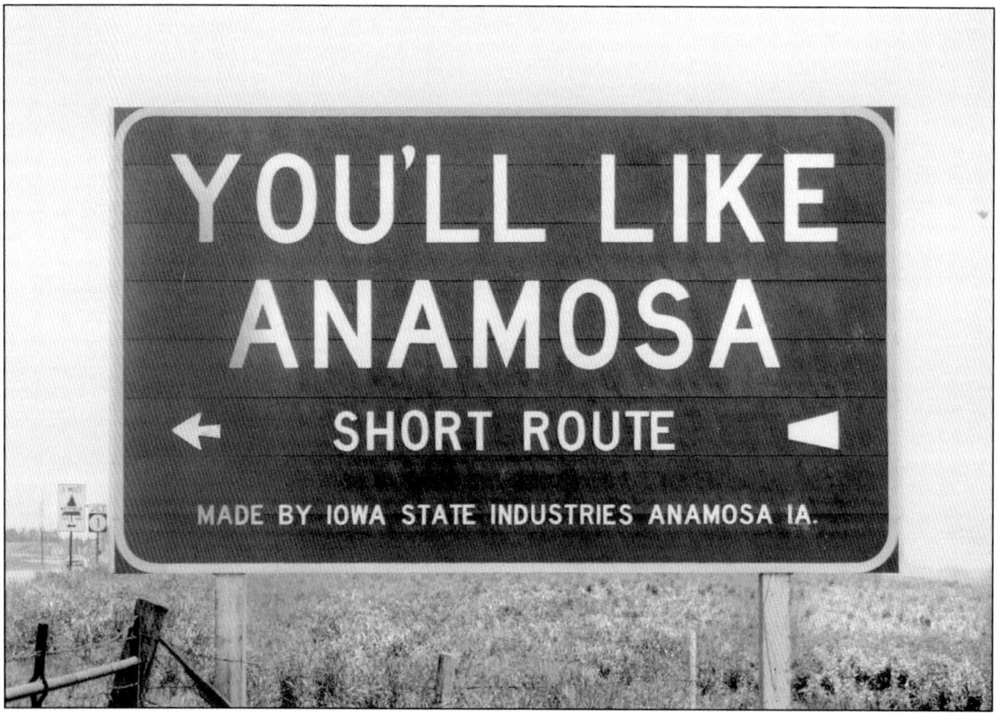

One wonders if the inmates who constructed this sign in the prison shop agreed with the sentiment expressed.

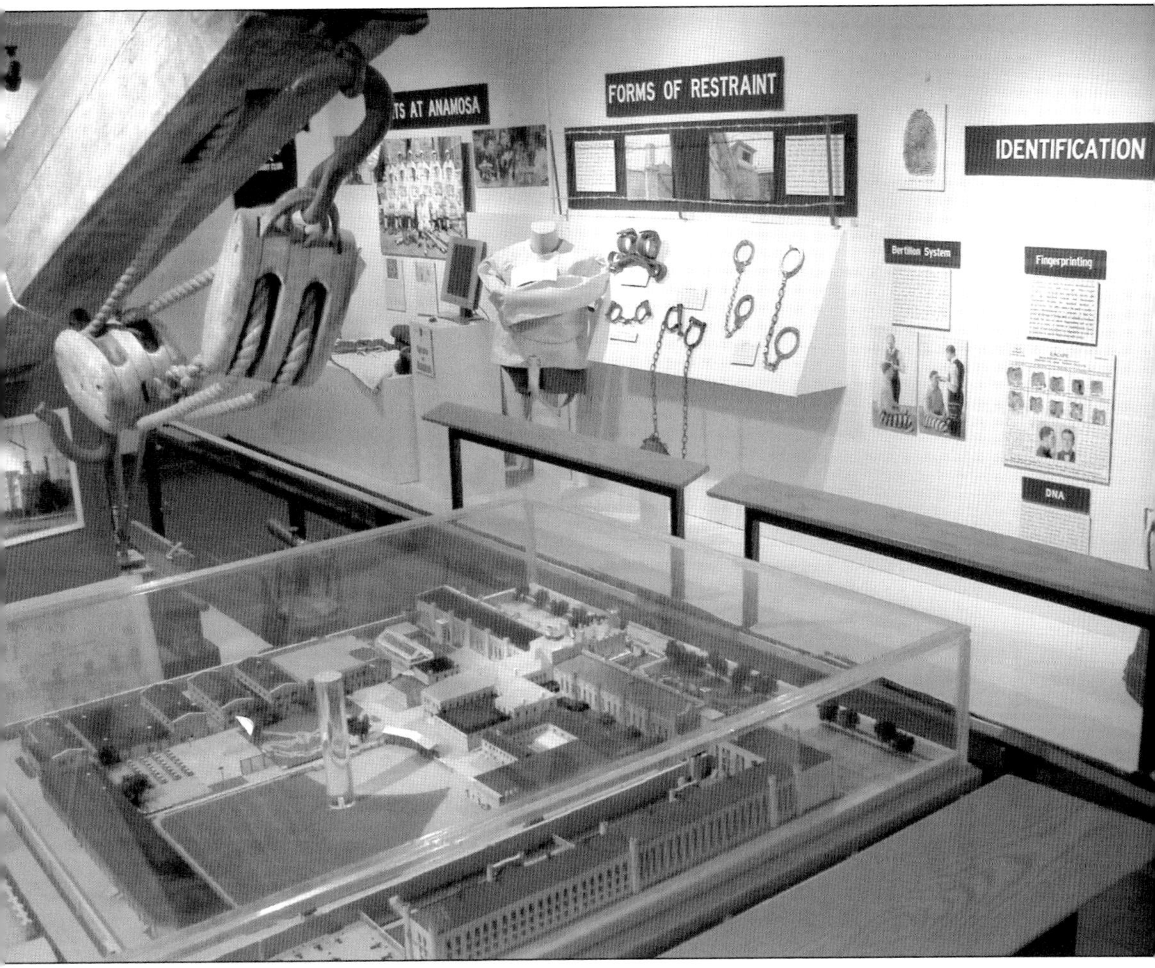

The Anamosa Penitentiary Museum presents the story of this 137-year-old correctional institution. Located at 406 North High Street in Anamosa, Iowa, the museum is operated by a nonprofit association using an all-volunteer staff. The museum is located in part of the former prison cheese factory in the shadow of the penitentiary's north wall. Visitors can see a video of prison inside views, view prison contraband, and see an inmate-made model of the prison. A mock cell and various photos and displays are also available. Students are admitted for free, while adults are currently charged $3. Summer hours are from 12:00 to 4:00 p.m. Friday through Sunday and other times throughout the year by appointment. Visitors are encouraged to call 319-462-2386 or email aspmuseum@mchsi.com for the latest information. A prison history Web site is also available at www.asphistory.com.

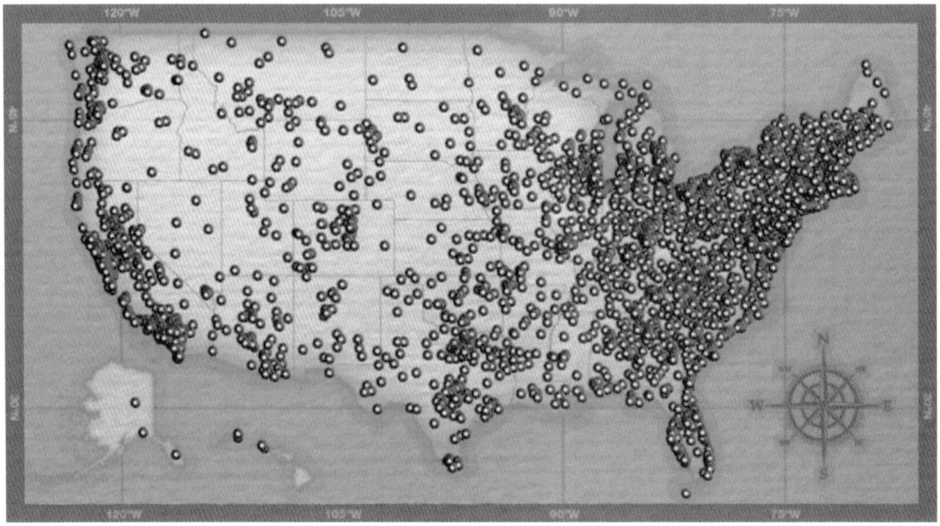